Communicating S

MW01059754

Science communication has become increasingly popular in journalism and mass communication as the media offer more scientific and technological information to the public. This volume explores the evolution of science communication, addressing key issues and offering substance for future study. Harnessing the energies of junior scholars on the forefront of science communication, this work pushes the boundaries of research forward, allowing scholars to sample the multiple paradigms and agendas that will play a role in shaping the future of science communication. Editors LeeAnn Kahlor and Patricia A. Stout challenge their readers to channel the energy within these chapters to build or continue to build their own research agendas as all scholars work together—across disciplines—to address questions of public understanding of science and communicating science.

These chapters are intended to inspire still more research questions, to help aspiring science communication scholars locate their own creative and original research programs, and to help veteran science communication scholars expand their existing programs such that they can more actively build interdisciplinary bridges. Crossing methodological boundaries, work from quantitative and qualitative scholars, social scientists, and rhetoricians is represented here.

This volume is developed for practitioners and scholars alike—for anyone who is concerned about or interested in the future of science and how communication is shaping and will continue to shape that future. In its progressive pursuit of interdisciplinary research streams—of thinking outside methodological and theoretical boxes—this book inspires science communication scholars at all levels to set a new standard for collaboration not just for science communication, but for communication research in general.

LeeAnn Kahlor (Ph.D., University of Wisconsin-Madison) is an Assistant Professor in the Department of Advertising and Public Relations at the University of Texas at Austin where she teaches courses in Public Relations, and Science and Health Communication. She is affiliated with UT's Center for Women's and Gender Studies and the university's Environmental Sciences Institute. Her work has appeared in *Science Communication, Public Understanding of Science, Health Communication, Risk Analysis, Communication Research, Human Communication Research, Media Psychology* and the *Journal of Broadcast and Electronic Media.*

Patricia A. Stout (Ph.D., University of Illinois Urbana-Champaign) is Professor and John P. McGovern Regents Professor in Health and Medical Science Communication in the Department of Advertising at the University of Texas at Austin. She teaches courses in Persuasive Communication and Health Communication. Stout is former co-director of the Center for Health Promotion Research (CHPR) in the School of Nursing at UT Austin.

New Agendas in Communication

A Series from Routledge and the College of Communication
at the University of Texas at Austin
Roderick Hart and Stephen Reese, Series Editors

This series brings together groups of emerging scholars to tackle important interdisciplinary themes that demand new scholarly attention and reach broadly across the communication field's existing courses. Each volume stakes out a key area, presents original findings, and considers the long-range implications of its "new agenda."

Interplay of Truth and Deception
Edited by Matt McGlone and Mark Knapp

Journalism and Citizenship
Edited by Zizi Papacharissi

Communicating Science
Edited by LeeAnn Kahlor and Patricia Stout

Political Emotions
Edited by Janet Staiger

Media Literacy
Edited by Kathleen Tyner

Communicating Science

New Agendas in Communication

Edited by LeeAnn Kahlor and
Patricia A. Stout

Routledge
Taylor & Francis Group

NEW YORK AND LONDON

First published 2010
by Routledge
711 Third Ave, New York, NY 10017

Simultaneously published in the UK
by Routledge
2 Park Square, Milton Park, Abingdon, Oxon OX14 4RN

Routledge is an imprint of the Taylor & Francis Group, an informa business

© 2010 Taylor and Francis

Typeset in Sabon by Wearset Ltd, Boldon, Tyne and Wear

Library of Congress Cataloging-in-Publication Data

Understanding and communicating science: new agendas in
communication/edited by LeeAnn Kahlor and Patricia A. Stout.
p. cm. – (A volume in the new agendas in communication series)
1. Communication in science. I. Kahlor, LeeAnn. II. Stout, Patricia
A.
Q223.U394 2009
501'.4–dc22

2009019017

ISBN10: 0-415-99958-8 (hbk)
ISBN10: 0-415-99959-6 (pbk)
ISBN10: 0-203-86763-7 (ebk)

ISBN13: 978-0-415-99958-8 (hbk)
ISBN13: 978-0-415-99959-5 (pbk)
ISBN13: 978-0-203-86763-1 (ebk)

Contents

Illustrations

Figures

Tables

Foreword

Building a Context for the Next Century of Science Communication Research

Sharon Dunwoody

Why Study the Popular Communication of Science?

I was well into my career as a science communication researcher before I asked myself this question. As a former science journalist who got into communication research in order to make sense of what I had been doing professionally for years, I assumed that a focus on science messages was a no-brainer. But then a number of things brought me up short.

One was that I could find few researchers working in this area when I began in the early 1970s. I knew of two senior colleagues—Hillier Krieghbaum at New York University and Joye Patterson at the University of Missouri—but was hard pressed to find others populating journalism and mass communication departments around the country. When I ventured to a meeting of the American Association for the Advancement of Science (AAAS) in the mid-1970s, I met two other young scholars: Rae Goodell at MIT and Sharon Friedman at Lehigh University. Rae had done her dissertation at Stanford University on scientists whose media visibility was generating both policy clout and intense peer criticism; that research became the classic book *The Visible Scientists*, published in 1977. And Sharon was beginning a lifelong study of media coverage of environmental issues, a program for which she remains internationally known. But even at this point, I could count the number of popular science communication scholars on the fingers of one hand.

Another unsettling clue came from science journalists with whom I interacted. I can still remember one AAAS meeting where Sharon Friedman, Carol Rogers (now at the University of Maryland) and I staged a standing-room-only session on science and the media. One of our speakers, *New York Times* reporter Nicholas Wade, opened his talk with a lament. Why, he opined, did this handful of communication researchers insist on focusing on science communication over other areas of journalism? What was so special about science, he asked, that it would draw such sustained analysis? He and his colleagues, he maintained, were beginning to feel like lab rats.

Why indeed? One part of the answer is that we are rewarded for this work in ways that other communication scholars may not be.

Legitimacy. Although professors fare reasonably well in comparative analyses of public confidence in and respect for occupations, scientists and physicians do even better. So by hitching our star to theirs, we gain cachet. Our studies—because they focus on public perceptions of stem cells or on framing patterns in media coverage of bioengineered foods or on scientists' perceptions of their communication activities—can legitimately compete for space in some of the world's top journals, such as *Science* and *Nature*. The intellectual legitimacy that derives from this coupling is worth its weight in gold.

Communication struggles to be a full partner among social science disciplines for funding purposes. We have yet to fit securely into funding categories employed by the National Science Foundation and National Institutes of Health. But when a major scientific grant opportunity comes along, the linkage between a science or health issue and communication scholarship can be sculpted in a vivid and fundable way. Thus, the "science" in science communication gives us a kind of external legitimacy that colleagues studying other areas of communication struggle to attain.

Interdisciplinarity. Science communication scholarship is inherently multidisciplinary, if not interdisciplinary. A decision to study mediated coverage of stem-cell research, for example, takes the principal investigation on a fascinating journey into not only conceptual frameworks governing patterns of narrative but also foundational work about stem cells themselves. A grant to better understand the role of information in public perceptions of a risk might well pair a communication scholar with an epidemiologist. And as federal funding moves to privileging larger, interdisciplinary initiatives, science and health communication scholars increasingly find themselves part of large, multidisciplinary and sometimes multi-*university* teams.

Clearer access to concepts and processes. Focusing on science also gives us a cleaner shot at a variety of communication concepts and processes. What we study is not conceptually unique. But I would argue that certain characteristics of science messages—as well as of scientists and those who communicate about them—are so potently present that they offer us natural laboratories where these characteristics are vivid and easier to study.

For example, scientists and physicians have higher status than any other occupations. This makes studies of the role of power in relationships illuminating, whether operating at the individual (reporter–source), organizational (media organization–science organization), or societal (journalism–science) level.

Another example: The sheer complexity and density of scientific knowledge—at least as it is generated and expressed within the disciplines—is a useful laboratory for exploring information processing and comprehension.

Most lay individuals tell us they know little about science but believe that science, nevertheless, is important and useful to society. These attitudes may minimize other contingencies (experiential knowledge, a false sense of efficacy) that could affect studies of how individuals use information to derive meaning.

One more example: Science is one of the few disciplines that have standardized ways of communicating what they DON'T know. As interest grows in understanding how individuals cope with uncertainty, science again offers a splendid laboratory in which to explore how both external uncertainty (perceptions of the uncertainty embedded in information and other aspects of the world "out there") and internal uncertainty (perceptions of one's own level of knowledge) influence our behaviors.

The potential to influence issues of importance. I do not mean to trivialize the importance of issues tackled by scholars who focus on other content areas, such as politics or the arts. But science and health issues sometimes come bearing a life-or-death quality that makes them not just compelling but globally critical. As countries move toward efforts to engage in large-scale actions to mitigate climate change, for example, communication scholars will be critical partners in catalyzing the kind of behavior change that will be crucial to success. Similarly, the impacts of global epidemics (AIDS, for example) are contingent on the evolution of knowledge and behaviors that are unpacked and facilitated by communication research.

We can only have that impact through the highest-quality scholarship. On that point, at least, I am sanguine. Any concerns about quality will be put to rest by this collection of studies by a group of young science communication scholars. The work you encounter here is well conceptualized, thoughtfully analyzed, and reflects a field well on its way to maturity. It represents a community of scholars that is a far cry from the small number of communication researchers whom I encountered wandering in the science wilderness in the 1970s. And I could not be happier.

Preface

The idea for this book grew from a solicitation issued by Rod Hart, Dean and Professor of Communication Studies, and Steve Reese, Associate Dean and Professor of Journalism, in the College of Communication at the University of Texas at Austin in spring of 2006. The college was sponsoring a series of conferences to highlight emerging intellectual trends in the field of Communication "writ large." Each conference would bring in around a dozen junior scholars whose work was poised to impact the field. After each conference, revised versions of the papers would become chapters in a series of books.

We immediately recognized the area of science communication as immensely fertile ground for promising new scholars and proposed a conference and volume that would focus on two main topics under that umbrella: (1) public understanding of science and (2) communicating science.

Under those two topics, we visualized potential manuscripts to cover science knowledge (and gaps), perceptions of/attitudes toward science, and science-related decision making and judgments (personal, social, policy, etc.), as well as science/medical journalism, issue advertising, and environmental policy. In soliciting chapter proposals for our volume, we cast our net widely—taking advantage of the networks that are the Science Communication Interest Group of the Association for Education in Journalism and Mass Communication and the Association for the Rhetoric of Science and Technology. Although we consider ourselves to be primarily quantitative social scientists, we wanted to hear from both quantitative and qualitative scholars, social scientists, and rhetoricians. And we did.

We heard from just under 30 scholars whose work covered exactly the topics we had hoped for, but with far more creativity and scope than we could have imagined. We reviewed the proposals and settled on 10 proposals that miraculously fell into three neat categories: merging theory and practice, characterization and meaning-making, and the future of science communication from an education perspective.

We brought the authors of those 10 proposals to Austin for a conference in spring of 2008. Our keynote speaker for the conference was Sharon

Dunwoody, who also stayed for the duration of the conference and participated fully (as only she can). Our scholars, whose work is of course showcased in this volume, flew in from across the country and spent two days reconnecting and forging new friendships, sharing ideas, reviewing each other's work, and otherwise making the most of this unique opportunity. There was a sense that those in the room formed an entity much larger than the individual research agendas being discussed that day. The details of the research agendas in this volume will be touched on in more detail in the Introduction. Suffice it to say, we anticipate that the work will indeed have an impact. To glimpse the weekend for yourself, you can visit http:// push.communication.utexas.edu/conferences/index.htm.

Of course, neither the conference nor the volume would have been possible without the help of a number of important people. First we want to thank Rod Hart and Steve Reese for their vision—without that vision, none of this would have happened. We also want to thank all of the authors who submitted proposals to us—it was a pleasure to sample your work. We would like to thank Anne Reed, Amanda Neuman, and Mark Rogers of the College of Communication for orchestrating the conference details, videography and support materials, and for helping us insure that the weekend went smoothly. We would like to thank Mike Mackert for helping get the videos on the Web for all to see.

We would like to thank Sharon Dunwoody, whose unflagging devotion to building science communication as a research program played a tremendous role in making this volume happen. The role she plays in mentoring junior scholars—some of whose work is showcased here—is truly a service to the larger field of communication research. In terms of mentoring, we also want to thank Susanna Priest, Katherine McComas, Dietram Scheufele, and Bruce V. Lewenstein, whose names came up repeatedly during our conference as the people who helped many of our authors begin building their own research agendas. We also want to thank Linda Bathgate, our editor at Erlbaum, for her support and patience as our deadlines pushed further into the future, and Dave Junker, Kelly Eidson, and Nam-Hyun Um for their assistance in copy-editing the chapters.

Finally, we want to thank our authors. Not only are they brilliant and motivated scholars, they are, quite simply, nice people. They are the kind of people with whom you can "talk theory," share a passion for science, and laugh. And so we did—and it was our pleasure. Thank you.

LeeAnn Kahlor and Patricia Stout
The University of Texas at Austin
April 1, 2009

Introduction

> It is increasingly difficult for Americans to be competent as citizens, workers, and consumers without some degree of competence in dealing with [science and technology].
>
> (Science and Engineering Indicators 2008, National Science Foundation, p. 7.5)

The National Science Foundation reported in 2006 that "although Americans express strong support for science and technology, most are not very well informed about these subjects. The public's lack of knowledge about basic scientific facts and the scientific process can have far-reaching implications" (NSF, 2006, p. 7.3). Such implications include the inability to evaluate scientific (and pseudoscientific) information that is presented daily by politicians, public health and environmental agencies, pharmaceutical companies, energy companies, journalists, bloggers, and medical practitioners. Science topics *du jour*—all rife with myriad health and policy implications—include alternative fuel development, stem-cell research, biotechnology, pharmaceutical risks, nanotechnology, climate change, and science education mandates legislated by state governments.

As a result, it is becoming increasingly difficult for communication researchers to ignore the flashing red light that is low science literacy and limited public understanding of science. Of course, communication researchers have a lot to contribute in terms of exploring why literacy is low and how it can rise—but the potential for contribution doesn't end there. They also stand poised to bring to the larger scientific endeavor an understanding of how communication works and doesn't work, who matters in the exchange of knowledge and why, and what the public brings to that exchange—with an emphasis on the fact that they do bring something, and we better start recognizing what that something is.

Thankfully, a fairly broad-based body of research on science communication has been coalescing for about 25 years. Now more than ever, research institutions (Cornell, Florida, Georgia, Maryland, South Carolina,

Texas, Wisconsin, etc.) are producing scholars dedicated to investigating public understanding and communication of the science that encompasses human and environmental health and public policy. These scholars are making important connections among science communication, public health and public policy; the research they are producing represents such areas as environmental science communication, medical science communication, technology and communication, and a host of other areas that fall under the umbrella of science communication.

As discussed in our preface, the purpose of this volume is to harness the momentum of the junior scholars who are now on the forefront, pushing the boundaries of science communication research further still. We see this volume as a handbook intended to appeal to practitioners and scholars alike—anyone who is concerned about or interested in the future of science and how communication is shaping and will continue to shape that future.

In her thoughtful foreword, Sharon Dunwoody discusses the interdisciplinary richness of conducting communication research related to science. Here we would like to touch on yet another source of interdisciplinary richness that can be found in this book through its showcasing of scholars who are approaching communication research from varied social scientific and rhetorical research paradigms. Interdisciplinary research is a term being touted at many universities these days. But what does it really mean? For us, it meant embracing disparate research methods and paradigms to capture a more holistic picture of science communication.

Scholarly texts that combine the work of social scientists and rhetoricians in one volume are not common; yet, we can think of no good reason for this division of communication scholarship. Still, the division exists and it is, regrettably, perpetuated in research training and execution. We assert that while quantitative and qualitative approaches must adhere to internal measures of consistency, neither the approaches nor insights of one should be closed to the other simply because rote orthodoxy dictates it. Thus, in some ways, this book issues a challenge to readers to reach outside their own disciplines and embrace the richness displayed in the varied ways in which our authors define and explore communication within the context of science.

That said, the interdisciplinary nature of this book will likely confront some readers with terms and methods that are somewhat unfamiliar. However, one of the things our authors noted after the conference (see Preface) that preceded this book was that we have much more in common as scholars than our preconceived notions had allowed. Regardless of how we go about answering our research questions, in many cases, we are asking the same questions. When we are not, we are discovering new ways to ask them, yielding a larger and more accurate range of the answers we all seek.

These chapters are each intended to inspire still more research questions, to help aspiring science communication scholars locate their own creative and original research programs, and to help veteran science communication scholars expand their existing programs such that they can more actively build interdisciplinary bridges. In its progressive pursuit of interdisciplinary research streams—of thinking outside methodological and theoretical boxes—the ultimate goal for this book is to inspire science communication scholars (junior and senior) to set new standards for collaboration not just for science communication, but for communication research in general.

In Part I, "Merging Theory and Practice: Models and Frameworks," we lead with a chapter by Dominique Brossard and Bruce Lewenstein in which the authors address whether practice can inform theory. The authors open with a discussion of four theoretical frameworks that have shaped the research on the public understanding of science, beginning with the public knowledge deficit model and leading up to the public participation model. The authors then test whether actual outreach efforts can be mapped onto those four models, or whether a newer model is needed to capture how outreach is currently practiced. Five case studies drawn from 94 outreach programs related to the Human Genome Program were employed in this task. Results indicate that outreach projects tend to make use of mixed approaches that blend models, rather than gravitate toward any one well-defined model. The chapter suggests that theoretical perspectives need to take into account the permeable boundaries between models and practice.

In Chapter 2, Matthew Nisbet argues that there is nothing essentially unique about science policy debates when compared to other political controversies—and that given this interpretative reality, scientists must strategically "frame" their communications in a manner that connects with diverse audiences. By synthesizing past research, Nisbet is able to identify a consistent set of frames that appear over and over again in science policy debates. He then explains how this research might be transformed into an innovative public engagement strategy to be used by scientists, press officers, and their institutions. Such engagement strategies would remain true to the underlying science, but would draw extensively from audience research in order to design messages that are personally relevant and meaningful to diverse publics. Nisbet draws on specific cases—nuclear energy, evolution, and climate change—to demonstrate the generalizable ways in which framing drives the dynamics of science controversies. Conceptualization and identification of campaign strategies, media messages, and their influence, as well as lessons related to public engagement strategies are discussed—although these lessons are not without several important ethical and normative considerations.

In Chapter 3, John Besley discusses past research on the social psychology of justice as fairness. He then argues that this research provides a promising theoretical basis with which to study direct and mediated engagement related to decision making about health and environmental risks. Justice as fairness is a concept posed by political philosopher John Rawls. While fairness has played an important role in science and risk research, most discussions of fairness fail to fully exploit social psychological theory to help explain how people perceive decision making related to Rawls' concept. The chapter outlines recent exploratory science communication research that explicitly uses a justice-as-fairness framework. This work argues that fairness perceptions—specifically sub-dimensions of fairness that address outcomes, procedures, interpersonal relations, and available information—are an important consequence of much official science communication. These perceptions of fairness result in outcomes such as satisfaction with decisions and perceptions of the legitimacy of authorities. Finally, areas where the justice-as-fairness framework could enhance science and risk communication research and practice are discussed.

In Chapter 4, Janas Sinclair and Barbara Miller focus on science information that enters the public domain from corporate sources, particularly in the case of technology advocacy campaigns. Technology advocacy campaigns are defined as attempts to persuade the public on issues related to science or technology with the goal of protecting an organization's interests and defending its current and future business activities. Advertising and public relations are typically used to accomplish this persuasive task. This chapter addresses how audiences respond to and interpret such strategic messages, and presents a theoretical model intended to explain public response to technology advocacy specifically. This model, which is based on the Persuasion Knowledge Model (Friestad & Wright, 1994), was developed through qualitative and quantitative research on audience perceptions of technology advocacy campaigns for the coal and crop biotechnology industries. According to the model, persuasion depends on audience perceptions of industry accountability, audience trust in the sponsor of the campaign, and audience motives to identify with or critique the technology advocacy message. Research directions for empirical tests of the proposed relationships among variables in the model, as well as implications for designing effective corporate advocacy campaigns, are also discussed.

Part I wraps up with a chapter by Bret Shaw in which the author discusses the intersections of social marketing and two temporally oriented social science models—Stages of Change and Diffusion of Innovations. Additional insights are drawn from the literature on persuasion and information campaigns. The intent is to generate a framework for researchers, natural resource educators, and outreach professionals to more effectively promote sustainable environmental behaviors. Although these models have achieved ample attention in the health communication literature, they have not received sufficient consideration from communication researchers and practitioners focused on conserving the environment. This chapter directs attention to the potential role of temporally oriented models to assist in audience segmentation efforts. The central argument made is that knowing where an audience segment is on a temporal basis, relative to that audience's understanding and adoption of a new behavior, has implications for addressing: (a) individual segment members' motivations, (b) perceived benefits and barriers, and (c) how to improve the likelihood of success for any social marketing campaign related to science communication.

Part II of this volume, "Characterization and Meaning-Making," shifts our focus to research agendas emerging from the area of science rhetoric. These next several chapters offer a closer look at scientists and audiences, particularly the negotiation of meaning and the very creation of scientific knowledge.

We lead this part of the book with a chapter by Lisa Keränen, who argues that the rhetorical concepts of *personae*, *ethos* and voice offer an analytical framework for the study of human character on display in scientific controversies. Keränen explicates these concepts and then applies them to the case of Bernard Fisher—the renowned cancer researcher whose career was momentarily tarnished by scandal in the mid-1990s. Her retelling of the Fisher controversy is as compelling as it is illustrative. The chapter argues that the three distinct *personae*—the swashbuckling revolutionary, the reluctant apologist, and the beleaguered administrator—emerged during the early months of the controversy. Together, these *personae* functioned to encourage policy outcomes focused on purging science of individual transgressions, while underplaying broader systemic reforms that could have addressed broader patient concerns. The chapter ultimately concludes that focusing on *personae*, *ethos* and voice provides a means of reconsidering the interrelatedness of character and knowledge, and of trust and truth in science-based controversies involving scientists and members of various publics. In the end, the reader is left with two rewards: a promising analytical framework and the feeling that comes with having read a good story.

In Chapter 6, John Lynch explores the topic of model organisms—particularly those that guide stem-cell research. By casting a spotlight on the role of model organisms in the larger scientific endeavor, Lynch allows us to glimpse how such organisms shape the dynamic process of doing science—from the lab, to discovery, to naming that discovery, and beyond. The chapter is guided by articulation theory and a three-component schema for understanding science—one that delineates the material, social, and rhetorical aspects of scientific programs. The chapter uses the case of stem-cell research to make three claims. The first claim is that communication is an essential component of scientific practice. The second claim is that the use of model organisms to define and organize stem-cell research illustrates the roles of each component of the tripartite schema in articulating science. The third claim is that these three components of science can interfere with or complement each other, as will be evidenced by the limitations exerted by the social/economic component of science on various concepts and definitions created by stem-cell models. In this chapter, scholars will glimpse how scientists connect the words "stem cell" to specific objects in the laboratory, thus altering the meaning and value of those words and the things related to them.

In Chapter 8, Danielle Endres explores the clashes between science, culture, and spirituality that often emerge in politically charged public debates over policies such as intelligent design, human genomics, and nuclear waste. This chapter engages the question: Are scientific arguments and spiritually/culturally based arguments mutually exclusive? Using the Yucca Mountain high-level nuclear waste siting controversy as a case study, this chapter focuses on how non-credentialed non-scientists simultaneously use both scientific claims and cultural/spiritual claims. In particular, arguments made by American Indian participants in the public comment period for the Yucca Mountain site authorization decision are analyzed. This chapter has implications for how public scientific controversy is understood. Specifically, it (a) shifts our focus from the arguments of scientists to scientific arguments made by the public; (b) reveals the fluidity of boundaries between scientific and non-scientific arguments in public scientific controversies; (c) has implications for public participation in environmental decision making; and (d) challenges misconceptions about the relationship between American Indian cultures and science.

In Chapter 9, Kristen Swain examines environmental justice debates between industries and communities and how debates are framed by the media. She begins with a discussion of the tendency to build landfills and factories in areas where ethnic minorities and low-income citizens live, which exposes residents to more pollution than the population as a whole. She then examines how industry rhetoric was framed in news coverage of such siting decisions during the 1990s, when the environmental justice movement first emerged and mobilized. Kohlberg's (1973) theory of moral development and a stage model of social movements were used as frameworks for analyzing dynamics between industries and the community. Content analysis of news stories indicated that coverage of commercial industries, new facilities, and early activism could be characterized preconventional (less moral) rhetoric. Swain argues that industries did not make a consistent effort to involve activists as stakeholders until weak public pressure evolved into organized protest. At that turning point, preconventional industry rhetoric, which reflected a disregard for citizens as stakeholders, evolved into post-conventional rhetoric, which reflected greater willingness to work with citizens and transparently evaluate public risk. The chapter also maps this media coverage onto the first three stages of social movement development, to examine the nature of industry rhetoric within distinct and critical periods of grassroots activism. Overall, framing defined the environmental justice movement as a larger social issue, interpreted causes of disease and disparity, provided moral evaluations of disproportionate burden, and offered possible solutions. The implications of these findings are then discussed.

Part III, "The Future," addresses the challenges faced as colleges and universities of all sizes seek to address low levels of science literacy in their own communities. While science communication programs are becoming more common at large flagship universities, there still exists the need to serve populations that reside near the nation's smaller state schools. In order to make real gains in training science communicators who can reach these populations, smaller schools across the country need to embrace the development of courses and programs that offer such training. In the sole chapter in Part III, Amy Pearce, Aldemaro Romero, and John Zibluk talk openly about the challenges they faced in implementing a science communication program at Arkansas State University—Jonesboro.

ASU—Jonesboro is a state agricultural school serving the Arkansas Delta region, a section of the state with marked poverty. Enrollment at the university is approximately 10,000 undergraduate and 1,500 graduate students. The Tobacco Settlement Proceeds Act of 2000 ushered in a new era for the university, including the inception of the collaborative Arkansas Biosciences Institute (ABI), a major research facility built to attract researchers, professors, and graduate students to that region of the country. In this chapter, these professors—one from journalism, one from biology, and one from psychology, offer a case study of how they came together against many odds to develop a successful science communication curriculum. Ultimately, their efforts were acknowledged by the Coalition for the Public Understanding of Science. The successes offered in this chapter, as well as the challenges, underscore the benefits of pooled resources and cross-disciplinary pollination in the development of science communication education initiatives.

In sum, the three-part focus of this book allows scholars to sample the multiple paradigms and agendas that will play a role in shaping the future of science communication. These agendas map theory onto practice (and practice onto theory), explore the very identity of science and scientists, and confront the challenges of training the next generation of science communicators who will do their part to end the science illiteracy that plagues this nation. It was mentioned above that communication researchers stand poised to bring to the larger scientific endeavor an understanding of how communication works, who matters in the exchange of knowledge, and what the public brings to that exchange. This volume is a start. We challenge our readers to channel the energy within these chapters to build or continue to build their own research agendas as we all work together—across disciplines—to address these driving questions.

References

Friestad, M., & Wright, P. (1994). The Persuasion Knowledge Model: How people cope with persuasion attempts. *Journal of Consumer Research, 21*(1), 1–31.

National Science Foundation. (2006). *Science and Engineering Indicators: 2006.* Publication No. NSB 06-01. Retrieved March 15, 2009, from www.nsf.gov/statistics/seind06.

National Science Foundation. (2008). *Science and Engineering Indicators: 2008.* Publication No. NSB 08-01. Retrieved March 15, 2009, from www.nsf.gov/statistics/seind08.

Part I

Merging Theory and Practice

Models and Frameworks

Chapter 1

A Critical Appraisal of Models of Public Understanding of Science

Using Practice to Inform Theory

Dominique Brossard and Bruce V. Lewenstein

Complex scientific issues are an inherent part of modern societies and are continuously debated in the public sphere. Stem-cell research, biotechnology, and global warming—these all require regulations and, as a result, necessitate scientific as well as societal considerations. Subsequently, a basic understanding of these complex issues should be made possible for all individuals living in societies that value and respect their citizens' views. In these democratic societies, public understanding of science is central to sound processes for policy making related to controversial scientific issues.

Recognizing the importance of the ethical, legal, and social dimensions of new scientific developments, the federal government over the last 20 years has made outreach activities and public understanding of science a mandatory component of federally funded projects. The essential assumption behind these outreach projects is that greater access to information will lead to more knowledge about ethical, legal, and social issues, which in turn will lead to enhanced ability on the part of individuals and communities to deal with these issues when they encounter them. Over the same period of time, new concepts of "public understanding of science" have emerged in the theoretical realm, moving from a "deficit" or linear dissemination of popularization, to models stressing lay-knowledge, public engagement, and public participation in science policy making (Lewenstein, 2003). In the public arena, calls for "better science communication" are routinely heard.

The present study turns to the Department of Energy-funded educational projects related to the Human Genome Project, specifically the Ethical, Legal, and Social Implications (ELSI) component of that research program, to explore the ways that information about a new and emerging area of science—one that is intertwined with public issues—has been used in educational public settings to affect public understanding of science. We aim to use real-world settings to investigate if discussions taking place in the theoretical realm can be translated into practice. In other words, we will use a case-study approach as a basis to test theoretical models of science outreach in order to assess to what extent those models accord with real-world outreach activities.

This chapter is organized in the following fashion: after placing theoretical models of public communication of science in a historical and conceptual context, we will discuss the methods we used to identify and analyze real-world outreach activities as related to these models. We will conclude by discussing the lessons to be learned from our investigation and their relevance to science communication research, and by challenging a strict use of the current theoretical models in public opinion and public understanding of science-related research.

Theoretical Background

"Public understanding of science," or PUOS, is a relatively new field of scholarly inquiry that has developed since the 1980s. PUOS-related projects can roughly be placed in two broad categories: (1) projects that aim at *improving* the understanding the public(s) have of a specific area of science; (2) projects that aim at *exploring* the interaction of the public and science.

Recent efforts have focused on integrating these two by linking research findings with outreach activities. Such efforts have aimed at building conceptual models of public communication of science that could give a comprehensive view of the frameworks that are at play for research in the field, one implicit goal of which is to implement these models systematically in the practical realm of outreach.

The Deficit Model

Not surprisingly, most discussions of public understanding of science emerge from within the scientific community itself. The primary concern there has been, since at least the middle of the 19th century, the lack of intellectual public support for scientific ways of thinking and material public support for scientific work—the funds for research (Burnham, 1987; LaFollette, 1990). By the mid-1970s, these concerns led to efforts by the National Science Board that attempted to measure public knowledge of and attitudes toward science and technology (Miller, 1983a, 1983b). These surveys show that in 2002, only 10% of Americans can define "molecule," and that more than half believe that humans and dinosaurs lived on the Earth at the same time (National Science Board, 2002). Combining these factual questions with ones about the process of science and the institutional place of science has yielded measures of "science literacy" that show, depending on the year and the particular method of interpretation, that only 5% of the American public is scientifically literate, and only 20% are interested and informed. The rest, by formal definition, are "residual" (National Science Board, 1991, 1993, 1996, 1998, 2000, 2002).

Studies such as these—along with anecdotes common among the scientific community about the public's inability to understand even basic ideas of probability, skepticism, and evidence—have led to cries about the lack of knowledge, and then to new programs for providing information to fill the gap of knowledge (Royal Society, 1985; U.S. National Commission on Excellence in Education, 1983). This approach has become known as the "deficit" model, since it describes a deficit of knowledge that must be filled, with a presumption that after fixing the deficit, everything will be "better" (whatever that might mean) (Ziman, 1991, 1992). Vast and important projects to address science literacy have emerged, perhaps most notably the National Science Education Standards in the United States (American Association for the Advancement of Science, 1993; National Research Council, 1996).

However, scholars have identified a series of difficulties with the Deficit Model. Most notably, many of the questions are asked without providing a context (Wynne, 1995). In what situation with personal relevance, for example, does a non-scientist need to know the definition of DNA? Learning theory has shown that people learn best when facts and theories have meaning in their personal lives (Bransford, National Research Council Committee on Learning Research and Educational Practice, 2000); for example, research has shown that in communities with water-quality problems, even people with limited education can quickly come to understand highly complex technical information (Fessenden-Raden, Fitchen, & Heath, 1987). In addition, the interpretation that labels many people "scientifically illiterate" or "residual," while based on good political theory, highlights the power relationships between those with the particular knowledge measured by the surveys and those without. There has been little attention to other forms of knowledge that may be relevant to individuals in their real, everyday lives (Irwin & Wynne, 1996). Another critique is that, after nearly 30 years of gathering data on the public understanding of science, and after many more years of active attempts to affect public knowledge, the numbers seem remarkably stable. Approaching the problem from the perspective of "filling the deficit" doesn't seem to have been a successful approach.

As a result of these concerns, at least three other models have been developed in response to the Deficit Model: the Contextual Model, the Lay Expertise Model and the Public Engagement Model. These models are frameworks for understanding what "the problem" is, how to measure the problem, and how to address the problem. Next, we discuss the Contextual Model of public communication of science.

The Contextual Model

The Contextual Model acknowledges that individuals do not simply respond as empty containers to information, but rather process information according to social and psychological schemas that have been shaped by their previous experiences, cultural context, and personal circumstances. One common area in which the Contextual Model has been applied is risk perception and risk communication (Krimsky & Plough, 1988; National Research Council (U.S.) Committee on Risk Perception and Communication, 1989; Slovic, 1987). The model acknowledges that individuals receive information in particular contexts, which then shape how they respond to that information. Personal psychological issues may affect the context, such as stage in life or personality type (fearful, aggressive), as may the social context in which information is received (a trusting relationship with an old friend versus a confrontational relationship with a distrusted employer, for example). The Contextual Model also recognizes the ability of social systems and media representations to either dampen or amplify public concern about specific issues (Kasperson et al., 1988).

Newer approaches to the Contextual Model have attempted to use modern marketing segmentation approaches to identify populations with differing underlying attitudes toward science, without necessarily tying those groups to particular risk contexts or to levels of "science literacy" (Office of Science and Technology & Wellcome Trust, 2000). At the practical level, the Contextual Model provides guidance for constructing messages about science relevant to individuals in particular contexts, such as using messages about addiction and brain structure as a vehicle for teaching reading to low-literacy adults (who often come from personal or social settings in which drugs and addiction are common) (Baker, 1995).

The Contextual Model has been criticized for being merely a more sophisticated version of the Deficit Model: it acknowledges that audiences are not mere empty vessels but nonetheless conceptualizes a "problem" in which individuals respond to information in ways that seem inappropriate to scientific experts (Wynne, 1995). The Contextual Model recognizes the presence of social forces, but nonetheless focuses on the response of individuals to information; it highlights the psychological component of a complex social psychological setting. The recent use of marketing and demographic approaches has also raised concern that Contextual Model research is intended as a tool for manipulation of messages to achieve particular aims; the goal might not be "understanding" but "acquiescence."

In response to the Deficit and Contextual Models, researchers expressed concern that perspectives for exploring public communication of science and technology were too tied to the interests of the scientific community, which almost by definition constitutes an elite group in society. The Deficit and Contextual Models often seemed to equate "public understanding of science" with "public appreciation of the benefits provided by science to society" (Lewenstein, 1992). They did not adequately address the social and political context in which the powerful social institutions of science use "science literacy" as a rhetorical tool to influence funding and policy decisions (Hilgartner, 1990), sometimes in political opposition to labor or local interests. Since the mid-1980s, these researchers have stressed the importance of recognizing local knowledge and commitments to political inclusion and participation. From these concerns have emerged two new models: the Lay Expertise Model and the Public Engagement Model.

The Lay Expertise Model

The Lay Expertise Model begins with local knowledge, sometimes called "lay knowledge" or "lay expertise" (Wynne, 1989). This is knowledge based in the lives and histories of real communities, such as detailed local farming or agricultural practices, or historical legacies such as the cultural heritage of African Americans for whom the Tuskegee syphilis experiments are a real antecedent to contemporary opinions about trust in scientific medicine. The Lay Expertise Model argues that scientists are often unreasonably certain—even arrogant—about their level of knowledge, failing to recognize the contingencies or additional information needed to make real-world personal or policy decisions. Basing their analyses largely on case studies (Irwin & Wynne, 1996), proponents of a lay knowledge approach argue that communication activities need to be structured in ways that acknowledge information and knowledge and expertise already held by communities facing scientific and technical issues (Wynne, 1996). While ideas about indigenous knowledge systems in developing countries have not been central to the intellectual development of the Lay Expertise Model, they clearly fit comfortably with that model, as they emphasize the importance of knowledge and expertise that is held and validated by social systems other than modern science (Ellen & Harris, 1996). However, unlike approaches to indigenous knowledge systems that attempt to use modern science methods to verify traditional beliefs, the Lay Expertise Model is explicitly targeted to valuing local knowledge as expertise in its own right (Centre for Study of Environmental Change, 2001; Grove-White, Macnaghten, Mayer, & Wynne, 1997).

Like other models, the Lay Expertise Model is subject to criticism. In particular, it privileges local knowledge over reliable knowledge about the natural world produced by the modern scientific system. For that reason, it can be called "anti-science," and certainly proponents of local knowledge approaches have been targets of some of the virulent "science wars" disputes of the 1990s (Labinger & Collins, 2001). It is clearly driven by a political commitment to empowerment of local communities. It is also not clear how a model of public understanding based on lay expertise provides guidance for practical activities that can enhance public understanding of particular issues, although it does suggest that activities designed to enhance trust among participants in a policy dispute are more important than specific educational or informational approaches.

More recently, a Public Engagement Model, which does not solely rely on lay expertise but rather aims to integrate citizens' views in public policy debates, has been put forward as the most appropriate framework for public communication of science.

The Public Engagement Model

The Public Engagement model focuses on a series of activities intended to enhance public participation in science policy. These activities include consensus conferences, citizen juries, deliberative technology assessments, science shops, deliberative polling, and other techniques (see, for example, Hamlett, 2002; Wachelder, 2003; International Science Shop Network, 2003). The public participation activities are often driven by a commitment to "democratizing" science—taking control of science from elite scientists and politicians and giving it to public groups through some form of empowerment and political engagement (Sclove, 1995), although the exact nature of this empowerment has yet to be clearly defined. Not all activities envisioned by supporters of public engagement necessarily require turning over control; in the United Kingdom, the Public Engagement Model is sometimes called the "dialogue" model and is intended to highlight the importance of seeking public input into science issues, without necessarily yielding control (House of Lords, 2000; Miller, 2001). Moreover, the Public Engagement Model appears to be similar to more established techniques such as public meetings and public hearings, although formal discussion of these links has not taken place (McComas, 2001).

Because the Public Engagement Model, like the Lay Expertise Model, carries with it a commitment to a particular stance about political relations, it can be criticized for addressing politics, not public understanding. Proponents of public participation, however, counter that the Deficit Model and Contextual Models are equally political, for they link the "problem" of public understanding to individuals rather than social relations (Dornan, 1990; Jasanoff, 1997). Still, the Public Engagement Model can be criticized for focusing on the process of science and not the substantive content (though some public engagement activities, especially consensus conferences, do commit significant resources to education), for serving only small numbers of people, and sometimes for having an "anti-science" bias.

In sum, the driving force behind these four theoretical models is different. As illustrated in Figure 1.1, two of the models thrive at *delivering information* to the general public or to a specific group (Deficit and Contextual Models), while the other two are about *actively engaging citizens* with science (Lay Expertise and Public Engagement Models). Although some overlap can be identified between the Contextual and the Deficit Models on the one hand, and the Lay Knowledge and Public Engagement

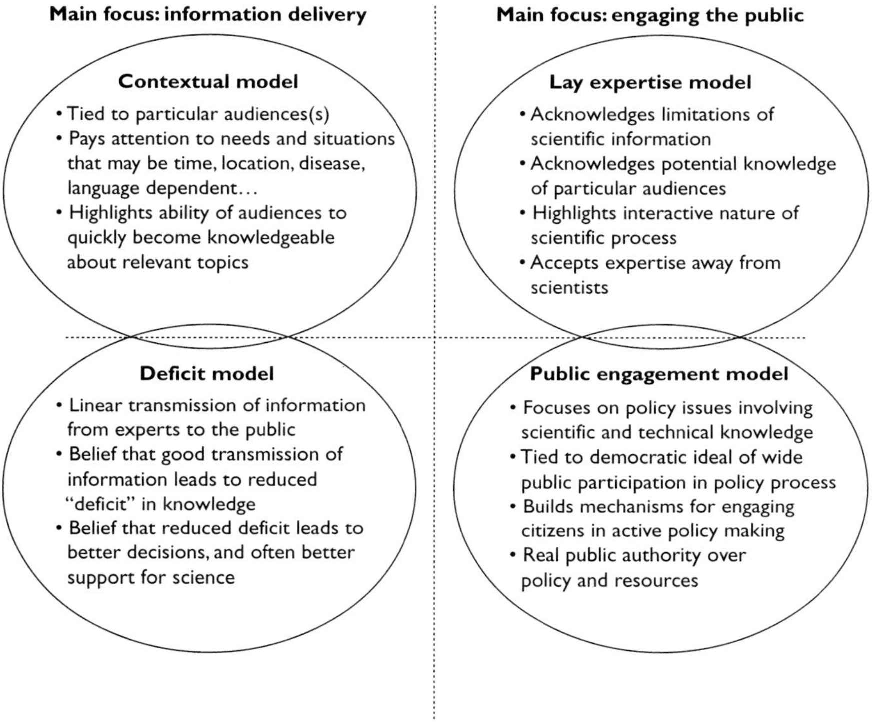

Main focus: information delivery

Main focus: engaging the public

Contextual model
- Tied to particular audiences(s)
- Pays attention to needs and situations that may be time, location, disease, language dependent…
- Highlights ability of audiences to quickly become knowledgeable about relevant topics

Lay expertise model
- Acknowledges limitations of scientific information
- Acknowledges potential knowledge of particular audiences
- Highlights interactive nature of scientific process
- Accepts expertise away from scientists

Deficit model
- Linear transmission of information from experts to the public
- Belief that good transmission of information leads to reduced "deficit" in knowledge
- Belief that reduced deficit leads to better decisions, and often better support for science

Public engagement model
- Focuses on policy issues involving scientific and technical knowledge
- Tied to democratic ideal of wide public participation in policy process
- Builds mechanisms for engaging citizens in active policy making
- Real public authority over policy and resources

Figure 1.1 Conceptual Models of Public Understanding of Science.

Models on the other, the Deficit and Contextual Models as described in the literature are conceptually distinct from the two other models presented in this chapter and described succinctly in Figure 1.1. In other words, the literature tends to describe these models as mutually exclusive and to present them as the backbone of different research and outreach paradigms of public communication of science.

In the present project, we will test whether actual outreach can be mapped onto these models as described schematically in Figure 1.1, or if other models need to be defined in order to capture the reality of practice. We will therefore use a case study method as a way to rebuild or improve theory (Burawoy et al., 1991), with the overarching goal to inform future science communication research. To do so, we will rely on a specific context: the ELSI Outreach Programs related to the Human Genome Project.

Case Study: The ELSI Outreach Programs Related to the Human Genome Project

Genomics is a good example of a context for which advances in science have implications for individuals and society at large and have to be taken into account at the policy level. Studies of ethical, legal, and social issues related to genomic research have therefore been integrated into the Human Genome Project (HGP) since the earliest days of the project at the beginning of the 1990s. Coordinated by the U.S. Department of Energy and the National Institutes of Health and concluded in 2003, the HGP aimed to:

> 1) identify all the approximately 20,000–25,000 genes in human DNA; 2) determine the sequences of the 3 billion chemical base pairs that make up human DNA; 3) store this information in databases; 4) improve tools for data analysis; 5) transfer related technologies to the private sector; and 6) address the ethical, legal, and social issues (ELSI) that may arise from the project.
>
> (U.S. Department of Energy, 2008)

Three to 5% of the Humane Genome Project's annual budget was therefore devoted to "public understanding of science" studies, under the umbrella of the Ethical, Legal, and Social Implications (ELSI) Programs of the National Human Genome Research Institute of the National Institutes of Health, and of the Office of Biological and Environmental Research of the U.S. Department of Energy (DOE). As part of the educational component, a significant portion of DOE-ELSI funds were dedicated to public outreach projects, with the underlying goal of promoting public awareness and ultimately public discussion of ethical, legal, and social issues surrounding availability of genetic information (D. Drell, personal communication).

According to grounded theory, case studies can form the basis for the development of general theories, the researcher approaching the case studies with no preconceived ideas of what they might encounter (Babbie, 2001; Strauss & Corbin, 1990). They can also be used to identify "theoretical gaps and silences" in existing theoretical frameworks (Burawoy et al., 1991, p. 10). Following this approach, our study will analyze the DOE-ELSI outreach projects to explore the following research question: Based on an assessment of how real-world outreach activities accord to the theoretical models, how can these models be refined?

Methods

Our preliminary step was to identify the projects funded by DOE-ELSI that had an outreach component (DOE-ELSI-funded programs were not exclusively outreach-related and could also tackle the following domains: privacy and fair use; clinical integration; and genetic research (ERPEG, 2000)). To do so, we downloaded from the DOE-ELSI website the abstracts of the 94 projects presented in the Human Genome Program Contractor–Grantee workshops in 1994, 1996, 1997, 1999, and 2000 (workshops IV to VIII; abstracts of projects funded prior to 1994 were not available). We then performed a content analysis of these abstracts to determine (1) the nature of the project (educational or other); (2) its primary intended audience; (3) the primary public communication of science model into which the project conceptually fitted; and (4) the main communication medium used for outreach in the project (for detailed methods, see DOE-ELSI, 2003).

To explore our research question, and based on the results of the content analysis, we selected from the educational-focused subsample four case projects that matched the following criteria: (1) the outreach project had an adult lay population as target audience (in other words, projects targeting professional groups were to be excluded since our goal was to discuss issues raised by public understanding of ethical, legal, and social issues related to genomics research in everyday life, i.e., outside a professional context); (2) the outreach project loosely fit within one of the four theoretical models of public communication of science presented earlier; (3) each outreach project selected used a different communication medium; (4) the selected project was completed, in order to be able to compare objectives and outcomes.[1]

Each of the four selected case projects was thoroughly analyzed (for detailed methods, see DOE-ELSI, 2003). First, we conducted 21 semi-structured interviews with project leaders and selected audience members. In this type of interview, the interviewer has a series of specific questions to be raised during an informal conversation with the interviewee (Leech, 2002). We analyzed the content of all outreach document drafts available following a chronological timeline, in order to identify if the project goals had evolved overtime. We also tracked and examined evaluative research that might have been performed on the project, and analyzed the final report submitted to DOE-ELSI officers. When applicable, we tracked public use of Web documents related to the project. Finally, we analyzed the final outreach materials used by each project to reach the target population (book chapters, articles, conference proceedings, emails, etc.) in order to identify the content themes tackled through the project.

Results and Discussion

In accordance with DOE-ELSI's stated goal of promoting education for genetic information-related issues, the majority of the 94 1994–2000

DOE-ELSI-funded projects had an educational component (76 of the 94 funded projects).

Among these 76 outreach projects, 23% were geared toward a youth audience, and/or specifically high school students. The same percentage of projects was geared toward professional groups (excluding teachers). Roughly 20% of the projects were designed for a general adult audience. Only 2.7% of the outreach projects targeted low-literacy adults. In line with conventional wisdom, a majority of the outreach projects (76%) fell within the Deficit Model. Roughly 20% loosely followed the Contextual Model. The "Lay Knowledge" and "Public Engagement" models were the main frameworks used by only 5% of the projects, respectively.

As a next step, and based on the above results, we chose four outreach case projects for in-depth analysis. Table 1.1 below presents these four projects and outlines the public communication of science model they seem to follow, their primary target audience, their main communication medium, and the project timeline. The following sections will discuss each of these projects in detail.

Table 1.1 Projects Selected for In-depth Analysis and Related Characteristics

Projects selected for case study	Public communication of science model*	Target audience*	Main communication medium	Timeline
The Geneletter	Deficit model	General public	Web newsletter	1996–1999
Challenges of Genome Research for Minority Communities	Contextual model	Minorities, mainly the African American community	Conferences	2001–2002
A Question of Genes	Lay knowledge model	General public	Television documentaries	Aired November 1997
The Hispanic Radio and Science Education Outreach	Contextual/ public engagement models	Hispanic community	Radio programs	1996–1999

Note
*As defined in the initial description of the project; these might have evolved over time.

Project 1—Deficit Model: the Geneletter

Case Background

Supported by DOE-ELSI funds from 1996 through April 1999, *Geneletter* intended to reach a broad public audience by reporting on scientific, ethical, legal, and social aspects of genetics through a Web-based newsletter. The idea of Phillip Reilly (Director of the Shriver Center at that time, and co-PI of the project with Dorothy Wertz), was that whoever used the Internet for public education about genetics and ethics would have power over public education. *Geneletter* published 10 issues on its site at www.geneletter.org, from July 1996 to February 1999. After that period (and ending with the DOE funding), the *Geneletter* was turned over to GeneSage (a California-based Internet start-up, aimed at genetic professionals) in return for a $20,000 donation to Shriver Center.

Each issue of the *Geneletter* included one or more of the following types of pieces: updates on scholarly conferences (5% of total pieces); updates on community events/community education/websites of interest (2.3%); book reviews (8%); new articles (79%); and case studies (5%).

A content analysis of the 196 pieces published between July 1996 and February 1999 confirmed that *Geneletter* addressed a wide range of issues, in line with the DOE-ELSI research agenda. Roughly 20% to 25% of the new articles had as main focus respectively "ethical issues," "legal issues," "social issues," and "scientific issues," indicating that the *Geneletter*'s content was in line with its stated objective.

Geneletter editors kept records of Web traffic statistics. According to the *Geneletter* final report, the average number of hits on the *Geneletter* webpage per day between September 18, 1996 and October 26, 1999 was 1,857. Starting with the March 1997 issue, which contained articles on the ethics of cloning, readership shot up to an average 5,000 site visits per week and remained there until the site was transferred from the Shriver Center in October 1999. The average user session lasted 7 minutes. The audience was broad, including a range from sixth-graders to college graduate individuals. According to the co-PI of the project Dorothy Wertz, "no visible difference in knowledge was apparent between the groups, as shown by the types of questions asked through e-mail or chatbox" (D. Wertz, personal communication).

Users' feedback was made possible through two channels: a chatbox and direct emails to the editors. The chatbox did not prove to be effective at promoting discussion, as numerous technical problems were encountered and only 200 items were posted in 3 years. As pointed out in the *Geneletter* final report, "it appears that although people were eager to seek information from the editors via email, comparatively few were eager to 'chat' about issues related to genetics."

Indeed, users did ask a wide variety of questions through the "Letter to the Editor" feature, i.e., emails. The editors received over 800 inquiries through this medium. A content analysis of a random sample of 177 emails sent to the editors produced the following results: 21% expressed support for the *Geneletter* webpage and 24% were related to education (i.e., school project, course content, graduate work). However, 12.4% addressed a theme not related to *Geneletter* content. As noted by Dorothy Wertz, "readers' queries focused on popular science issues (cloning, Jurassic Park) rather than on ethical concerns" (D. Wertz, personal communication).

Whenever possible, the editors made a point of answering readers' queries. Many of the emails, however, asked very broad questions (and were therefore hard to answer, according to the editors) such as "Tell me everything you know about the Human Genome Project." One may therefore wonder to what extent the content of the *Geneletter*'s articles was appropriate for the knowledge level of a fraction of the readership.

The initial project ended with DOE-ELSI funding in October 1999. *Geneletter* resumed its publication in February 2000, with a new editor, Paul Billing, and with financial support from GeneSage, Inc. *Geneletter* had lost a lot of readership by then, but eventually got back on track. *Geneletter*'s targeted audience shifted to primary-care physicians. Articles were written by staff and freelance writers, and the format of the letter changed. According to Dorothy Wertz, the quality of articles varied. Sixteen issues were published between February 2000 and May 2001 (one per month). The project ran out of funds in January 2001, and the last four issues ran previously used material. Dorothy Wertz did want to insure the continuation of the project as it was initially set up (and geared toward a broad audience), but was unsuccessful at getting *Geneletter* back to the Shriver Center.

Case Study in Relationship with the Theoretical Models

Geneletter essentially followed the Deficit Model, at least in principle. *Geneletter* aimed to increase public understanding of ethical, legal, and social issues related to genomics, the editors defining the themes to be covered and addressing a broad range of ethical, legal, and social issues related to genomics research. No specific audience was targeted, the editors aiming to reach all interested individuals. This approach seemed to be successful: (1) readership of the newsletter was broad, and included a range from sixth-graders to college graduate individuals; (2) the site had 5,000 visits per week (after March 1997), the average user session lasting 7 minutes, a reasonably high number for a specialized newsletter; (3) the themes raised by the readership in the "Letters to The Editor" were in line with the content of the articles posted online. However, the content of the emails did raise the question of the level of information that should be provided to a broad audience.

Still, although at first glance *Geneletter* broadly followed the Deficit Model of public communication of science, it did provide information in context, which critics often claim deficit approaches do not attempt to do. Most of the articles (particularly those using a "case study" format to address ethical issues) provided information in a clear and simple way and made this information as relevant as possible to readers' lives. In other words, *Geneletter* displayed some characteristics usually not outlined in theoretical accounts of Deficit Model approaches and were actually in line with the Contextual Model.

Another feature of the project illustrates that the Deficit Model label does not accurately describe the *Geneletter*. Project leaders and readership did interact through emails, and readership was, to some extent, encouraged to "engage" with science, to use the project leaders' own words. As pointed out earlier, "engagement" and public empowerment are the main goals of the Public Engagement Model. We did mention earlier how this term is conceptually vague, because it can range from sparking interest among the public, to engaging citizens in decision-making procedures related to science. Although obviously we do not know to what extent *Geneletter* did spark public participation in decisions related to scientific issues, the project does suggest that the boundaries between the Deficit model and the Public Engagement models may not be as drastic as sometimes described in academic realms.

In sum, the analysis of the *Geneletter* shows that the Deficit Model does not fully capture the reality of this type of outreach. A project that, at first glance, might have appeared to be a traditional deficit approach had characteristics that made it fit in several theoretical models.

Project 2—Contextual Model: "The Challenges and Impact of Human Genome Research for Minority Communities Conferences"

Case Background

The National Educational Foundation of Zeta Phi Beta Sorority, Inc. received support from DOE-ELSI to sponsor conferences specifically geared toward minority communities. Five major conferences took place between 1999 and 2001 in New Orleans, Philadelphia, Atlanta, and Washington, DC, three of them funded by DOE-ELSI.

The conferences broadly aimed to involve minorities with science and genetics. The goals were to provide minority community members with information about the Human Genome Project and to find out minorities' concerns related to current genomic research. The conferences also aimed at getting minority college students interested in the areas of genetics, biotechnology, and related sciences.

We focused our in-depth analysis on the Philadelphia (July 7–8, 2000) conference. Leaders of the conference were Issie L. Jenkins, Esq., Zeta Foundation chair and Kathryn Malvern, conference project director. A planning committee developed the program for the conference. An advisory council (composed of around 25 representatives from minority organizations, governmental agencies, health organizations, churches, and educational institutions) provided feedback during program development and was in charge of information dissemination to communities.

According to Jenkins,

> the committee advisory groups [were] very instrumental in identifying people in that community who could be a part of the program ... and in raising questions that might be of interest to them so that [they] might be included in the program.
>
> (I.L. Jenkins, personal communication)

They were also instrumental in getting community members to attend the conference because community leaders, such as ministers, could encourage individuals to attend who might otherwise be left out of the process.

The conference combined experts' presentations and panel discussions, workshops, and public discussions. Organizers succeeded in creating a very mixed group of presenters (researchers, DEO representatives, private researchers, sociologists, anthropologists, educators). According to the organizers, general scientific information and terminology (e.g., genes, proteins) was first provided in order to make the presentation of the Human Genome Project—and its potential benefits and ethical, legal, and social implications—easier to understand. Follow-up workshops covered a variety of topics related to minorities and genetics and aimed at producing a list of concerns and recommendations. Handouts and free copies of the book *Your Genes, Your Choices: Exploring the Issues Raised by Genetic Research* (Baker, 1997) (both provided by DOE) were made available to conference participants. The conference proceedings were posted online on the DOE-ELSI webpage.

There was very little newspaper, television, or radio coverage prior to the conference, with advertising restricted to flyers and mailings. The organizers reached out to the community members by contacting organizations directly, and by providing them with materials and registration forms to give to their members. Kathryn Malvern reported the following story (K. Malvern, personal communication):

> So I was telling you the story about the judge in PA, she said, "Dr. Malvern, you are not going to get the Chinese community this time, because they are all focused on Chinatown." [The judge] said, "I will be the conduit," and she was for what was happening, and she would

be part of whatever happened later. She was there at the conference, she had all the material.... So I am saying, you must have a true leader ... she has kept that community involved.

Attendance exceeded expectations. The conference was attended each day by 250 individuals representing, among others, minority organizations, civic groups, religious groups, leaders in health communication, local government officials, and students. Roughly three-quarters of the audience was composed of African Americans.

Some 55 attendees requested to serve as future community liaison coordinators, and signed up to be trained as such at the end of the conference. Participants were also asked to fill out evaluation surveys, which was done by 83 attendees. Of those, 88% felt the conference was very successful at imparting useful information to members of their groups (8.4% somewhat useful; 2.4% don't know), 67.5% felt they had learned a great deal about the science being done on the HGP (25% a little). Roughly 55% of respondents said that they learned a great deal about the ethical implications of the HGP, about the potential harmful effects of the HGP for minority groups, about the social implications of the HGP, and about the potential benefits of the HGP for minority groups (35% a little).

As far as attitudes toward the potential effects of the HGP, 48.7% felt that the benefits would be greater than the harmful effects, while 15.4% felt the harmful effects would be greater than the benefits; 80.8% were concerned about the availability of genetic information to employers; 79.7% were concerned about the availability of genetic information to insurers; 78.9% were concerned that HGP benefits would be available only to privileged groups.

The conference seemed therefore to have achieved the goal of informing its audience and raising awareness of the potential benefits and harmful effects of the HGP for minority communities. However, the percentages reported above should be interpreted with caution, because only 33% of the attendees (assuming that the same 250 people attended the conference every day) filled in the evaluation survey. The project did succeed in initiating the propagation of HGP-related information to minority communities beyond the conference itself. The fact that 55 of the conference attendees signed up to become community liaison coordinators demonstrates that the conference motivated some individuals to reach out to their communities, which was ultimately the goal of the conference.

Case Study in Relationship with the Theoretical Models

The project broadly followed the "Contextual Model" of public communication of science. As explained in an earlier section, according to this model, researchers identify populations that might have different underlying

ing attitudes and concerns related to genomics research without necessarily tying those groups to particular risk contexts or to levels of "science literacy." Outreach projects are then built in a way that is relevant to these audiences. The conference focused on minority needs and concerns.

What is particularly interesting is that the conference was used as a setting not only for the dissemination of relevant information, but also to find out the characteristics of the particular context at play. For instance, the Rev. Dr. Deborah Wolfe, a conference panelist, produced 14 questions for which she requested answers at the conference. As she put it:

> Since, as you know, I did not participate in bringing about this great discovery [the genetic code] and since I really know so little about the details of the study, all I can do as a teacher, as a preacher, as an interested citizen is to raise questions to you who are specialists.
>
> (Jenkins, personal communication)

The meetings with the community liaisons were also a place where specific minority concerns could be identified. Kathryn Malvern synthesized this point in the following way:

> You see, we don't necessarily know all minority issues. Take for instance the Hispanics, their morals and culture can be different and when we think in terms of something that happens in the community, we could think that it is negative when for them it is a positive thing. Therefore it is important to get their leaders involved, so that we can more easily understand [the context] and get into those communities.
>
> (K. Malvern, personal communication)

Philadelphia conference organizers and community liaisons did share the goal of providing useful information to their community through outreach. But as David Lieu (from the organization State of the Arts Inc. and one of the community liaisons) put it, "the challenge was that people [had] a different interpretation of outreach. Everybody was going towards a goal, but using different ways to get there" (D. Lieu, personal communication).

Not surprisingly, the project borrowed some features of the Deficit Model, by providing background knowledge a priori defined by experts. The goal was to help the audience grasp the basic scientific content needed to be able to constructively discuss ethical, legal, and social issues related to genomic research and its applications. As discussed previously, critics have argued that the Contextual Model is at best an "improved" Deficit Model, since it still posits expert knowledge to be the correct one and conceptualizes a "problem" in which individuals respond to information in ways that seem inappropriate to scientific experts. However, as our case study points out, the community members themselves seek scientists' input, based on the assumption that some scientific knowledge was necessary for conference participants to be able to raise meaningful questions. In this case, the goal was not, as argued by critics of the Contextual Model, to fix lack of knowledge among lay publics, but rather to bring all audience members to a shared level of basic knowledge before discussing specific concerns. One may argue then that the conference was more of an "empowerment" tool, following the philosophy of the Public Engagement Model, since it broadly aimed to involve minorities with science and genetics. However, the goals of the organizers were very pragmatic and did not seem to have political motivations: to help minority members understand the science behind the genome project, to allow them to raise their concerns, and to get answers, if any, from a group of experts from various backgrounds.

Project 3—Lay Expertise Model: "A Question of Genes"

Case Study Background

On September 16, 1997, a special program developed with funds from DOE-ELSI, entitled "A Question of Genes: Inherited Risks," aired on national public television. Through case studies, this documentary aimed at exploring the dramatic social and ethical dilemmas raised by genetic testing, and at appealing to a broad audience. The general philosophy of the documentary was "to tell what the technology [meant], not what it [did]" (N. Schwerin, personal communication).

The project was developed at the initiative of the filmmaker Noel Schwerin, who had worked previously on science-related documentaries (for programs such as NOVA, in particular) and who performed all the background research necessary for the program. Schwerin then brought the project to an executive producer, Angier Production, to work on a proposal to be submitted to DOE.

Two types of outreach materials were developed in the context of the project: first, the documentary that was aired on national television, and second, a website developed concurrently to provide additional information and links relevant to the topic at hand.

The documentary provided a series of seven profiles, or case studies, of people "like you and me" that had had to deal with issues related to genetic testing in the course of their lives. The filmmaker had the individuals directly share their personal experiences—there was no narrator. As Schwerin put it: "I believe that they are the experts... They had the real data" (N. Schwerin, personal communication).

The seven profiles presented in the documentary were given equal weight, although they did not all present the same point of view. The goal was to get the audience to think about the issue and the ethical implications of such situations, while presenting only the science that was needed to understand the case study. Schwerin pointed out that it was often "tricky to give just enough information as not to get confused" (N. Schwerin, personal communication). In some cases, the individual recounted his/her experience and provided necessary scientific information. In others, a doctor or expert presented relevant background information. In some instances, additional information was provided at the end of the case study through a scroll-down text.

The seven case studies were also presented on the website related to the project, giving interested viewers the opportunity to find out more about the issues at hand. Video clips with audio were posted for each case study—users could also read transcripts of the scripts. Each case study was also accompanied by a link to an educator's guide specific to that topic, as well as links to a discussion forum. Users could post comments and questions to the discussion forum from September 16 to October 13, 1997. During this period, users were able to interact with a panel of participants from the TV program, which included physicians, patients, and researchers.

It is hard to assess the size of the audience that viewed the program when it aired on national television, although it did have the potential to reach millions of individuals. It seems reasonable to assume that the audience was typical for such TV shows broadcast on PBS in the late 1990s. PBS reached at that time 90 million viewers a week, an audience that reflected the U.S. population in terms of race/ethnicity, education, and income (PBS, 2009).

The educator's guides (provided through the website) were distributed to 66,000 professionals in genetics, ethics, biology, public health, and related fields. Results from a bounced-back survey card (223 responses) provided with the educator guide indicated that 63% of the respondents were professors or teachers. Additionally, the website had 40,000 hits in its first 3 months, very high traffic for such a show. Some evaluation of the TV program was provided through the bounce-back survey cards and through phone interviews with a sample of those who had been provided with the education guide (94 interviews). Respondents, overall, gave very positive feedback on "A Question of Genes," 92% of the respondents indicating that the program was excellent. More than 85% of the respondents indicated that they had or would use "A Question of Genes" as an educational resource; 92% videotaped the program for future use; of those, 80% said that they would recommend it to their students.

The timing of the project was perfect for the format used in the program. Since media coverage about these issues was still minimal, people were more genuine and more eager to share their experiences. According to Schwerin, "it was an amazing opportunity to find out how people felt about these issues" (N. Schwerin, personal communication).

As shown by the evaluation data and the press coverage, "A Question of Genes" was a highly successful documentary that won several awards. Not only was the documentary used as a TV program and discussed through the website; anecdotal evidence shows that it is also in demand for use in high schools and other educational settings. Schwerin has been invited to talk about the film at the University of California at Berkley and Stanford University, and a screening of sections of the film were shown at a meeting of the American Association for the Advancement of Science, for an audience of bioethicists.

Case Study in Relationship with the Theoretical Models

"A Question of Genes" exemplifies how the Lay Expertise Model for public communication of science can be used in an outreach setting. As we discussed earlier, proponents of a lay knowledge approach argue that communication activities need to be structured in ways that acknowledge information, knowledge, and expertise already held by communities or individuals about science and technology issues they face. Despite criticisms of this model, this case study demonstrates that it might be a good way to approach issues that do have high relevance in people's lives and that might provoke strong feelings. In other words, as Schwerin argued, having "real people" explain how they dealt with genetic counseling will explain "what the technology means, not what it does." If this is the goal of the outreach, a "lay knowledge" approach might be the way to go.

In line with the conclusions reached for the other projects, this case study also reveals some overlaps between the theoretical models we presented earlier, by fostering participants' engagement with science. Showing overlap between the lay knowledge and public engagement models, the TV program led viewers to go to the website and to get the educators guide, likely in order to use it in other settings. The project also provided the scientific information necessary for the audience to be able to understand the case studies. In that sense it did share some of the characteristics usually attributed to the "Deficit Model" of public communication of science. Finally, the project displayed some characteristics of the Contextual Model, in that it paid attention to the needs of particular audiences, the people for whom genetic counseling might be particularly relevant. By emphasizing what the technology meant and what it did, i.e., by focusing on attitudes rather than on knowledge, the project successfully went beyond the Deficit Model.

Project 4—Contextual/Public Engagement Models: "The Hispanic Radio and Science Education Outreach"

Case Background

In 1998, the Self Reliance Foundation (SRF), a nonprofit organization connecting Hispanics in the United States with informational resources, got three years of funding from DOE-ELSI to develop a series of radio shows focusing on the HGP, its scientific, medical, and ELSI implications, and complementary outreach projects. The shows were to be broadcast on the Hispanic Radio Network (a Spanish-speaking radio network). The overall goal was to "help inform the Spanish-speaking population in the U.S. about the HGP and its ELSI implications, and motivate them to access the resources available for further education and information on these issues" (Self Reliance Foundation Robert Purcell, personal communication).

From February 1998 to February 2000, the project developed more than 75 brief (1–2-minute) radio programs that were broadcast on three radio shows of the Hispanic Radio Network: 30 programs through "Fuente de Salud" (carried by 36 station affiliates); 10 programs though "Planeta Azul" (carried by 96 station affiliates); and 10 programs through "Saber is Poder" (carried by 31 station affiliates). These programs covered the following themes: Hispanic individuals involved in aspects of genome research and its implications; economic implications of genome science; bio-industry involvement in the genetic revolution; and encouragement of Hispanic students to pursue science and biotechnology careers. The project also developed three hour-long shows for the radio talk show "Mundo 2000" (carried by 17 affiliates), in which Spanish-speaking experts in genetics discussed a number of issues and answered audience questions.

An 800 telephone number was listed at the end of the radio programs. A bilingual operator would answer the call and use a database of over 15,000 local organizations, ranging from health clinics to science museums, to provide additional referral information. The goal of the 800 number was to link people to information sources useful to their needs. Finally, the project used the syndicated newspaper column "La Columna Vertebral," syndicated in 82 Spanish-language newspapers, to provide information about genomics and its implications.

Although no data are available concerning the audience for DOE-funded programs, general information about the syndicated programs is: "Fuente de Salud" reaches an estimated 48.9% of the Hispanic population of the United States, "Planeta Azul" 86.4%, "Saber es Poder" 46.2%, and "Mundo 2000" 20.9%. The column reaches 2.5 million readers overall.

In 2001, SRF started to broaden its outreach to involve a greater mix of components. Its new philosophy was to use the radio program to get people interested in a specific topic, and help them follow up on their interests. One of SRF's most recent projects is "Celebre la Ciencia" (celebrate the science), which is funded by the National Science Foundation. For that project, SRF tries to combine traditional media (radio, newspapers, etc.) and high-profile events, like community festivals. Information on why science is important and how families can get involved is presented in the media, with examples of science museums, zoos, and other family-friendly settings. In recent years, SRF had six science-related organizations represented at the Mount Pleasant festival in Mount Pleasant, MD. Notices were posted on the radio, and local TV news programs announced the event.

Case Study in Relationship with the Theoretical Models

The project clearly fits into the Contextual Model of public communication about science, because it was specifically geared toward the Hispanic population and tailored to their needs and attitudes. Because Hispanics made up 12.5% of the population in 2000, and were the fastest growing minority in the United States (U.S. Census Bureau, 2006), the project intended specifically to reach and inform that audience. According to the organizers, data had also shown that a significant fraction of this minority felt discriminated against by the U.S. health-care system. Radio seemed an appropriate medium since it appears that most of the Latino population has good access to it—greater access than lower-income African American families (Arbitron, 2005).

The project also had a public engagement component. The purpose of using the toll-free number was to promote a self-informational process for the audience of the radio shows. The SRF clearly intended to go beyond informational engagement, as the follow-up projects demonstrated, by promoting active participation of Hispanic families in science activities, such as the ones displayed in science museums, and therefore increase general interest in scientific issues and, potentially, policy-making involvement. In short, the project clearly did not fit exclusively into one of the theoretical models as presented in the academic literature.

Conclusion and Lessons for Research Agendas

The goal of the present study was to assess whether theoretical models routinely discussed in the public communication literature are a good reflection of outreach efforts in the public realm. Our objective was to use practice to inform theory and to identify areas of research that should be integrated in new agendas for science communication research.

Our analysis of specific outreach projects related to the ELSI of genome research showed that although the scholarly literature tends to present the theoretical models outlined in our first section as incommensurable and as reflecting different research and outreach paradigms, practice is likely to be more pragmatic, with projects adopting parts of each model to suit different contexts. We found that a "contextual project" does attempt to provide information and to promote understanding of a scientific issue. It can also aim more particularly at shifting attitudes toward using scientific knowledge, rather than at specifically increasing knowledge. Alternatively, a project that fit the "lay knowledge" approach did display characteristics compatible with the "public engagement" model, by actively encouraging participants to seek more information about genetic counseling and by encouraging involvement in science.

In sum, we argue that theoretical approaches to public communication of science do not capture the complexity of the reality of informal science education projects. Our somewhat limited analysis (we focused on four projects) did unveil an overlap between models traditionally presented as incommensurable in theoretical discussions. Projects tended to use mixed approaches that blended models, rather than gravitating toward any one well-defined framework.

Figure 1.2 presents the public communication of science models as experienced in the outreach settings. All outreach projects tended to use the Deficit Model approach as a backbone, even if they seemed to follow other theoretical approaches. Contextual projects aim not only at increasing knowledge, but also at discussing the audience's attitudes toward science and scientists. Public engagement with science was fostered at different levels: (1) through a simple interaction between citizens and scientific experts; (2) through the empowerment of citizens to voice their viewpoints; and (3) by providing real public authority over policy.

Several of our findings have important implications for science communication research. First, our analysis highlighted the importance of defining the public(s) of interest for any type of communication effort (and by extension any type of science communication research context). This might at first glance seem like a given, since as discussed previously, theoretical models do acknowledge that science audiences differ on a number of characteristics and do give different weight to these audiences. But it is important to reiterate that a crucial element of science communication resides in the level of commitment of the publics under consideration. Not all citizens want to be involved in science decision making, nor should they be; nor do all scientists want to participate in the communication of science. In short, research should not rely on a priori characterizations of science audiences and should carefully assess all contexts of inquiry.

Second, all case studies shared the goal of communicating accurate scientific information to an audience (whether this audience was the general public or a specific group), even when lay expertise or public engagement were put forward as the focus of the project. However, although all project organizers acknowledged that an understanding of scientific concepts was a prerequisite to any type of discussions about the ELSI of genomics research,

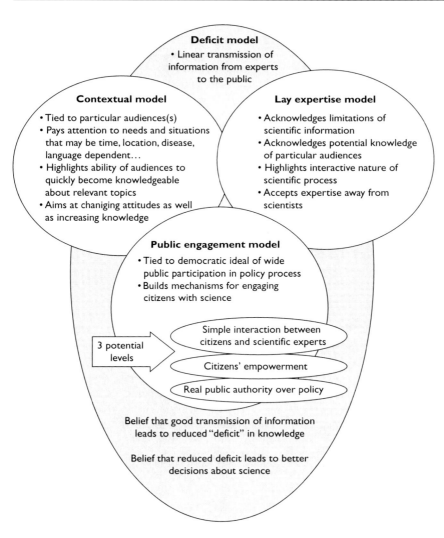

Figure 1.2 Public Communication Models in the Outreach Setting.

there was no consensus among project organizers about the level and type of knowledge to be fostered. In fact, this was reflective of the lack of consensus at that time about what constitutes an "adequate" knowledge of genetics, a point that was brought up in 2000 by the ELSI Research Planning and Evaluation Group (ERPEG). The ERPEG report noted, "a major gap in DOE-ELSI education and resources portfolio is the absence of studies that examine basic issues such as what each audience (students, teachers, nurses, judges, lay public) actually needs to know about genetics and ELSI" (ERPEG, 2000).

This conclusion, reached in 2000, is still valid today and has implications for science communication research agendas. We live in a world in which "scientific citizens," to borrow a term coined by Alan Irwin (2001), are increasingly expected to express viewpoints on a variety of controversial topics having technological dimensions (such as stem-cell research, biotechnology, nanotechnology, biofuels), while what constitutes scientific literacy and how to measure it is still under debate. Understanding this dynamic should continue to be a major priority of research agendas in science communication (for a recent discussion on scientific literacy, see Brossard & Shanahan, 2006).

More broadly, the relationship between levels of understanding of technological innovations and public attitudes toward these issues should also continue to be analyzed. Recent research has shown that levels of knowledge do indeed matter, but in a more complex way than previously thought. Individuals are likely to use their existing knowledge to form attitudes, but will tend to interpret scientific information differently by relying on pre-existing value predispositions as filtering tools (Brossard, Kim, Scheufele, & Lewenstein, 2008; Ho, Brossard, & Scheufele, 2008). Most of the research exploring the link between knowledge and attitudes has traditionally been performed in predominantly quantitative methodological settings, while relying on measures of knowledge that were for the most part conceptualized by experts. This line of research would benefit from insights provided by the Lay Expertise Model, while integrating qualitative and quantitative methods of inquiry. In a nutshell, we should develop measures of scientific knowledge that take into account relevance and context (time and place) and that relate to a specific objective, and we should continue to research scientific literacy and knowledge-production mechanisms. This will be made possible by building bridges between research paradigms.

Third, our analysis highlighted a concept often put forward in recent debates related to public communication of science, the notion of "public engagement." What is "public engagement" in the context of science-related activities, and what type of engagement can these projects reasonably aim at increasing are both questions worth asking in science communication research. Although educators (and outreach specialists) might conceptualize "engagement in science" very pragmatically as "interest" and "involvement," academics and policy makers tend to give the term a political dimension. The analysis of our case studies demonstrates that citizens can be engaged in science (and ultimately in science policy) at different levels. First, individuals can engage in a simple interaction with experts to discuss scientific issues and their ethical implications (e.g., *Geneletter* emails). Second, individuals can be empowered through different public participation processes (e.g., "A Question of Genes" project; the minority conferences). Third, citizens can be given authority for decision making about science policy. In this case, scientific experts are to some extent disempowered. This form of engagement is the one traditionally put forward through the Public Engagement Model. Although it is encountered in some public communication of science instances (e.g., consensus conferences), we did not identify it within the DOE-ELSI educational portfolio. This is interesting considering the fact that wide public engagement is the ultimate goal in current discussions related to nanotechnology and other controversial innovations.

As science communication researchers, we need to acknowledge that citizens can indeed become engaged, but not always when we want them to (for a discussion, see Brossard & Shanahan, 2003). Research on public engagement in science within different contexts (conceptualization and operationalization) should therefore be one of our priorities. Political science has for decades examined the concept of public engagement. Here again, science communication research will be fruitful if it builds bridges between different research paradigms.

Finally, science communication research should focus on interpersonal processes. The minority conferences used in this chapter relied on community opinion leaders to build effective communication contexts and on different discussion settings to foster dialogue and shared understanding. Methodologically sound research on the role of interpersonal discussions in science communication is yet to be published, although it has been the focus of numerous research studies in other fields of inquiry. The role of opinion leaders in science communication is also ripe for focus in our field.

In sum, theoretical perspectives in science communication research need to take into account the permeable boundaries between theoretical models and continue to reach toward other fields of inquiry. Practice may be achieving what academics and researchers still need to accomplish: breaking down the walls that separate paradigms and building bridges between them where useful and effective.

Acknowledgment

This material is based upon work supported by the U.S. Department of Energy under Grant No. DE-FG02-01ER63173. Any opinions, findings, and conclusions or recommendations expressed in this material are those of the authors and do not necessarily reflect the views of the U.S. Department of Energy.

Note

1. It should be noted that no formalized sampling methodology was applied to the selection of the case projects, since we were not aiming to generalize conclusions to other projects.

References

American Association for the Advancement of Science (AAAS). (1993). *Benchmarks for science literacy*. New York: Oxford University Press.

American Association for the Advancement of Science (AAAS). (2003). *Featured projects: Science + Literacy for Health; The Human Genome Project*. Retrieved April 10, 2003, from http://ehrweb.aaas.org/ehr/3_1_0.html.

Arbitron. (2005). *Ethnic time spent listening*. Retrieved October 1, 2008, from www.Arbitron.com/advertisers/home.htm.

Babbie, E. (2001). *The practice of social research*. Belmont, CA: Wadsworth.

Baker, C. (1995). *The brain book: Your brain and your health*. Washington, DC: American Association for the Advancement of Science.

Baker, C. (1997). *Your genes, your choices: Exploring the issues raised by genetic research*. Washington, DC: American Association for the Advancement of Science.

Bransford, J., Brown, A. L., National Research Council (U.S.) Committee on Developments in the Science of Learning, Cocking, R. R., & National Research Council (U.S.) Committee on Learning Research and Educational Practice. (2000). *How people learn: Brain, mind, experience, and school* (expanded ed.). Washington, DC: National Academy Press.

Brossard, D., Kim, E., Scheufele, D. A., & Lewenstein, B. V. (2008). Religiosity as a perceptual filter: Examining processes of opinion formation about nanotechnology. *Public Understanding of Science*. Retrieved April 10, 2009, from http://pus.sagepub.com/cgi/rapidpdf/0963662507087304v2.pdf.

Brossard, D., & Shanahan, J. (2003). Do citizens want to have their say? Media, agricultural biotechnology, and authoritarian views of democratic processes in science. *Mass Communication and Society, 3*(6), 291–312.

Brossard, D., & Shanahan, J. (2006). Do they know what they read? Building a scientific literacy measurement instrument based on science media coverage. *Science Communication, 28*, 47–63.

Burawoy, M., Burton, A., Ferguson, A., Fox, K. J., Gamson, J., Gartrell, N., et al. (Eds.). (1991). *Ethnography unbound: Power and resistance in the modern metropolis*. Berkeley, CA: University of California Press.

Burnham, J. (1987). *How superstition won and science lost: Popularizing science and health in the United States*. New Brunswick, NJ: Rutgers University Press.

Centre for Study of Environmental Change. (2001). *Public attitudes to agricultural biotechnologies in Europe: Final report of PABE project*. Lancaster: Centre for Study of Environmental Change, Lancaster University.

Department of Energy. (2003). *Assessing models of public understanding in ELSI outreach material: Final report*. U.S. Department of Energy Grant DE-FG02-01ER63173.

DOE-ELSI. (2003). Ethical, legal, and social issues research: ELSI research funded by the U.S. Department of Energy—Abstracts from DOE Human Genome Program contractor–grantee workshops. Retrieved April 10, 2009, from www.ornl.gov/TechResources/Human_Genome/research/elsi.html.

Dornan, C. (1990). Some problems in conceptualizing the issue of "science and the media." *Critical Studies in Mass Communication, 7*(1), 48–71.

Ellen, R. F., & Harris, H. J. (1996). Concepts of indigenous environmental knowledge in scientific and development studies literature: A critical assessment. Retrieved 27 March, 2003, from http://lucy.ukc.ac.uk/Rainforest/SML_files/ Occpap/indigknow.occpap_TOC.html.

ERPEG. (2000). The ELSI Research Planning and Evaluation Group (ERPEG) report. Retrieved June 5, 2009, from www.genome.gov/10001727.

Fessenden-Raden, J., Fitchen, J., & Heath, J. (1987). Providing risk information in communities: Factors influencing what is heard and accepted. *Science, Technology & Human Values, 12*(3/4), 94–101.

Grove-White, R., Macnaghten, P., Mayer, S., & Wynne, B. (1997). *Uncertain world: Genetically modified organisms, food and public attitudes in Britain* (in association with Unilever). Lancaster: IEPPP, Lancaster University.

Hamlett, P. W. (2002). Technology theory and deliberative democracy. *Science, Technology & Human Values, 28*(1), 112–140.

Hilgartner, S. (1990). The dominant view of popularization: Conceptual problems, political uses. *Social Studies of Science, 20*(3), 519–539.

Ho, S., Brossard, D., & Scheufele, D. (2008). Effects of value predispositions, mass media and knowledge on public attitudes toward embryonic stem cell research. *International Journal of Public Opinion Research, 20*(2), 171–192.

House of Lords. (2000). *Science and society.* London: House of Lords.

Human Genome Project. (2003). *Human Genome Project information, ethical, legal and social issues.* Retrieved March 27, 2003, from www.ornl.gov/ TechResources/Human_Genome/research/elsi.html.

International Science Shop Network. (2003). *Living knowledge: Building partnerships for public access to research.* Retrieved March 27, 2003, from www. scienceshops.org.

Irwin, A. (2001). Constructing the scientific citizen: Science and democracy in the biosciences. *Public Understanding of Science, 10*(1), 1–18.

Irwin, A., & Wynne, B. (Eds.). (1996). *Misunderstanding science? The public reconstruction of science and technology.* Cambridge: Cambridge University Press.

Jasanoff, S. (1997). Civilization and madness: The great BSE scare of 1996. *Public Understanding of Science, 6*(3), 221–232.

Kasperson, R. E., Renn, O., Slovic, P., Brown, H. S., Emel, J., Goble, R., et al. (1988). The social amplification of risk: A conceptual framework. *Risk Analysis, 8,* 177–187.

Krimsky, S., & Plough, A. (1988). *Environmental hazards: Communicating as a social process.* Dover, MA: Auburn House.

Labinger, J. A., & Collins, H. M. (2001). *The one culture? A conversation about science.* Chicago, IL: University of Chicago Press.

LaFollette, M. C. (1990). *Making science our own: Public images of science, 1910–1955.* Chicago, IL: University of Chicago Press.

Leech, B. L. (2002). Asking questions: Techniques for semi-structured interviews. *Political Science and Politics, 35*(4), 665–668.

Lewenstein, B. V. (1992). The meaning of "public understanding of science" in the United States after World War II. *Public Understanding of Science, 1*(1), 45–68.

Lewenstein, B. V. (2003). Popularization. In J. L. Heilbron (Ed.), *Oxford companion to history of modern science.* Oxford and New York: Oxford University Press.

McComas, K. (2001). Theory and practice of public meetings. *Communication Theory, 11*, 36–55.

Miller, J. D. (1983a). *The American people and science policy: The role of public attitudes in the policy process*. New York: Pergamon Press.

Miller, J. D. (1983b). Scientific literacy: A conceptual and empirical review. *Daedalus, 112*(2), 29–48.

Miller, S. (2001). Public understanding of science at the crossroads. *Public Understanding of Science, 10*(1), 115–120.

National Research Council. (1996). *National science education standards*. Washington, DC: National Academy Press.

National Research Council (U.S.) Committee on Risk Perception and Communication. (1989). *Improving risk communication*. Washington, DC: National Academy Press.

National Science Board. (1991). Public science literacy and attitudes towards science and technology. In National Science Board (Ed.), *Science & engineering indicators—1991* (pp. 165–191). Washington, DC: U.S. Government Printing Office.

National Science Board. (1993). Science and technology: Public attitudes and public understanding. In National Science Board (Ed.), *Science & engineering indicators—1993* (pp. 193–215). Washington, DC: U.S. Government Printing Office.

National Science Board. (1996). Science and technology: Public attitudes and public understanding. In *Science & engineering indicators—1996* (chapter 7). Washington, DC: U.S. Government Printing Office.

National Science Board. (1998). Science and technology: Public attitudes and public understanding. In *Science & engineering indicators—1998* (chapter 7). Washington, DC: U.S. Government Printing Office.

National Science Board. (2000). Science and technology: Public attitudes and public understanding. In *Science & engineering indicators—2000* (chapter 8). Washington, DC: U.S. Government Printing Office.

National Science Board. (2002). Science and technology: Public attitudes and public understanding. In *Science & engineering indicators—2002* (chapter 7). Washington, DC: U.S. Government Printing Office.

Office of Science and Technology, & Wellcome Trust. (2000). *Science and the public: A review of science communication and public attitudes to science in Britain* (Vol. 2001). London: Wellcome Trust.

PBS. (2009). *PBS 2001–2002 season celebrated the diversity of America*. Retrieved January 5, 2009, from www.pbs.org/aboutpbs/news/20010816_diversity.html.

Royal Society. (1985). *The public understanding of science*. London: Royal Society.

Schiele, B. (Ed.). (1994). *When science becomes culture: World survey of scientific culture* (Proceedings I). Boucherville, Quebec: University of Ottawa Press.

Sclove, R. (1995). *Democracy and technology*. New York: Guilford.

Slovic, P. (1987, April 17). Perception of risk. *Science, 236*, 280–285.

Strauss, A., & Corbin, J. (1990). *Basics of qualitative research: Grounded Theory procedures and techniques*. Newbury Park, CA: Sage.

U.S. Census Bureau. (2006). *Hispanic population of the United States*. Retrieved October 16, 2008, from www.census.gov/population/www/socdemo/hispanic/hispanic.html.

U.S. Department of Energy. (2008). *Human genome information*. Retrieved September 30, 2008, from www.ornl.gov/sci/techresources/Human_Genome/home.shtml.

U.S. National Commission on Excellence in Education. (1983). *A nation at risk: The imperative for educational reform—A report to the nation and the Secretary of Education, United States Department of Education*. Washington, DC: The Commission.

Wachelder, J. (2003). Democratizing science: Various routes and visions of Dutch Science Shops. *Science, Technology & Human Values, 28*(2), 244–273.

Wynne, B. (1989). Sheep farming after Chernobyl: A case study in communicating scientific information. *Environment Magazine, 31*(2), 10–15, 33–39.

Wynne, B. (1995). Public understanding of science. In S. Jasanoff, G. E. Markle, J. C. Petersen, & T. Pinch (Eds.), *Handbook of science and technology studies* (pp. 361–388). Thousand Oaks, CA: Sage.

Wynne, B. (1996). May the sheep safely graze? A reflexive view of the expert–lay knowledge divide. In S. Lash, B. Szerszynski, & B. Wynne (Eds.), *Risk, environment and modernity: Towards a new ecology* (pp. 44–83). London: Sage.

Ziman, J. (1991). Public understanding of science. *Science, Technology & Human Values, 16*(1), 99–105.

Ziman, J. (1992). Not knowing, needing to know, and wanting to know. In B. V. Lewenstein (Ed.), *When science meets the public* (pp. 13–20). Washington, DC: American Association for the Advancement of Science.

Chapter 2

Framing Science

A New Paradigm in Public Engagement

Matthew C. Nisbet

In January 2008, an interdisciplinary committee of leading scientists gathered for a news conference at the National Academies headquarters in Washington, DC. The purpose of the conference was to release *Science, Evolution, and Creationism* (National Academy of Science and the Institute of Medicine, 2008).[1] As the news conference participants described, the booklet had been carefully designed to provide an updated account of evolutionary science that would be accessible to a diverse audience of school board members, journalists, teachers, activist parents, and clergy. Its contents covered three main topics: "Evolution and the Nature of Science," "The Evidence for Biological Evolution," and "Creationist Perspectives," with the last section focusing on the scientific and legal arguments against the teaching of creationist perspectives in public schools. Committee member Bruce Alberts, editor of *Science* and past president of the National Academy of Science (NAS), told the audience, "Where evolution debates occur in the country, scientists and others call us for help and the major tool we provide is this booklet."

In an effort to ensure that the booklet would be accessible to diverse audiences, the committee commissioned focus groups and a national survey to gauge the extent of citizens' understanding of the processes, nature, and limits of science. The committee also tested various "frames" or interpretative storylines that served as explanations for why alternatives to evolution were inappropriate for science classes (Labov & Pope, 2008). Although the committee had expected to find the most convincing storyline to be the authority of past legal decisions and the constitutional separation of Church and state, the data revealed that audiences were not as persuaded by this framing of the issue. Instead, somewhat surprisingly, the committee discovered that emphasizing evolutionary science as the modern building block for advances in medicine was the most effective frame for translating the importance of teaching evolution. The research also pointed to the effectiveness of reassuring the public that there was no conflict between teaching evolution and the beliefs of many religious traditions. Taking careful note of this feedback, the committee structured the 2008 revision of the booklet to emphasize these two central frames; they also highlighted these frames in subsequent efforts to publicize the new edition (Labov & Pope, 2008).

The National Academies' innovative "audience-based" approach is part of an emerging paradigm shift in how the scientific community in the United States views public engagement. Left behind is the assumption that simply "informing the public" of scientific facts will meaningfully alter the perceptions of either policy makers or citizens. Instead, one can detect a growing recognition that communication is not simply a translation of facts—it is a negotiation of meaning (for more on this shift, see Chapter 1 of this book). In this light, science and its policy implications need to be communicated in ways that address an intended audience's values, interests, and world views.

Several decades of social science research on framing underpin this paradigm shift. On the topic of science communication in particular, work by Nisbet and colleagues has argued that there is nothing essentially unique about science policy debates, when compared to other political controversies. Given this interpretative reality, scientists—like any other actor in the policy process—must strategically "frame" their communications in a manner that connects with diverse audiences (cf., Nisbet, Brossard, & Kroepsch, 2003; Nisbet & Huge, 2006; Nisbet & Mooney, 2007).[2] In that body of research, a consistent set of frames are identified and appear over and over again in science policy debates. The research suggests that these recurring frames offer an innovative public engagement technology to be harnessed by scientists, press officers, and organizations. As in the National Academies' case, when target audiences have been carefully researched, the resulting messages can be true to the science, but also personally relevant and meaningful to a diverse array of publics.

The purpose of this chapter, therefore, is to synthesize findings from previously published studies and articles that have focused on the framing of science for public consumption. Drawing on the cases of nuclear energy, evolution, and climate change, the chapter demonstrates the generalizable ways in which framing can drive the dynamics of science controversies. For researchers, the chapter offers careful conceptualization and identification of campaign strategies, media messages, and their influence. For scientists and communication professionals, the chapter highlights lessons for effective public engagement strategies—although these lessons are not without several important ethical and normative considerations.

A Scientific Approach to Public Communication

Historically, a prevailing assumption has been that ignorance is at the root of social conflict over science. As a solution, after formal science education ends, the popular science media should be used to educate the public about the technical details of the matter in dispute. Once citizens are brought up to speed on the science, then they will be more likely to judge scientific issues as scientists do; as a result, the controversy will go away. In this traditional "deficit" model, communication is defined as a process of transmission from experts to the public with the goal of "filling in" the deficits in knowledge. The facts are assumed to speak for themselves and to be interpreted by all citizens in similar ways. If the public does not accept or recognize these facts, then the failure in transmission is blamed on the inadequacies of journalists, the "irrational" beliefs of the public, or both (Bauer, Allum, & Miller, 2007; Nisbet & Goidel, 2007; Wynne, 1992). The heavily referenced symbols in this traditional science communication paradigm are popular media such as *Scientific American* or PBS's *Nova* and popular icons such as American physicist Richard Feynman and American astronomer Carl Sagan.

Rhetorically speaking, whenever the relationship between science and society breaks down, science illiteracy is blamed, the absence of quality science coverage is bemoaned, and there is a call put out for "the next Carl Sagan." Of course, in the context of these controversies, such condescending claims only risk further alienation of key audiences. Moreover, by emphasizing what is wrong with the public and the media, many scientists ignore the possibility that their communication efforts might be part of the problem or that there might be legitimate reasons fueling public concern or controversy (Irwin & Wynne, 1996).

Not only does this traditional paradigm unfairly blame the media and the public, arguments in favor of this decades-old model are not very scientific. Deficit model assumptions cut against more than 60 years of research in social psychology and political communication—a body of work that depicts citizens as preferring to be miserly and strategic in their information seeking rather than fully informed on all the facts (Downs, 1957; Fiske & Taylor, 1991; Popkin, 1991). Science debates are little different from political controversies. Instead of weighing and deliberating all issues, citizens rely heavily upon their social values to pick and choose among ideologically friendly interpretations offered up in news coverage; indeed, citizens often make up their minds about a topic in the absence of complete knowledge (Ho, Brossard, & Scheufele, 2008; Nisbet, 2005).

The deficit model also does not hold up well against the realities of the modern digital age. The great paradox of today's media environment is that, by way of cable television and the Internet, a wider public has greater access to quality science information than at any other time in history—yet public knowledge of science remains modest (National Science Board, 2008). One major reason that the science knowledge gap remains is the problem of choice: citizens not only select media content based on ideology or religious views (Mutz, 2006), but also based on their preference (or lack thereof) for public affairs and science-related information (Prior, 2005). In today's fragmented media system, information-rich science enthusiasts become even more informed while the broader American audience remains disengaged.

Thus, although continued investments in formal education and traditional science media are likely to remain centrally important to science education efforts, a substantial increase in public engagement will also require outreach strategies that work with audiences and respond to their values. As an example of such outreach strategies, public dialogue settings such as deliberative forums, science cafes, and town meetings appear to be particularly effective at addressing activists and stakeholders (see Brossard & Lewenstein, this volume; Besley, this volume). However, beyond the issues of media diversity and strategic outreach, there is still the issue of message. To truly maximize the potential of both traditional and more strategic science communication efforts, scientists and their organizations must also learn to "frame" their messages in ways that engage specific audiences and fit with the constraints of a diversity of media outlets and communication forums.

Media effects research, particularly in the area of framing, offers a rich explanation of how various actors in society define issues in politically strategic ways, how journalists from various beats selectively cover these issues, and how diverse audiences differentially perceive, understand, and participate. Perhaps even more importantly, this basic research can be applied to effective public communication. As the cases and research reviewed in this chapter will show, effective framing can result in a range of outcomes. Scientists can use framing to motivate greater interest and concern; to shape preferences for policies informed by or supportive of science; to influence political or personal behavior; to go beyond polarization and unite various publics around common ground; to define policy choices or options; and/or to rally fellow scientists around shared goals or strategy.

Although framing has been explored in the research on science communication, those studies have tended to "reinvent the wheel" in identifying and labeling the frames that exist in science-related debates. Not only has this led to inconsistencies in understanding the nature of disputes over science, it has also led to major differences in the measurement of media trends and in the observation of framing influence. Currently, the field of science communication lacks a generalizable typology for the study of framing in science-related issues. Drawing from the current research on framing, this chapter will explicate such a typology and offer evidence supporting its robustness and its promise for researchers and practitioners.

Framing and Media Influence

The earliest formal work on framing traces back four decades to the anthropologist Erving Goffman (1974). In his ethnographic research, he described frames as "schemata of interpretation" that allow individuals to "locate, perceive, identify, and label" issues, events, and topics. Words, according to Goffman, are like triggers that help individuals negotiate meaning through the lens of existing cultural beliefs and world views. In the 1970s and 1980s, cognitive psychologists Daniel Kahneman and Amos Tversky applied a similar concept of framing in experimental designs to understand risk judgments and consumer choices (cf., Kahneman & Tversky, 1972, 1979, 1984; Tversky & Kahneman, 1981). The two psychologists discovered in their Nobel Prize-winning research that the different ways in which a message is presented or "framed"—apart from the content itself—can result in very different responses, depending on the terminology used to describe the problem or the visual context provided in the message (Kahneman, 2003).

Over the past two decades, research in political communication and sociology has started to explain how media portrayals, in interaction with other cultural forces, shape public views. Frames are defined in this body of research as organizing central ideas on an issue. They endow certain dimensions of a complex topic with greater apparent relevance than the same dimensions might appear to have under an alternative frame (Gamson & Modigliani, 1989). Echoing the earlier work of Goffman (1974), frames are said to be used by audiences as "interpretative schema" to make sense of and discuss an issue; but they are also employed by journalists to condense complex events into interesting and appealing news reports and by policy makers to define policy options and reach decisions (Pan & Kosicki, 1993; Scheufele, 1999). For each of these stakeholders— citizens, journalists, and policy makers—frames help simplify complex issues by lending greater weight to certain considerations and arguments over others. In the process, frames help distill why an issue might be a problem, who or what might be responsible, and what should be done (Ferree, et al., 2002).

Frames are also a useful tool for managing (or attempting to manage) policy attention to an issue, including the "scope of participation" within a given policy arena such as Congress. For example, frames can influence the types and numbers of groups who are involved in decision making. In fact, across the history of many science debates, frames have empowered some groups to not only control attention to an issue across policy arenas, but also to simultaneously define the nature of the problem and what should be done about it (Nisbet & Huge, 2006; Nisbet et al., 2003).

A Frame Typology for Science

Previous studies describe a set of frames that appear to re-occur across science-related policy debates. Originally identified by the sociologists William Gamson and Andre Modigliani (1989) in an examination of nuclear energy, this typology was further developed in studies of food and medical biotechnology in Europe and the United States (Dahinden, 2002; Durant, Bauer, & Gaskell, 1998; Nisbet & Lewenstein, 2002). Before elaborating further on the typology, however, two key characteristics of frames need to be highlighted.

First, frames as general organizing devices should not be confused with specific policy positions. As the sociologist William Gamson and his colleagues describe, individuals can disagree on an issue but share the same interpretative frame (Ferree et al., 2002). As several examples in this chapter will demonstrate, a frame serves as a valence-neutral organizing device for arguments and interpretations, meaning that it may lead to pro-issue, anti-issue, and neutral positions. However, it should also be noted that for some frames one position might be expected to surface with more frequency. The second characteristic that needs to be highlighted here is that the latent meaning(s) of any frame can be translated instantaneously through frame devices such as catchphrases, metaphors, sound bites, graphics, and allusions to history, culture, and/or literature (Ferree et al., 2002).

Consider the controversy over embryonic stem-cell research, which several studies have detailed (Nisbet et al., 2003; Nisbet & Scheufele, 2007). A dominant frame suggested by that research is one of "morality/ethics." Both sides use this frame—which, on its own is valence-neutral—to argue their case in the debate. For example, research opponents say it is morally wrong to destroy embryos, since they constitute human life, while research supporters say it is morally wrong to hold back on research that could lead to important cures. Like all frames, the morality/ethics frame is communicated by the use of several kinds of frame devices. Unlike frames, these devices are typically not neutral and connote a specific position. In the case of the embryonic stem-cell debate, such devices have included: (a) metaphors such as "scientists are playing God," or "scientists racing to find a cure"; (b) comparisons to historical exemplars such as the Holocaust or discovering the cure for polio; (c) catchphrases such as "respect for life," "crossing an important moral boundary," or "it is pro-life to be pro-research"; and (d) photo-ops such as President George W. Bush posing with "snowflake" babies, children born from adopted frozen embryos. Ultimately, these devices work to shape and define the issue.

Table 2.1 outlines the generalizable typology put forth in this chapter; it lists eight frames and their various latent meanings.[3] These are the frames that consistently appear in science policy debates, though as the case of climate change will show, unique issue-specific frames can also emerge. To further explicate this typology let us first review then take an updated look at Gamson and Modigliani's (1989) classic framing analysis of the longest and most durably intense debate in science policy.

Table 2.1 Frames that Consistently Appear Across Policy Debates

Frame	Defines science-related issue as...
Social progress	... improving quality of life, or solution to problems. Alternative interpretation as harmony with nature instead of mastery, sustainability.
Economic development/ competitiveness	... economic investment, market benefits or risks; local, national, or global competitiveness.
Morality/ethics	... in terms of right or wrong; respecting or crossing limits, thresholds, or boundaries.
Scientific/technical uncertainty	... a matter of expert understanding; what is known versus unknown; either invokes or undermines expert consensus, calls on the authority of "sound science," falsifiability, or peer-review.
Pandora's box/ Frankenstein's monster/ runaway science	... call for precaution in face of possible impacts or catastrophe. Out-of-control, a Frankenstein's monster, or as fatalism, i.e., action is futile, path is chosen, no turning back.
Public accountability/ governance	... research in the public good or serving private interests; a matter of ownership, control, and/or patenting of research, or responsible use or abuse of science in decision making, politicization.
Middle way/alternative path	... around finding a possible compromise position, or a third way between conflicting/ polarized views or options.
Conflict/strategy	... as a game among elites; who's ahead or behind in winning debate; war; battle of personalities or groups (usually journalist-driven interpretation).

The Rise and Fall of Nuclear Energy

Few Americans are likely to associate nuclear energy with slogans like "Atoms for peace" or "electricity too cheap to meter." Yet before the 1970s, nuclear energy production was framed almost exclusively in these terms, with the technology defined as leading to *social progress, economic development,* and a better way of life (Gamson & Modigliani, 1989; Weart, 1988). In 1953, when President Dwight Eisenhower delivered his "atoms for peace" speech before the United Nations, demand for electricity in the United States was doubling each decade and Europe faced severe energy shortages. In that speech, the construction of nuclear power plants at home was defined by the president as giving the United States an important economic advantage, and the promotion of civilian nuclear technology abroad was heralded as a key diplomatic tool in winning allies against the Soviet Union (Eisenhower, 1953).

As Gamson and Modigliani (1989) describe, frames changed in the mid-1970s, however, as Ralph Nader and other consumer advocates reinterpreted nuclear energy in terms of *public accountability*, arguing that the industry had become a "powerful special interest." Environmentalists also began to emphasize a *middle way* frame, focusing on alternative paths to energy independence, advocating energy conservation, and solar, hydro, and wind generation. Other groups such as the Union of Concerned Scientists turned the *economic competitiveness* frame *against* nuclear power, emphasizing that production was simply not "cost-effective." At this time, civilian nuclear energy production was linked to the larger "nuclear freeze" movement, as President Jimmy Carter's administration limited the export of civilian technology abroad and protestors swarmed nuclear power plants at home.

The tipping point for the image of nuclear energy was the Three Mile Island (TMI) accident in Middletown, PA, in 1979.[4] Several weeks before the TMI incident, the popular *China Syndrome* movie was released. With its focus on industry secrecy and incompetence, the film emphasized an interpretation of *public accountability*. More importantly, with the film's reactor meltdown climax, the movie amplified a new frame focusing on the *Pandora's Box* or *runaway* nature of the technology. In this interpretation, the risks of nuclear power were portrayed as a Frankenstein's monster beyond the ability of citizens to control. When news reports of TMI galvanized national attention, these frames became the major modes of interpretation (Gamson & Modigliani, 1989). In a classic example of a frame device instantly signaling a *runaway technology*, *Time* magazine featured a cover with an ominous picture of the TMI reactor and the headline "Nuclear Nightmare" (A Nuclear Nightmare, 1979).[5]

That accident helped set in motion a dominant media narrative of lingering *scientific uncertainty* that went on to spotlight additional examples of construction flaws, incompetence, faulty management, and potential risks at nuclear power plants across the country. The frames of *public accountability*, *runaway technology*, and *scientific uncertainty* were only strengthened in 1986 with the Chernobyl disaster. The event generated worldwide attention, with few media providing context on the comparative safety record of the American nuclear energy industry, effectively leaving the frames unchallenged (Friedman, Gorney, & Egolf, 1992; Gamson & Modigliani, 1989). The last nuclear power plants to be built in the United States were constructed in the 1970s, though more than 100 power plants remain in operation (U.S. Nuclear Regulatory Commission, n.d.).

At the start of this decade, however, new focusing events began to shift the interpretative packages and mental categories applied to nuclear energy. In 2001, against the backdrop of rising energy costs and rolling black outs in California, the newly elected President George W. Bush administration launched a communication campaign to promote nuclear power as a *middle way* path to energy independence (Ackman, 2001). The terrorist attacks of September 11, 2001 dampened the viability of this frame package, as subsequent media reports focused on nuclear power plants as potential terrorist targets (Council on Foreign Relations, 2006). But since 2004, as energy prices have climbed and as the dependence on overseas oil has been defined as a major national security issue, a renewed emphasis on the energy independence interpretation has surfaced. As of 2007, more than 20 applications have been submitted to the U.S. Nuclear Regulatory Commission by utility companies proposing to build additional nuclear reactors across the country (Department of Energy, 2008).

This renewed framing effort has been complemented by an attempt to sell nuclear energy as a *middle way* technofix for greenhouse gas emissions. Former EPA administrator Christine Todd Whitman and Greenpeace co-founder Patrick Moore are among the sponsors of this interpretative package. Their tagline is that nuclear energy is "cleaner, cheaper, and safe." According to their argument, if Americans are going to satisfy their energy demands while achieving the goal of cutting greenhouse gas emissions, the country needs to reinvest in nuclear energy (Whitman & Moore, 2006). Former President George W. Bush and 2008 presidential candidate Senator John McCain argued a similar *middle way* interpretation. McCain declared in a 2008 campaign speech, "If we're looking for a vast supply of reliable and low-cost electricity, with zero carbon emissions and long-term price stability, that's the working definition of nuclear energy" (Real Clear Politics, 2008).

However, several opposition frames invoked in the 1970s still resonate. Groups like the Union of Concerned Scientists now favor *uncertainty* and *public accountability* interpretations, demanding that nuclear plants be tightly regulated in light of safety problems, the "public's right to know," and a "failure of regulators to take effective action" (UCS, n.d.). Other environmental groups emphasize in their opposition not only the potential *runaway* dangers, but also the absence of cost-effectiveness. They emphasize that nuclear power is not safe, not cost-effective, and not needed (NIRS, 2005).

In sum, it is argued here that the typology reflected in Table 2.1 captures the dominant frames that have surfaced among the media, policy makers, and public-interest groups across the history of nuclear energy. To further illustrate the generalizability of this typology, the next section provides a detailed analysis of the frames at play in the debate over the teaching of evolution in public schools.

Conflict and Consensus in Communicating about Evolution

In the evolution debate, as in the case of nuclear energy, strategic messaging has been used to trigger favorable interpretations among key stakeholders and audiences. In fact, framing has been the central tool used by anti-evolutionists to gain traction among opinion leaders, journalists, and a swing public of Americans. It is only recently that the scientific community has begun more aggressively responding to the realities of the modern interpretive landscape, as is the case in the audience research that informed the update of the National Academies (2008) booklet, *Understanding Our Audiences: The Design and Evolution of Science, Evolution, and Creationism*.

For 150 years, Charles Darwin's original theory of evolution has served as the basis for major advances in the sciences—and these breakthroughs have only further strengthened the evidence in support of evolution. Based on these discoveries, along with corroborating evidence from the fossil record and comparative anatomy, the National Academies call evolutionary biology the "cornerstone of modern science" (National Academy of Science and Institute of Medicine, 2008, p. xi). As is the case with most scientific theories, questions remain in the particulars; still, the vast majority of scientists maintain that the theory is the best available tool for understanding lingering uncertainties. Furthermore, most scientists agree that there is no scientifically credible alternative explanation for the vast diversity of organisms that exist today.

Despite overwhelming evidence in support of evolution, cultural conservatives in the United States have long opposed the teaching of the theory in public schools. Fundamentalist Christian activists first proposed "creation science" decades ago—a doctrine that claimed archeological evidence for Noah's flood and other biblical stories (for a current example of this doctrine see Brown, 2002). Defining the issue in terms of so-called educational balance, these creationists framed the matter in terms of *public accountability*, calling for "equal time" in public schools and decrying the issue as a matter of "free speech." Yet court decisions have repeatedly ruled that creation science was a religious doctrine and that its inclusion in public school curricula violated the Constitutional separation of church and state.

In response to these legal defeats, during the late 1990s, creation science itself evolved by way of a modern repackaging and reframing. A small group of conservative intellectuals came together to develop a new account of the origins of life called intelligent design (ID), which argues that the complexity of life on earth is best explained by the intervention of an intelligent force, rather than the process of macro-evolution. With this premise as their foundation, ID proponents set about to reframe the validity of one of the most widely supported theories in science by offering up what appeared to be their own scientifically valid compromise. The ID public relations campaign proved politically successful, at least initially. In less than 10 years, ID earned endorsements from President George W. Bush (Bumiller, 2005), Senate majority leader Bill Frist (MSNBC, 2005), state and local school boards, political reporters, pundits, and a notable number of Americans (Nightline, 2005).

Redefining Evolution as a Social Problem

The origins of the ID movement can be traced to a document labeled "The Wedge" (Downey, 2006). This document was issued in 1999 by the Center for the Renewal of Science and Culture of the Discovery Institute, a Seattle-based conservative Christian think-tank. With clearly stated Christian motives, the document lays out a multi-pronged strategic communication campaign for replacing the theory of evolution with "the theistic under-standing that nature and human beings are created by God" (Discovery Institute, 2003, p. 15). In order to mobilize a base of Christian conserva-tives, the ID movement drew heavily upon the *social progress* and *moral-ity/ethics* frames, emphasizing that evolution is responsible for moral decay in society. According to the original Wedge document, the "proposition that human beings are created in the image of God ... came under whole-sale attack by intellectuals drawing on the discoveries of modern science" (Discovery Institute, 2003, p. 12). Such "wholesale attack" led to "devas-tating" consequences because proponents of evolution "denied the exis-tence of objective moral standards" (Discovery Institute, 2003, p. 12).

Despite the focus in this doctrine on *social progress* and *morality*, these frames were not the interpretations offered by the ID movement to the mainstream media or the wider American public. To these audiences, the so-called social problem of evolution was communicated around other dimensions. In a somewhat ironic approach, ID proponents attempted to use the authority of science to argue their case to journalists and swing publics. First, the ID movement promoted a *scientific uncertainty* frame, insisting that there are holes in the theory of evolution, and therefore, by default, ID must be true. The movement relied (and still relies) heavily on the reasoning of scientists and scholars such as Michael Behe, a biochemist at Lehigh University in Pennsylvania; William Dembski, a philosopher at Southwestern Baptist Theological Seminary who holds a doctorate of mathematics from the University of Chicago; Paul Chien, a biology profes-sor at the University of San Francisco; and Robert Kaita, a physicist at Princeton University.

In his top-selling book, *Darwin's Black Box*, Behe (1998) argued that certain features of organisms are "irreducibly complex," meaning that some form of supernatural intelligence must have intervened to create them. Playing on the vernacular meaning of the term "theory," ID proponents further translated this uncertainty motif by way of the slogan: "Evolution is a theory, not a fact." In other words, argued ID proponents, if the theory of evolution could not account for irreducible complexity or other so-called holes in the science, then rival interpretations need to be taught in class (see Forrest & Gross, 2004 for an overview).[6]

Second, ID proponents paired their manufactured uncertainty message with an equally effective *public accountability* frame that played on public belief in critical thinking as a cornerstone of education. In 2005, President George W. Bush echoed this theme in public statements supporting the teaching of ID. Asked about his views, Bush told a political reporter,

> Both sides ought to be properly taught, so people can understand what the debate is about. Part of education is to expose people to different schools of thought.... You're asking me whether or not people ought to be exposed to different ideas, and the answer is yes.
>
> (Bumiller, 2005)

By 2005, the merits of ID as an addition to science curricula had been discussed by several local school boards and states across the country. Indeed, that same year in Dover, Pennsylvania, parents filed suit in opposition to the local school board's resolution that students be read a statement in science class asserting that evolution was a theory and not a fact. That statement also declared that ID was a scientifically credible alternative account of life's origins, and that students wanting more information could turn to an ID textbook available in the school library (Powell, 2005).

Balance as Bias

Local and national political leaders were not the only important publics adopting the ID movement's preferred framing of the issue. As school boards, state legislatures, and the courts paid increasing attention to intelligent design, journalists relied heavily on the agenda of these political venues to guide coverage. In 2004 and 2005 there was a major spike in national and regional media attention to ID. Perhaps more importantly, as science was debated within these political contexts, the topics of evolution and ID moved from the exclusive domain of science-beat reporters to the domains of political reporters, opinion writers, and cable TV news. According to Mooney and Nisbet (2005), coverage on the political and opinion beats de-emphasized the technical background favored by science writers and replaced it with the type of *strategy and conflict* frame more familiar to election coverage or issues such as abortion. Though these types of stories provided important details about the tactics, fundraising, and campaign activities of the ID movement, they also tended to ignore scientific context. Instead, they would carefully balance arguments from both sides, thereby lending credibility to the claim by ID proponents that there was a growing "scientific controversy" over evolutionary theory, when in fact, there was none (Mooney & Nisbet, 2005).

Given the strong paired messages of uncertainty and critical thinking that were pushed by elected officials, pundits, and political journalists, national surveys showed that the American public remained unsure about the scientific basis of both evolution and intelligent design (cf., Newport, 2006a, 2006b). In one national survey study, only a slight majority of adult Americans (56%) agreed that an overwhelming body of scientific evidence supported evolution, while a sizable proportion (44%) thought precisely the same thing about ID. Additionally, roughly 60% of the public believed intelligent design should be taught as an alternative to evolution in public school science courses (Nisbet & Nisbet, 2005). The ID movement, through careful tailoring and targeting of their message, had literally created a public perception wedge, defining intelligent design as the compromise between teaching "atheistic evolution" and constitutionally unacceptable biblical doctrine.

The initial response to the ID movement from many evolution defenders was to simply repeat technical and detailed arguments in favor of evolution and against ID—the assumption was that the factual basis of evolutionary science would simply win out without any concerted effort to tailor messages to specific segments of the public. While these technical arguments are objectively true and may be persuasive to a highly attentive and informed audience, they are likely to be ignored by a wider public and/or interpreted as a confusing fight among dueling experts.

For those scientists who did challenge ID publicly, their often awkward communication posture was a sharp contrast to the seductive style of many ID proponents. Filmmaker Randy Olson's 2006 documentary, *Flock of Dodos,* powerfully depicted that contrast. Indeed, by putting on display the inherent weaknesses in scientists' traditional thinking about public communication, Olson's film served as a catalyst for self-reflection among some scientists. In what has become a heavily referenced scene, Olson gathered biologists together for poker, beer, and an informal discussion of the ID challenge. One participant's comments capture perfectly the faulty instincts of some evolution defenders:

> It's not my position, it's not my position to persuade people, you shouldn't believe in god, or you should believe in god. But, when they come into the scientific arena, and they start saying things that are manifestly wrong, that are manifestly ignorant, I think people have to stand up and say, you know, you're an idiot.
>
> (Olson, 2006)

Such condescending statements played directly into the perceptual trap set by the ID campaign, reinforcing the movement's preferred message that allegedly dogmatic scientists were in favor of censoring alternative explanations in public schools.

Although evolution defenders may have been losing the battle in the court of public opinion, Federal Judge John E. Jones' December 2005 decision in the aforementioned Dover, Pennsylvania case appeared to turn the tables (at least temporarily) on the ascent of the ID movement (Powell, 2005). Jones' ruling redefined the controversy away from the ID movement's preferred emphasis on critical thinking and free speech, toward a new *public accountability* frame that portrayed the movement as the work of a powerful special interest group seizing power and promoting its religious agenda. According to Jones' interpretation of the evidence, a small group of Christian conservatives had been elected to the school board in Dover and had proceeded to pass the curriculum change as a way to push their preferred religious beliefs on a community of diverse faith. Jones concluded that this was an unconstitutional act.

In the wake of the Dover case, the emphasis on the wrong-headedness of a special interest group pushing their religious values on students, combined with the fear of lawsuits, appeared to spill over to affect the moderate members of the Ohio school board. In February 2006, these board members voted against their Christian conservative counterparts and reversed a 2002 policy that allowed the teaching of ID in Ohio schools. "We allow a Dover risk to remain if we leave this lesson plan on the shelf," Robin C. Hovis, a board member, told the *New York Times* (Rudoren, 2005).

An Expert Consensus on Communication Strategy?

Motivated by the public communication failures that preceded the Dover case, the National Academies, as described at the opening of this chapter, decided to carefully explore the types of frames that might best translate evolution for an ambivalent public. Indeed, somewhat surprisingly, the Academies' focus group and survey research revealed that a *social progress* emphasis on evolutionary science as the building block for medical advances was the most effective frame among swing publics. Moreover, the research also concluded that by emphasizing the *middle way* interpretation of science and religion as compatible, scientists could begin to reduce audience reservations and confusion.

Reinforcing these twin frames, the National Academies booklet was co-sponsored by the NAS and the Institute of Medicine (IOM), with the authoring committee chaired by Francisco Ayala, a biologist who had once trained for the Catholic priesthood. The booklet opens with a compelling detective story narrative of the supporting evidence for evolution. Placed prominently in the first few pages is a call-out box titled "Evolution in Medicine: Combating New Infectious Diseases," featuring a picture of passengers on a plane wearing SARS masks (NAS & IOM, 2008). A lead quote in the booklet's press release echoed this dual emphasis: "Understanding evolution is essential to identifying and treating disease," said Harvey Fineberg, president of the Institutes of Medicine (National Academies, 2008, p. 1). He further explained in that document,

> For example, the SARS virus evolved from an ancestor virus that was discovered by DNA sequencing. Learning about SARS' genetic similarities and mutations has helped scientists understand how the virus evolved. This kind of knowledge can help us anticipate and contain infections that emerge in the future.
>
> (National Academies, 2008, p. 1)

To communicate the *middle way* frame, at the end of the first chapter of the National Academies booklet, following a definition of science and how it is different from religion, there is a prominent three-page special color section that features testimonials from religious scientists, religious leaders, and official church position statements, all endorsing the teaching of evolution in schools. As the booklet states and as quoted in the press release: "The evidence for evolution can be fully compatible with religious faith. Science and religion are different ways of understanding the world. Needlessly placing them in opposition reduces the potential of each to contribute to a better future" (NAS & IOM, 2008; National Academies, 2008, p. 1.).

Mixed Messages and Maverick Communicators

While the National Academies have taken the lead in providing a carefully researched resource for scientists and others to rely on when communicating about evolution, the seemingly loudest voice of science on this matter invokes a decidedly different framework. Most notably, Richard Dawkins (2006) argues in his best-selling book, *The God Delusion*, that religion itself is a scientific question and that evolution in particular undermines not only the validity of religion but also respect for all religious faith. Maverick communicators such as Dawkins fuel the *conflict frame* that is often favored by the news media; as a result, it generates magazine covers, sound bites, and other frame devices such as "God vs. Science," or "Science vs. religion," to name just a few examples. The underlying message for the wider public is that science—exactly as the ID proponents claim—does indeed undermine religious values.

This conflict frame is powerfully employed in the 2008 documentary *Expelled: No Intelligence Allowed* (Frankowski, 2008). By relying exclusively on interviews with outspoken atheist hardliners such as Dawkins, *Expelled* reinforces the false impression that evolution and faith are inherently incompatible and that scientists are openly hostile to religion. In the film, the comedic actor Ben Stein plays the role of a conservative Michael Moore, taking viewers on an investigative journey into the realm of "Big Science," an institution where Stein concludes that "scientists are not allowed to even think thoughts that involve an intelligent creator." The film goes so far as to outrageously suggest that "Darwinism," as Stein calls evolution, led to the Holocaust, and that today scientists have been denied tenure and that research has been suppressed, all in the service of an atheist agenda to hide the supposedly fatal flaws in evolutionary theory.[7]

By the end of its Spring 2008 run in theaters, *Expelled* ranked as one of the top-grossing public affairs documentary of all time.[8] Even more troubling have been the advanced screenings of *Expelled* for policy makers, interest groups, and other influentials. These screenings have been used to promote "Academic Freedom Acts" in several states, legislation that would encourage teachers (as a matter of "academic freedom") to discuss the alleged flaws in evolutionary science. In June 2008, an Academic Freedom bill was successfully passed into law in Louisiana with similar legislation under consideration in other states (see Nisbet, 2008 for a more in-depth essay on *Expelled*).

Clearly, the public debate over evolution offers a productive context for studying the frames that have been generated (and responded to) by the media, religious groups, scientists, the public, and policy makers. Furthermore, as just reviewed, this debate offered a context for applying the typology in Table 2.1 as a means of decoding the message strategies of competing camps and arriving at clues about how audiences are likely to make sense of a science-related debate. The next section reviews how these same generalizable frames and latent meanings played out in the debate over climate change.

Climate Change: A Consistent Pattern of Strategies and Meanings

By the end of 2007, conventional wisdom had pegged the year as a major breakthrough for mobilizing the public on climate change. As evidence, many journalists, bloggers, and advocates pointed most notably to former Vice President Al Gore and his Nobel Prize-winning efforts at communicating about the "climate crisis." Perhaps more importantly, Gore's *An Inconvenient Truth* (Guggenheim, 2008) media campaign had been backed up by ever stronger and louder expert agreement from the Intergovernmental Panel on Climate Change (IPCC).[9] The key message emanating from this crescendo of public outreach was that man-made global warming posed serious environmental and societal consequences.

Conventional wisdom, however, cut against the reality of public opinion. Despite the strongest conclusions to date by the scientific community about the urgency of the issue, polling revealed that global warming still scored consistently as a bottom-tier political priority for the public (Nisbet & Myers, 2007). Partisan judgments of the objective reality of global warming also varied widely. According to Gallup surveys, between 2006 and 2008, worry about global warming grew to a record high of 85% among Democrats, while the percentage of concerned Republicans remained unchanged at less than 50% (Dunlap, 2008). When factoring in education, an even deeper chasm is revealed. According to recent Pew surveys, less than one-quarter of college-educated Republicans believe that global warming is due to human activities compared to more than three-quarters of their Democrat counterparts (Pew, 2008).

So by 2008, although Gore and the sharp increase in mainstream media attention had intensified the beliefs of Americans who were already concerned about climate change, it appears that a deep opinion divide between partisans remained. What explains, then, this perceptual gridlock? Nisbet and Mooney (2007) argue that if mainstream news attention and expert consensus alone drove public responses, one would expect increasing public confidence in the validity of the science, and decreasing gridlock. However, instead of focusing on scientific reality, much of the media coverage has offered audiences more ideologically focused frames.

The Climate Skeptic Playbook

Several conservative think tanks, political leaders, and commentators continued to hew closely to the decade-old playbook on how to downplay the urgency of the issue. Moreover, even as Republican leaders such as Senator John McCain and California Governor Arnold Schwarzenegger asserted the need for action on global warming (Elsworth, 2008), the strength of these decade-old frames appeared to linger as salient in popular culture, political discourse, and the memory store of many citizens. During the 1990s, the climate skeptic message strategy was in part devised by Republican pollster Frank Luntz. Based on focus groups and surveys, Luntz recommended emphasizing repeatedly that the "scientific debate remains open," that further research is needed before government action is taken, and that any U.S. policy action would lead to "unfair" economic burden on Americans since countries like China and India were not also taking action. This "paralysis by analysis" emphasis on *uncertainty* and *economic development* was effectively implemented by conservative think tanks and members of Congress to defeat adoption of the Kyoto Protocol (which was adopted by other developed nations in December 1997) and other major policy proposals (McCright & Dunlap, 2003). The strategy also led to distortions in news coverage. As political reporters applied their preferred *conflict and strategy* frame to the policy debate, they engaged in the same type of false balance that was common to their coverage of intelligent design (Boykoff & Boykoff, 2004). That is, the media presented two equal sides to these issues, when only one side had garnered an overwhelming majority of scientific consensus and evidence.

A Pandora's Box of Looming Disaster

Al Gore, many environmentalists, and even some scientists have attempted to counter the *uncertainty* and *economic development* frames with their own emphasis on a looming "climate crisis." For example, environmentalists have relied on depictions of specific climate impacts including powerful hurricane devastation, polar bears perched precariously on shrinking ice floes, earth scorched from drought, blazing wildfires, or a future where a rising sea level has put prominent cities or landmarks under water. With an accent on the visual and the dramatic, this strategy has been successful in triggering similarly framed media coverage. Most prominently, a much talked about *Time* magazine cover from 2006 featured the image of a polar bear on melting ice with the tagline: "Be worried, be *very* worried" (*Time*, 2006).[10] Yet given that the uncertainty for each of these climate impacts is greater than the general link between human activities and global warming, these claims are quickly challenged by climate change skeptics as liberal "alarmism," shifting debate back into the mental box of *scientific uncertainty* and partisanship (Brainard, 2006).

The "War on Science"

A second preferred frame by environmentalists, liberals, and many scientists resonates with a larger political debate over the use of expertise and evidence in the Bush administration. To these claimants, President George W. Bush and Republican leaders in Congress have created a culture of "anti-science" that favors populism and ideology over expertise (Mooney, 2005). In the 2004 election, Democrats attempted to make strategic use of this *public accountability* frame, connecting climate change to a wider debate over the president's decision making on Iraq and other issues (Reynolds, 2004). The following year, Mooney's best-selling book, *The Republican War on Science*, helped crystallize the *public accountability* train of thought among scientists, turning the book's title into a rallying cry. In 2007, the lingering resonance of this frame device was evident in candidate Hillary Clinton's speech marking the 50th anniversary of Sputnik, with the Senator promising to end the "war on science" in American politics (Clinton, 2008).

Switching Trains of Thought on Climate Change

Not every citizen cares about the environment or defers to the authority of science, yet among climate change advocates, these mental points of reference continue to be the dominant emphasis. In order to generate widespread public support for meaningful policy action, the communication challenge is to figure out how to shift the climate change focus away from the traditional frames and devices—such as *scientific uncertainty*, "unfair economic burden," a *Pandora's Box* of disaster, or a "war on science"—toward a new perceptual context that resonates with the current values and understanding of a specific intended audience.

Such a shift might look something like the debate Nordhaus and Schellenberger (2007) have stirred among fellow environmentalists with their book *Break Through: From the Death of Environmentalism to the Politics of Possibility*. The book advocates a move away from what they call the "pollution paradigm," which offers a familiar storyline of dire environmental consequences if greenhouse gas emissions are not radically reduced. Nordhaus and Schellenberger (2007) offer an alternative communication strategy, which is to turn the traditional *economic development* frame in favor of action on climate change by redefining policy action not as an "unfair economic burden" or a response to pollution, but as an energy challenge. Their goal in reframing the debate is not just to engage the wider public, but also to catalyze a more diverse social movement—perhaps even engaging support for energy policies among Republicans who think predominantly in terms of market opportunities, or labor advocates who value the possibility of job growth. Nordhaus and Schellenberger (2007) argue that only by refocusing messages and building diverse coalitions in support of "innovative energy technology," "green collar jobs," and "sustainable economic prosperity" can meaningful action on climate change be achieved.

A second potentially unifying interpretation is offered by scientist and atheist E. O. Wilson in his top-selling book *The Creation: An Appeal to Save Life on Earth* (2006). Wilson frames environmental stewardship as not only a scientific matter, but also one of *morality and ethics*; in doing so, he has engaged a religious audience that might not otherwise pay attention to popular science books or appeals related to climate change. Paralleling Wilson's interpretation, an increasing number of religious leaders, including Pope Benedict XVI and best-selling author and pastor Rick Warren, are emphasizing the religious duty to be "stewards" of God's creation (Goodstein, 2006; Vidal & Kington, 2007).

The *morality/ethics* frame also resonates in Gore's $300 million dollar *We Can Solve It*, or "WE" campaign, which was launched in launched in Spring 2008. The WE campaign is a call to arms for the country to unify behind solving a moral challenge; it also serves as a replacement frame for

An Inconvenient Truth's storyline of looming disaster. In television and print advertisements titled "strange bedfellows" and "unlikely alliances," the WE campaign tries to break through partisan perceptions by pairing spokespeople such as Democratic House Speaker Nancy Pelosi with Republican Newt Gingrich, and the Reverend Al Sharpton, a liberal, and Pat Robertson, a conservative religious broadcaster. Other ads compare action on global warming to the Civil Rights movement, the Space Race, World War II, and the recovery from the Great Depression.[11] Importantly, these ads are placed during day-time talk shows, entertainment programming, and in leisure magazines, all of which reach non-news audiences who might not otherwise be paying attention to news coverage of the issue (Eilperin, 2008).

Similar to the *Pandora's Box* emphasis of 2006, journalists have also started to echo this *morality frame* in their coverage of climate change. For example, *Time* magazine devoted its 2008 Earth Day cover to that interpretation. Using special effects to shape-shift the iconic Iwo Jima flag-raising photograph, the cover featured an illustration of soldiers struggling to plant a tree and the tagline "How to Win the War on Global Warming."[12] Managing editor Richard Stengel described the cover as: "Our call to arms to make this challenge—perhaps the most important one facing the planet—a true national priority" (Stengel, 2008).

Over the past few years, the public health implications of climate change have also emerged as a potentially powerful interpretative resource for advocates. This trend is an example of how a unique issue-specific frame may emerge that is not predicted by the generalizable typology outlined in Table 2.1 and reviewed thus far in this chapter. The public health frame emphasizes the potential of climate change to increase the incidence of infectious diseases, asthma, allergies, heat stroke, and other salient health problems. Importantly, not only does the public health frame make climate change personally relevant to new audiences, it also adds a new "public face" to the debate, shifting the visualization of the issue away from remote Arctic regions, peoples, and animals to more socially proximate neighbors and places. In the process, not only do the symbols of global warming change, but the issue begins to cut across media zones, triggering coverage at local television news outlets and specialized urban media.

Conclusion

The Future of Public Engagement

For researchers, framing offers a powerful theoretical tool for understanding the dynamics of science debates and their relationship to public opinion, media coverage, and policy decisions. Additionally, given the recent work by the National Academies to ensure the appeal of their evolution booklet (NAS & IOM, 2008), it appears that the framing research presented here may already be catalyzing new approaches to public engagement. This suggests that leading science organizations and industry members are aware of the principles reviewed here and are actively trying to harness the potential power of frames in their communication goals. Still, by bringing together in one place the implications of multiple published research studies and news articles, popular books and websites, this chapter offers researchers, communication professionals, and scientists a clearer path forward.

The typology described herein—this generalizable set of frames, devices, and social meanings, appeared repeatedly across the science debates outlined in this chapter. These generalizable features of framing reveal important clues about the intersection between media frames and audience dispositions, the role of journalistic routines in altering the definition of an issue, and how science policy decisions are made. However, to put theory and principles into practice—which happened with the National Academies' booklet on evolution—science organizations and communication researchers should continue with surveys, focus groups, and other analyses that can help identify audience values, as well as effective frames, devices, messages, and media platforms. Drawing on the typology of frames presented here, research needs to pinpoint the mental associations and cognitive schema that make a complex science topic accessible and personally meaningful for a targeted audience along with the particular frame devices that instantly translate these intended meanings. For experimental researchers, the typology can additionally serve as a deductive source for developing and testing competing frames on science-related issues. This would not only bolster consistency in research, but also external validity, matching frames as they are tested in the lab with the reality of how they appear in public discourse and the news media.

Finally, critics argue that framing on the part of scientists means engaging in false spin, as intelligent design proponents and climate skeptics have done in the past (Holland et al., 2007). However, if scientists have a duty to figure out what is approximately true about the world, they also have a responsibility to communicate this truth effectively. Framing is a tool for doing this. As the cases of intelligent design and climate change underscore, it is literally a matter of "frame" or be "framed." Critics have also argued that scientists should stick to research and let media relations officers and science writers worry about translating the implications of that research (Holland et al., 2007). This is certainly ideal, but in the real world, when controversies erupt or when new issues emerge, it will be scientists, because of their authority and expertise, that will end up giving the media interviews, testifying before Congress, addressing community groups, writing blog posts, or authoring popular books, op-eds, and magazine articles. Perhaps even more importantly, as senior decision makers, many scientists are ultimately responsible for setting communication policy at scientific institutions, universities, agencies, and organizations. These leaders need to understand the research, its implications, and how framing can impact public perceptions about its value.

Of course, as an innovative new public engagement method, strategic framing needs to be used responsibly. For example, scientists must respect the uncertainty that is inherent to any technical question and resist engaging in hyperbole or offering concrete answers when there are none. If they stray from the science, they risk losing public trust. Moreover, if framing appears to serve political purposes, there is the risk that the science will be quickly and easily reinterpreted by the public through partisan lenses. The result will be increased polarization, rather than increased engagement.

The ethics of framing is also central to the future of science journalism. Faced with a profusion of think tanks and maverick experts, many journalists seek ways to move beyond the trap of "false balance," even if it jeopardizes their perceived non-partisan objectivity (Cunningham, 2003). Like scientists, they are discouraged that the public still fails to accept the urgency of climate change and the validity of evolution (Mooney, 2004). In addition, as victims of market forces, veteran science writers have been forced to leave their jobs at major news organizations while early-career journalists encounter limited job prospects (Russell, 2006). As an alternative career path, some science reporters have joined with universities or foundations to forge a new brand of not-for-profit journalism where reporting and commentary merge in outlets such as blogs, interactive websites, books, and documentary films. The focus at these outlets is not only to inform but also to alert and mobilize the public (Brainard, 2008).

Given these shifting roles for scientists and journalists, there is more work to be done in applying the relevant work on ethical persuasion. Still missing from the new "framing science" paradigm is an ethics of science communication that is as solid as the research fueling these important innovations in public engagement strategy.

Notes

1. *Science, Evolution, and Creationism* is the third edition of a booklet originally published in 1984 in response to several states having passed legislation mandating the teaching of creationism in public schools.
2. The mark of any paradigm shift is controversy. Indeed, the chapter by Keränen in this volume covers the topic of scientific revolutionaries—and controversy—in great detail. In the case of framing research as applied to science communication, Nisbet and Mooney's (2007) article in the journal *Science* generated more than a half dozen published letters in reply (Brewer & Lakoff, 2007; Holland et al., 2007; Kolmes & Butkus, 2007; Kronje, 2008), sparked a global blog debate involving more than 50 bloggers (Science & Politics, 2007), garnered considerable media attention (On the Media, 2007; Boyle, 2007), and prompted invited lectures at more than four dozen universities and venues across North America and Europe.

3. With the reader in mind, throughout this section and others, references to frames from the typology are italicized and frame devices are in quotes.
4. A fact sheet on the Three Mile Island accident can be found on the website of the United States Nuclear Regulatory commission at www.nrc.gov/reading-rm/doc-collections/fact-sheets/3mile-isle.pdf.
5. An image of the magazine's cover—and a link to the full story—is available online at www.time.com/time/coversearch.
6. Despite making for a great catchphrase and a deceptively compelling argument, Behe's claims, however, have never been published in the peer-reviewed literature, the process by which scientific claims are tested and validated. More importantly, as the National Academies recently summarized, the peer-reviewed research has shown that each of these "design" examples can in fact be explained by natural selection alone.
7. For detailed responses to the film's claims, see the special report by *Scientific American* at www.sciam.com/article.cfm?id=sciam-reviews-expelled and the website maintained by the National Center for Science Education at www.expelledexposed.com.
8. Only Al Gore's *An Inconvenient Truth*, Morgan Spurlock's *Super Size Me*, and Michael Moore's *Fahrenheit 9/11*, *Sicko*, and *Bowling for Columbine* have grossed more than *Expelled*. (After controlling for inflation, add Moore's 1989 *Roger & Me*.)
9. Information on this international panel and its views on climate change can be found at www.ipcc.ch/.
10. The *Time* cover is archived at: http://www.time.com/time/covers/0,16641, 20060403,00.html.
11. These ads can be viewed at www.wecansolveit.org/content/videos.
12. To see the *Time* cover, see: www.time.com/time/covers/0,16641,20080428,00. html.

References

Ackman, D. (2001, May 8). A phantom energy crisis. *Salon.com*. Retrieved December 11, 2008, from http://archive.salon.com/politics/feature/2001/05/08/energy/index.html.

Bauer, M., Allum, N., & Miller, S. (2007). What can we learn from 25-years of PUS research? Liberating and expanding the agenda. *Public Understanding of Science, 16*(1), 79–95.

Behe, M. J. (1998). *Darwin's black box: The biochemical challenge to evolution.* New York: Free Press.

Boykoff, M., & Boykoff, J. (2004). Bias as balance: Global warming and the U.S. prestige press. *Global Environmental Change, 14*(2), 125–136.

Boyle, A. (2007, April 5). Framed or be framed? MSNBC.com. Retrieved December 11, 2008, from http://cosmiclog.msnbc.msn.com/archive/2007/04/05/113609.aspx.

Brainard, C. (2006, September 28). Inhofe, climate change and those alarmist reporters. *Columbia Journalism Review Online*. Retrieved December 11, 2008, from www.cjr.org/behind_the_news/inhofe_climate_change_and_thos.php.

Brainard, C. (2008, December 8). A one-stop shop for climate information? *Columbia Journalism Review Online*. Retrieved December 11, 2008, from www.cjr.org/the_observatory/climate_central.php?page=all.

Brewer, J., & Lakoff, G. (2007, August 29). The science behind framing. *Science*, E-letters. Retrieved December 11, 2008, from www.sciencemag.org/cgi/eletters/316/5821/56#9909.

Brown, W. (2002). *In the beginning: Compelling evidence for creation and the flood* (7th ed.). Retrieved November 15, 2008, from www.creationscience.com/onlinebook/index.html.

Bumiller, E. (2005). Bush remarks roil debate on teaching of evolution. *New York Times*. Retrieved November 15, 2008, from www.nytimes.com/2005/08/03/politics/03bush.html?ex=1181102400&en=c05617bb5a86470e&ei=5070.

Clinton, H. (2008, October 4). Ending the war on science. *Hillary Clinton for President campaign*. Retrieved December 11, 2008, from www.hillaryclinton.com/news/release/view/?id=3566.

Council on Foreign Relations. (2006, January). Backgrounder: Targets for terrorism: Nuclear facilities. Retrieved December 11, 2008, from www.cfr.org/publication/10213/targets_for_terrorism.html.

Cunningham, B. (2003, July/August). Rethinking objectivity. *Columbia Journalism Review*. Retrieved December 11, 2008, from http://cjrarchives.org/issues/2003/4/objective-cunningham.asp.

Dahinden, U. (2002). Biotechnology in Switzerland: Frames in a heated debate. *Science Communication, 24*, 184–197.

Dawkins, R. (2006). *The God delusion.* New York: Houghton Mifflin.

Department of Energy. (2008, October 9). *Status of potential new commercial nuclear reactors in the United States*. Retrieved December 11, 2008, from www.eia.doe.gov/cneaf/nuclear/page/nuc_reactors/reactorcom.html.

Discovery Institute. (2003, February 3). *The "Wedge Document": So what?*. Retrieved November 17, 2008, from www.discovery.org/scripts/viewDB/filesDB-download.php?id=349.

Downey, R. (2006, February 1). Discovery's creation. *Seattle Weekly*. Retrieved November 15, 2008, from www.seattleweekly.com/2006-02-01/news/discovery-s-creation.

Downs, A. (1957). *An economic theory of democracy.* New York: Harper.

Dunlap, R. E. (2008, May 29). Climate-change views: Republican–Democratic gaps expand. *Gallup News Service*. Retrieved November 15, 2008, from www.gallup.com/poll/107569/ClimateChange-Views-RepublicanDemocratic-Gaps-Expand.aspx.

Durant, J., Bauer, M. W., & Gaskell, G. (1998). *Biotechnology in the public sphere: A European sourcebook.* Lansing, MI: Michigan State University Press.

Eilperin, J. (2008, March 31). Gore launches ambitious advocacy campaign on climate. *Washington Post*, p. A04.

Eisenhower, D. (1953). Atoms for peace: Address before the General Assembly of the United Nations on peaceful uses of atomic energy. Retrieved November 15, 2008, from www.eisenhower.archives.gov/All_About_Ike/Speeches/Atoms_for_Peace.pdf.

Elsworth, C. (2008, February 4). Arnold Schwarzenegger to back John McCain. *Daily Telegraph*. Retrieved February 4, 2008, from www.telegraph.co.uk/news/worldnews/1577193/Arnold-Schwarzenegger-to-back-John-McCain.html.

Ferree, M. M., Gamson, W. A., Gerhards, J., & Rucht, J. (2002). *Shaping abortion discourse: Democracy and the public sphere in Germany and the United States.* New York: Cambridge University Press.

Fiske, S. T., & Taylor, S. E. (1991). *Social cognition* (2nd ed.). New York: McGraw-Hill.

Forrest, B., & Gross, P. R. (2004). *Creationism's Trojan horse: The wedge of intelligent design.* New York: Oxford University Press.

Frankowski, N. (2008). *Expelled: No intelligent allowed.* Dallas, TX: Premise Media Productions.

Friedman, S. M., Gorney, C. M., & Egolf, B. P. (1992). Chernobyl coverage: How the U.S. media treated the nuclear industry. *Public Understanding of Science, 1,* 305–323.

Gamson, W. A., & Modigliani, A. (1989). Media discourse and public opinion on nuclear power: A constructionist approach. *American Journal of Sociology, 95,* 1–37.

Goffman, E. (1974). *Frame analysis: An essay on the organization of experience.* New York: Harper & Row.

Goidel, K., & Nisbet, M. C. (2006). Exploring the roots of public participation in the controversy over stem cell research and cloning. *Political Behavior, 28*(2), 175–192.

Goodstein, L. (2006, February 8). Evangelical leaders join global warming initiative. *New York Times.* Retrieved November 15, 2008, from www.nyt.com.

Guggenheim, D. (2008). *An inconvenient truth.* Los Angeles, CA: Lawrence Bender Productions.

Ho, S. S., Brossard, D., & Scheufele, D. A. (2008). Effects of value predispositions, mass media use, and knowledge on public attitudes toward embryonic stem cell research. *International Journal of Public Opinion Research, 20*(2), 171–192.

Holland, E. A., Pleasant, A., Quatrano, S., Gerst, R., Nisbet, M. C., & Mooney, C. (2007). Letters: The risks and advantages of framing science. *Science, 317*(5842), 1168b.

Irwin, A., & Wynne, B. (1996). Introduction. In A. Irwin & B. Wynne (Eds.), *Misunderstanding science? The public reconstruction of science and technology* (pp. 1–19). Cambridge: Cambridge University Press.

Kahneman, D. (2003). Maps of bounded rationality: A perspective on intuitive judgment and choice. In T. Frängsmyr (Ed.), *Les Prix Nobel: The Nobel Prizes 2002* (pp. 449–489). Stockholm: Nobel Foundation.

Kahneman, D., & Tversky, A. (1972). Subjective probability: A judgment of representativeness. *Cognitive Psychology, 3,* 430–454.

Kahneman, D., & Tversky, A. (1979). Prospect theory: An analysis of decisions under risk. *Econometrica, 47,* 313–327.

Kahneman, D., & Tversky, A. (1984). Choices, values and frames. *American Psychologist, 39,* 341–350.

Kolmes, S. A., & Butkus, R. A. (2007). Science, religion, and climate change. *Science 316*(5824), 540.

Kronje, R. (2008). Going public with the scientific process. *Science, 319*(5869), 1483.

Labov, J., & Pope, B. K. (2008). Understanding our audiences: The design and evolution of science, evolution, and creationism. *CBE-Life Sciences Education, 7*(1), 20–24.

McCright, A. M., & Dunlap, R. E. (2003). Defeating Kyoto: The conservative movement's impact on U.S. climate change policy. *Social Problems, 50*(3), 348–373.

Mooney, C. (2004, November/December). Blinded by science. *Columbia Journalism Review.* Retrieved December 11, 2008, from http://cjrarchives.org/issues/2004/6/mooney-science.asp.

Mooney, C. (2005). *The Republican war on science.* New York: Basic Books.

Mooney, C., & Nisbet, M. C. (2005, September/October). When coverage of evolution shifts to the political and opinion pages, the scientific context falls away, unraveling Darwin. *Columbia Journalism Review,* 31–39.

MSNBC. (2005). Frist voices support for "intelligent design." MSNBC.com. Retrieved December 11, 2008, from www.msnbc.msn.com/id/9008040.

Mutz, D. (2006). How the mass media divide us. In P. Nivola & D. W. Brady (Eds.), *Red and blue nation?* (vol. 1, pp. 223–263). Washington, DC: The Brookings Institution.

National Academies. (2008, January 3). Scientific evidence supporting evolution continues to grow; nonscientific approaches do not belong in science classrooms. Retrieved November 18, 2008, from http://www8.nationalacademies.org/onpinews/newsitem.aspx?RecordID=11876.

National Academy of Sciences and Institute of Medicine. (2008). *Science, evolution, and creationism.* Washington, DC: The National Academies Press.

National Science Board. (NSB). (2008). *Science and engineering indicators 2008.* NSB 08-01; NSB 08-01A. Arlington, VA: National Science Foundation.

Newport, F. (2006a, March 8). American beliefs: Evolution vs. Bible's explanation of human origins. *Gallup News Service.* Retrieved November 15, 2008, from www.gallup.com.

Newport, F. (2006b, June 5). Almost half of Americans believe humans did not evolve. *Gallup News Service.* Retrieved November 15, 2008, from www.gallup.com.

Nightline. (2005, August 10). *Despite criticism, "intelligent design" finds powerful backers, Seattle group works to create national debate where scientists say none exists.* Retrieved November 15, 2008, from http://abcnews.go.com/Nightline/story?id=1027129&page=1.

Nisbet, M. C. (2005). The competition for worldviews: Values, information, and public support for stem cell research. *International Journal of Public Opinion Research, 17*(1), 90–112.

Nisbet, M. C. (2008, September/October). Ben Stein's Trojan Horse: Mobilizing the state house and local news agenda. *Skeptical Inquirer, 32*(5), 16–18.

Nisbet, M. C., Brossard, D., & Kroepsch, A. (2003). Framing science: The stem cell controversy in an age of press/politics. *Harvard International Journal of Press/Politics, 8*(2), 36–70.

Nisbet, M. C., & Goidel, K. (2007). Understanding citizen perceptions of science controversy: Bridging the ethnographic-survey research divide. *Public Understanding of Science, 16*(4), 421–440.

Nisbet, M. C., & Huge, M. (2006). Attention cycles and frames in the plant biotechnology debate: Managing power and participation through the press/policy connection. *Harvard International Journal of Press/Politics, 11*(2), 3–40.

Nisbet, M. C., & Lewenstein, B. V. (2002). Biotechnology and the American media: The policy process and the elite press, 1970 to 1999. *Science Communication, 23*(4), 359–391.

Nisbet, M. C., & Mooney, C. (2007). Policy forum: Framing science. *Science, 316*(5821), 56.

Nisbet, M. C., & Myers, T. (2007). Twenty years of public opinion about global warming. *Public Opinion Quarterly, 71*(3), 444–470.

Nisbet, M. C., & Nisbet, E. C. (2005). Evolution and intelligent design: Understanding public opinion. *Geotimes, 50*(8), 28–33.

Nisbet, M. C., & Scheufele, D. A. (2007, October). The future of public engagement. *The Scientist.*

Nordhaus, T., & Schellenberger, M. (2007). *Break through: From the death of environmentalism to the politics of possibility.* New York: Houghton Mifflin.

Nuclear Information and Resource Service. (2005). *Environmental statement on nuclear energy and global warming.* Retrieved December 11, 2008, from www.nirs.org/climate/background/nuclearglobalwarmingstatement6162005.pdf.

Olson, R. (2006). *Flock of dodos: The evolution–intelligent design circus.* Los Angeles, CA: Prairie Starfish Productions.

On the Media. (2007, April 13). *Blinded with science.* Retrieved December 11, 2008, from www.onthemedia.org/transcripts/2007/04/13/04.

Pan, Z., & Kosicki, G. M. (1993). Framing analysis: An approach to news discourse. *Political Communication, 10,* 55–75.

Pew. (2008, May 8). A deeper partisan divide on global warming. *Pew Research Center for the People and the Press.* Retrieved November 15, 2008, from http://people-press.org/report/417/a-deeper-partisan-divide-over-global-warming.

Popkin, S. L. (1991). *The reasoning voter.* Chicago, IL: University of Chicago Press.

Powell, M. (2005, December 21). Judge rules against intelligent design. *Washington Post.* Retrieved November 15, 2008, from www.washingtonpost.com.

Prior, M. (2005). News v. entertainment: How increasing media choice widens gaps in political knowledge and turnout. *American Journal of Political Science, 49,* 577.

Real Clear Politics. (2008, June 18). McCain's speech on energy independence. Retrieved December 11, 2008, from www.realclearpolitics.com/articles/2008/06/mccains_speech_on_energy_secur.html.

Reynolds, P. (2004, September 15). Bush and Kerry battle over science. Retrieved December 11, 2008, from http://news.bbc.co.uk/2/hi/science/nature/3660276.stm.

Rudoren, J. (2005, February 15). Ohio Board undoes stand on evolution. *New York Times.* Retrieved December 11, 2008, from www.nytimes.com/2006/02/15/national/15cnd-evolution.html.

Russell, C. (2006). Covering controversial science: Improving reporting on science and public policy. Working Paper, Joan Shorenstein Center on the Press, Politics, and Public Policy, Harvard University. Retrieved December 11, 2008, from www.hks.harvard.edu/presspol/research_publications/papers/working_papers/2006_4.pdf.

Scheufele, D. A. (1999). Framing as a theory of media effects. *Journal of Communication, 29,* 103–123.

Science & Politics blog. (2007). A one-stop shop for the framing science debate. Retrieved December 11, 2008, from http://sciencepolitics.blogspot.com/2007_04_01_archive.html.

Stengel, R. (2008, April 17). Why we're going green. *Time.* Retrieved November 20, 2008, from www.time.com/time/magazine/article/0,9171,1731899,00.html.

Time. (1979, April 9). A nuclear nightmare. Retrieved November 15, 2008, from www.time.com/time.

Time. (2006, April 3). Global warming: Be worried. Be very worried. Retrieved November 15, 2008, from www.time.com/time/covers/0,16641,20060403,00. html.

Tversky, A., & Kahneman, D. (1981). The framing of decisions and the psychology of choice. *Science, 211*, 453–458.

Union of Concerned Scientists (n.d). Position on nuclear power and energy. Retrieved December 11, 2008, from www.ucsusa.org/nuclear_power/nuclear_ power_and_global_warming/ucs-position-on-nuclear-power.html.

United States Nuclear Regulatory Commission (n.d). *Our History: The NRC Today*. Retrieved November 15, 2008, from www.nrc.gov/about-nrc/history.html.

Vidal, J., & Kington, T. (2007, April 27). Protect God's creation: Vatican issues new green message for world's Catholics. *Guardian*. Retrieved June 5, 2009, from www.guardian.co.uk/world/2007/apr/27/catholicism.religion.

Weart, S. R. (1988). *Nuclear fear: A history of images*. Cambridge, MA: Harvard University Press.

Whitman, C., & Moore, P. (2006, May 15). Nuclear should be part of our future. *Boston Globe*.

Wilson, E. O. (2006). *The Creation: An appeal to save life on earth*. New York: W.W. Norton.

Wynne, B. (1992). Misunderstood misunderstanding: Social identities and public uptake of science. *Public Understanding of Science, 1*, 281–304.

Chapter 3

Focusing on Fairness in Science and Risk Communication

John C. Besley

Introduction

At some point while growing up, most children are told that life is not fair. Communication scholars, too, can look to our field and see instances where fairness has become crucial due to concerns about its absence. Media historians can point to the emergence of the Federal Communication Commission's Fairness Doctrine, mandating honest, equitable, and balanced coverage of political issues; those interested in the sociology of the news can point to the idea of fairness as a norm meant to guide journalists in their work. Fox News has co-opted the word "fairness" as the slogan for its conservative news channel, while the media watchdog Fairness & Accuracy in Reporting (FAIR) criticizes the shift toward ideology-slanted programming that organizations like Fox create.

While most individuals recognize the futility of expecting fair treatment in many aspects of their lives, they also view the fair treatment of citizens as essential to what makes the democratic process superior to other forms of decision making (Hibbing & Theiss-Morse, 2002). In political theory, Rawls (1971, 2001) uses the thought-experiment of a "veil of ignorance" as a means to encourage readers to contemplate how society might create governance procedures that ensure political justice. In this well-known idea, fairness is achieved by forcing participants to design a political system without knowledge of their eventual place in that system. According to Ryan (2006), Rawls' theory has led to more than 2,000 follow-up books, articles, and other pieces of commentary.

Similar, and perhaps most relevant to communication scholars, is the work of Habermas (e.g., Habermas, 1989) from whom many have drawn guidance in describing a normative ideal for the public sphere against which to compare contemporary politics (e.g., Norris, 2000; Scheufele & Nisbet, 2002). Habermas' discussion of a hypothetical ideal speech situation serves as a means of assessing the quality of democratic processes in terms of the degree to which they are fairly and competently enacted. In addition to political philosophy, social theory has also shown a keen interest in understanding the idea of fairness in how humans interact. For example, a recent issue of *Social Research* (Humphrey, 2006) was dedicated to the topic, some of which focused on the potential biological and evolutionary roots of fairness (de Waal, 2006).

The core idea of this chapter is that fairness matters: it is a theoretically rich concept around which to build research and evaluation of any situation where citizens have direct or mediated communication with decision makers. This chapter begins with an outline of social psychological research on justice as fairness and a discussion of the relevance of this research tradition to science communication scholarship and practice. The discussion focuses on existing research on public participation and the concept of trust, arguing that both traditions draw on concepts related to justice without explicitly drawing on this body of research. It further argues that focusing research on known sub-dimensions of fairness—which include outcome or distributive fairness, procedural fairness, interpersonal fairness, and informational fairness—could enhance existing science communication research and evaluation efforts. To support this assertion, several specific science communication projects that have successfully integrated justice as fairness research into their design and provided meaningful results are presented.

Social Psychological Research on Justice as Fairness

The centrality of fairness in how people think has led to an active body of social psychological research on fairness that began with a focus on perceived fairness of outcomes. This stream of research began in the 1940s with classic research on why some soldiers felt they were receiving adequate levels of promotion and reward while other soldiers who were actually moving up the ranks faster felt less satisfied. The results of this work showed that absolute outcome was less important to a sense of fairness than perceived outcome such that soldiers who experienced an environment of rapid promotion (e.g., airmen) were less happy than those who experienced a more stable environment (e.g., military police) (Stouffer, Schuman, DeVinney, Star, & Williams, 1949). Researchers built on this work over the next couple of decades until, in the mid-1970s, two legal scholars used a series of experiments to assess which court procedures people felt were most effective (Thibaut & Walker, 1975). The findings of this research emphasized the importance of fair procedure and shifted the fairness discussion from an exclusive focus on outcomes to a discussion that included both outcomes and procedures. Indeed, the ground-breaking aspect of this research by Thibaut and Walker was the finding that those who received unfavorable outcomes might still be kept satisfied if they perceived that the procedures leading to those outcomes were fair (see also

Leventhal, 1976, 1980). Thibaut and Walker (1975) argued that their research presented a challenge to rational choice models which argued that individuals act primarily based on outcomes. The research on fair procedure during this era primarily focused on the idea of "voice," which was the idea that individuals would be more likely to perceive a process as fair if they felt they had an appropriate voice in that decision-making process (Folger, 1977; Folger, Rosenfield, Grove, & Corkan, 1979). Voice, in this regard, resembles the concept of external efficacy which is used in much of the political communication research (Rosenstone & Hansen, 1993; Verba, Schlozman, & Brady, 1995).

Having differentiated between distributive (outcome) and procedural fairness, it was not long before justice research began to show that fairness included additional dimensions. Initial interest focused on showing that interpersonal fairness—also called relational or interactional justice (Bies & Moag, 1986; Lind & Tyler, 1988; Tyler & Lind, 1992)—is separate from the voice component of procedural justice. Interpersonal fairness includes factors such as a sense that a decision maker is unbiased, truthful, and respectful. More recently, a dimension called informational justice (Colquitt, 2001; Greenberg, 1993) has emerged that emphasizes the importance individuals place on feeling that authorities have provided adequate information needed to make a decision. Overall, current research seems to suggest the presence of four fairness dimensions—distributive, procedural, interpersonal, and informational—that individuals use to assess decision makers (for reviews, see Colquitt, Conlon, Wesson, Porter, & Ng, 2001; Colquitt, Greenberg, & Zapata-Phelan, 2005; Colquitt & Shaw, 2005; Tyler, 2000; Tyler, Boeckmann, Smith, & Huo, 1997). While justice researchers have not generally focused on the communicative aspects of their model, justice perceptions in the studies above reflect experience with an authority figure with whom individuals have direct (e.g., through the court system or at work) or mediated (e.g., through scenario-oriented descriptions similar to news stories) communication (also see Gangl, 2003).

In addition to studying the dimensions of fairness, researchers have also sought to determine what makes fairness matter. Evidence for two non-mutually exclusive reasons dominates: Tyler and his research collaborators (e.g., Tyler & Lind, 1992), in particular, have argued that fair procedures and treatment have an impact on variables like individual satisfaction because they communicate to individuals a respect for group identity. In this regard, when individuals are dealing with out-groups (e.g., foreigners), the influence of perceived outcomes overwhelms the influence of process (Huo, Smith, Tyler, & Lind, 1996; Tyler et al., 1997). In more recent work, Tyler has turned to demonstrating that fair treatment can also lead to group identity formation (Tyler & Blader, 2003). Lind, Kulik, Ambrose, and Deverapark (1993) and van den Bos (van den Bos, 2001; van den Bos

& Miedema, 2000) have further shown that individuals use their sense of whether a process has been fair as a heuristic decision tool when they are uncertain about what would constitute a correct outcome.

The following section focuses on the argument that the breadth and depth of the social psychological literature on justice as fairness warrants greater consideration by science communication researchers (Besley & McComas, 2005; Joss & Brownlea, 1999). While a substantial body of research involving fairness does exist in science and risk communication, that research, which is discussed below, does not consider social psychological theories of justice.

Fairness in Research on Citizen Engagement about Science and Risk

While science communication researchers have not specifically taken heed of the social psychological research described above, they have included the concept of fairness in research assessing public decision making. As will be described more fully below, an examination of the science communication literature demonstrates that fairness has been included as either an assessment criteria for citizen engagement or as a specific component of a measurement index for constructs such as trust and credibility. The discussion of these concepts extends far beyond the scholarship of science communication, but the focus here is limited to how the field of science communication has dealt with the concept of fairness. In lieu of a full review of engagement assessment criteria (see, however, Fiorino, 1990; McComas, 2001; Rowe & Frewer, 2000, 2004) or trust measures (see, however, Allum, 2007; Metlay, 1999), only discussions related specifically to fairness are included here.

In their book *Fairness and Competence in Citizen Participation*, a seminal collection on assessing public engagement, Renn, Webler, and Wiedemann (1995) argue that "the results that emerge from a review of the public participation literature … is that public participation must be fair and competent. These are principles that are widely agreed upon" (Renn et al., 1995, p. 11). In one of those chapters, Webler (1995) recognizes Habermas' efforts to encourage citizen engagement proponents to create procedures that are fair by allowing participants to self-identify (and have the opportunity to self-identify) and then take part in the development of agendas, rules, and discussion formats from the beginning to the end of a decision-making process. To a student of procedural justice research, these fairness criteria would appear to reflect a primary concern for adequate voice, as well as concerns about interpersonal treatment. Webler further describes competence in a way that appears to correspond with the concept of informational justice. For example, his criteria focus attention on the degree to which participants in decision making are given access to the best available information, as well as guidance about how that information was obtained.

Fairness also appears as a concept in a series of essays and research related to assessment by Rowe and Frewer. While highlighting the work of Renn and his colleagues, these authors do not provide an expansive discussion of fairness in the evaluation framework that they propose for assessing public participation methodologies (Rowe & Frewer, 2000, 2004). The criteria they describe do, however, touch on many of the same issues studied by social psychologists interested in justice. For example, they focus on issues related to voice and the likelihood that citizens have an opportunity for their perspectives to be heard based on a number of factors: the degree to which participants in decision making are representative of the affected public, the degree to which citizens are involved early enough in a decision-making process to affect the decision, and the actual influence that such citizens can actually have on the decision. Rowe and Frewer also include criteria related to informational justice, such as the degree to which citizens have access to resources necessary to understand the issue at hand and whether information is provided to explain the relationship between decisions and evidence.

Elsewhere, Rowe and Frewer (2004) call attention to the need to recognize that any citizen engagement can be evaluated by both its outcomes and its procedures (see also Chess & Purcell, 1999). However, whereas research on justice as fairness suggests looking at whether people believe they received a fair outcome, the outcomes discussed by Rowe and Frewer seem relevant primarily to the sponsor of the participation. For example, the outcomes evaluated involved whether decisions were reached to participants' satisfaction and whether satisfaction in decision makers increased, which do not correspond clearly with distributive justice outcomes. Some outcome criteria, such as whether a diverse group of stakeholders became engaged, seem relevant to what has been described here as procedural justice. The process criteria, inasmuch as they are met, often touch on issues related to procedural (i.e., voice), interpersonal, and informational justice.

While assessment of engagement is a complex undertaking, it is noteworthy that, in the work described, much of the language touches on similar subjects: outcomes, process, fairness. However, the science communication literature on engagement has not benefited from the efforts of this previous research to explicate and measure these concepts regarding attitudes toward authority.

Fairness in Research on Trust and Credibility

A similar use of the language of fairness can be seen in research aimed at measuring the contested constructs of trust and credibility. Several studies have sought to include fairness in the context of a single trust or credibility measure. For example, Trumbo and McComas used a credibility index initially designed to assess newspaper credibility (Meyer, 1988) to evaluate the credibility of government environmental and health agencies (McComas, 2003; McComas & Trumbo, 2001; Trumbo & McComas, 2003). The index itself includes five questions that use semantic differential scales to assess how respondents assessed government's (1) fairness, (2) bias, (3) trustworthiness, (4) accuracy, and (5) willingness to tell the whole story.

By and large, researchers have found that trust needs to be measured using at least two types of questions (i.e., trust consists of two factors). For example, one study differentiates social trust from neighborhood trust, with the second construct including a question about whether the news media report fairly about the respondents' neighborhood (Greenberg & Williams, 1999). Metlay (1999) found that questions focused on openness, reliability, integrity, credibility, fairness, and caring seemed to fit together as a single construct, whereas questions assessing trust as competence represented a second, unique concept. In another study, however, trustworthiness, caring, and competence questions appeared to measure the same "source expertise" construct, with a separate "source trustworthiness" factor emerging related to issues of vested interests, willingness to sensationalize, protecting themselves, and being held accountable (Frewer, Howard, Hedderley, & Shepherd, 1996).

A shortened version of Frewer et al.'s 1996 measures was used in a later study (Frewer, Scholderer, & Bredahl, 2003).[1] In this case, no specific mention of fairness was made, but it is relevant because it includes a number of survey questions that seem directly related to fairness dimensions as described by justice researchers. Moreover, similar dimensions were obtained by Poortinga and Pidgeon (2003) using a series of questions that included a specific question about perceived government fairness, which seemed to share substantial variance with questions about competence, caring, and openness. A second dimension emerged that was similar to the one found by Frewer, with underlying questions about distortion of information and industry interests. The authors called this trust dimension "skepticism."

Several other studies, although not explicitly mentioning fairness, have included various questions addressing elements that are often included in interpersonal fairness measures such as honesty (Allum, 2007; Jungermann, Pfister, & Fischer, 1996; Lang & Hallman, 2005; Sjoberg, 1999; Viklund, 2003) and caring (Allum, 2007; Siegrist, Cvetkovich, & Roth, 2000), as well as questions addressing potential informational fairness issues such as willingness to disclose information (Jungermann et al., 1996; Lang & Hallman, 2005). Johnson (1999) provides a thoughtful discussion of some of the problems of conceptualizing trust in terms of competence and caring,[2] but he does not provide a suggestion for alternative dimensions. He also discusses potential sub-dimensions of caring, such as process control, an approach that is not consistent with contemporary approaches to conceptualizing justice.

From the perspective of this chapter, the problem that Johnson describes may originate with attempting to conceptualize trust as a unique variable rather than as a component of something broader that matters to citizens. From the perspective of justice research, fairness is what matters to individuals, and the trustworthiness of decision makers is but one aspect of determining if a procedure is likely to be fair. It is equally possible to say that witnessing a fairly enacted procedure can tell a person something about the trustworthiness of a decision maker (and this almost certainly happens), but the main reason such knowledge would matter is to know whether one should expect fair treatment from that authority. The practical and theoretical goal is the perception of a fair process, not trust. Trusting an official means being able to expect fair treatment, particularly fair interpersonal treatment.

Allum (2007) also points out that competence, often included in measures of trust, has no necessary relationship with trust. In other words, it should be possible to design (as he does) a measure of competence that includes only questions about whether a decision-making authority has the expertise and knowledge necessary to make an appropriate decision. There is no reason to think that an individual could not believe that an expert has all the expertise needed to be fair, but fails to act because he or she simply does not care enough to deploy that expertise on behalf of the affected individual. The research described below, consistent with past justice research, also argues that while measurement difficulties will always create some intercorrelation, it should be possible to separate out the degree to which a person sees a process as fair in terms of providing a voice for individual concern, whether that person sees officials as interpersonally trustworthy and respectful, and whether that person feels that he or she has access to needed information. Competence, it will be argued, must be considered, but not necessarily in the context of fairness.

In summary, just as the evaluation-oriented research has recognized the importance of fairness without placing the concept into a broader body of theory, so too has the trust literature used many concepts that are linked to fairness research without strong connections to social psychological justice theories.

Recent Science Communication Research on Fairness as Justice

In this section, three recent, multi-method science communication projects that attempted to integrate the social psychology of justice research are described. Efforts to consider the impact of distributive, procedural, inter-personal, and informational fairness on outcomes such as decision satisfaction and perceived legitimacy of authority provide the focus. Each project grew from a model that, simply put, posits a relationship between communication behavior—whether direct or mediated—and justice perceptions; and a relationship between justice perceptions and outcome variables, such as satisfaction with a decision or support for decision makers (see Figure 3.1). Direct communication includes any activity that brings an individual into contact with a decision maker, such as a traditional public meeting or information session (Creighton, 2005; Gastil & Levine, 2005). Mediated communication would include any exposure to decision-making processes or authorities that occurs through interpersonal conversation with non-decision makers or, most commonly, via the news media.

In an effort to learn more about the relationship between fairness and outcome, three projects, addressing multiple research questions, are detailed. The Cancer Cluster Project examines public engagement in communities with possible elevated rates of cancer. The Perceptions of Local Scientists Project examines what residents of two communities think about local scientists conducting research related to agriculture biotechnology, nanotechnology, and gene technology. Finally, the Citizens' School Project

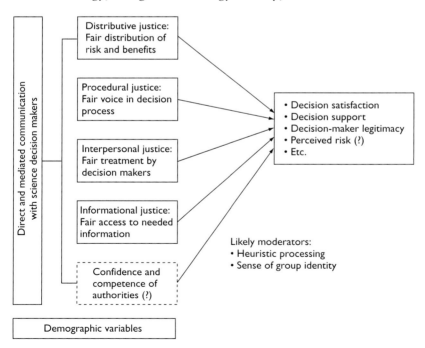

Figure 3.1 Hypothesized Relationships between Communication, Justice, and Civic Outcomes Related to Science and Risk Decision Making.

evaluates a citizen engagement exercise. In each of these projects, the central focus is on exploring how the sub-dimensions of fairness are associated with outcomes such as satisfaction.

Cancer Cluster Project

This initial project, focused on using justice as fairness variables to explain views about authority, was undertaken through public health investigations of elevated, community-level cancer rates. A portion of the project looked at six communities where there was an active attempt on behalf of public health officials to host some type of public forum to discuss the design of epidemiological investigations into high cancer levels or to host meetings to report the results of such investigations. The information presented here is part of a larger project involving 30 suspected "cancer cluster" communities (Trumbo, McComas, & Besley, 2008).

For the six-community project, mail surveys were sent to individuals who attended a public meeting as well as to a random sample of non-attendees. The attendee surveys (n = 133) included variables designed to assess distribution of risks, voice (procedural), and interactional (interpersonal and informational) fairness, as well as standard justice-related dependent variables such as meeting satisfaction, willingness to accept a decision, and willingness to attend future meetings. This study did not separate informational and interpersonal fairness components.

As a first attempt to use justice concepts in the context of risk, hypotheses were based primarily on the work of Tyler et al. (e.g., 1997). Analyses were run on the close-ended questions for the attendees. The results largely met expectations with perceived voice and interactional variables explaining the largest proportion of the dependent variables as measured using ordinary least squares (OLS) regression. The only exception was a dependent variable aimed at assessing post-meeting risk perceptions. In this case, perceived distribution of risks and benefits of the cluster research was the most substantive predictor of post-meeting risk perceptions, though perception of voice was still a significant predictor. In general, those who believed they had more voice indicated the meeting made them feel less concerned. This study provided preliminary evidence as to the potential of adapting concepts used in previous justice research to risk research while also highlighting the important role that non-outcome-oriented variables (voice and interactional justice) may play in explaining the impacts of activities such as public meetings.

In addition to meeting attendees, the cancer-cluster project also sent surveys to individuals in each of the potentially affected areas who had not attended the meeting, resulting in a total of 582 completed surveys for both attendees and non-attendees across the six communities. Both the attendee and non-attendee surveys included an open-ended question asking respondents why he or she did or did not attend the public meeting. As an additional analysis, the open-ended questions were content analyzed using a coding scheme that differentiated among several different explanations for decisions whether or not to attend. Open-ended responses were coded for rational decisions (i.e., the respondent wanted to get information, or ask a question, or the meeting seemed irrelevant). The coding scheme also captured SES/mobilization explanations meant to tap the degree to which respondents' life situations affected participation, including codes for explanations such as whether respondents indicated they attended because a friend/neighbor invited them or that they did not attend because they were busy with a competing activity. Finally, the coding scheme captured non-outcome justice explanations such as whether respondents decided to attend or not attend because they thought authorities were biased (interpersonal justice) or likely to be unresponsive to community concerns (procedural justice). The fairness-oriented explanations were evident in responses of only about 5% of attendees and 5% of non-attendees. Rational explanations were given by at least 60% of attendees and 15% of non-attendees. SES/mobilization explanations were given by 5% of attendees and at least 40% of non-attendees.[3] Whereas analysis of the close-ended question on the survey supported the notion that fairness represents a useful way to understand risk, the analysis of open-ended responses underscored the importance not to underestimate the critical role that practical considerations play in individual decision making about citizen engagement.

Three additional studies related to the Cancer Cluster Project also touch on justice as fairness concepts, including an analysis of survey data related to justice perceptions of meeting attendees (McComas, Trumbo, & Besley, 2007), data related to content analysis focus on cancer cluster news coverage (Besley, McComas, & Trumbo, 2008), and a series of qualitative interviews with journalists about the role of procedural fairness by decision makers as a component of their stories (Besley & McComas, 2007).

Perceptions of Local Scientists Project

This project attempted to better understand the relationship between media use and independent variables assessing sub-dimensions of justice perceptions. Specifically, it assessed how residents of two university-affiliated counties felt about scientists conducting research in their community in controversial areas such as agricultural biotechnology, gene therapy, and nanotechnology. A survey was mailed to 5,000 individuals across the two counties, resulting in a final sample of 1,306 respondents. The survey included a full set of media exposure and attention measures (Chaffee & Schleuder, 1986) for both regular news and science news. It also included updated measures of justice based on the work of Colquitt

(2005), including measures for science-oriented distributional, procedural, interpersonal, and informational justice.

The first analysis of these data examined the relationships between media use and justice perceptions using OLS regression (Besley, McComas, & Waks, 2006). Results indicated that exposure to television, national newspapers, and local newspapers are poor predictors of the perceived fairness of local scientists. Attention to science news, however, was generally a reasonable predictor of distributive, procedural, and interpersonal justice, but not of informational fairness. Of a range of variables, only community attachment predicted perceived informational fairness. The data best explained the distributive fairness of risk and benefits (as captured by the r-squared statistic). In this case, attention to news and science media both predicted increased sense of fair outcomes.

A second analysis sought to build models to assess how various perceptions of justice actually influence perceptions of the risks and benefits of three emerging technologies; it also sought to assess overall satisfaction with local research activities (McComas, Besley, & Yang, 2008). In this case, the distributional justice measure, consisting of questions about the relative risks and benefits of research to the community, was the only fairness-oriented predictor of support for technology. All four of the justice measures, however, predicted overall satisfaction, although the relationship between interpersonal justice and satisfaction was relatively weak. The media-use variables did not appear to be significant predictors of views about emerging technologies, although a negative relationship emerged between satisfaction and science media use. Also, even though the recent history of justice research emphasizes the importance of non-outcome-oriented fairness, these two analyses highlight the apparent importance of outcomes when it comes to thinking about risk.

This project was the first attempt by science communication scholars to use the full range of justice dimensions, but the adaptation of these dimensions for use in science communication research turned out to be somewhat problematic. Only the questions meant for measuring interpersonal justice had high enough levels of intercorrelation to have a Cronbach's *alpha* above 0.90. The other three variables had alphas between 0.67 and 0.68, somewhat less than is desirable (DeVellis, 2003). These difficulties highlight the need for research aimed at formally designing and testing improved measures for justice as fairness in science communication contexts.

Citizens' School Project

Justice concepts were also examined in the evaluation of a science outreach project hosted by the University of South Carolina (Toumey, 2007; Toumey & Baird, 2006). Citizens' Schools are a form of engagement that involve having members of the public take part in evening sessions for approximately two months that involve a combination of learning about emerging technologies and dialogue with working scientists and fellow citizen participants. In one investigation of these schools, the key sub-dimensions of justice were integrated into the analysis of open-ended comments provided by participants in "citizens' schools" discussing nanotechnology. The goal here was to understand what lay participants involved in the outreach project told others, if anything, about the experts who took part in the program. The survey found that 18% of participants said they discussed the quality of the discussion (procedural justice/voice) and 8% said they discussed experts' interpersonal behavior (interpersonal justice) during the program. In contrast, 17% said they discussed the utility of their participation, 26% said they discussed experts' presentation skills, and 17% said they discussed the depth of knowledge and competence possessed by expert presenters (Besley, Kramer, Yao, & Toumey, 2008). In addition to the analysis of why people attend (McComas, Besley, & Trumbo, 2006), described above, this represented a further attempt to use justice concepts in the analysis of text. Similar to the previous content analysis, the results pointed to the utility of justice concepts in understanding views about science and technology while also highlighting the need to consider non-justice concepts such as the utility of an experience and the competence of experts.

A second endeavor undertaken with two groups of participants in citizens' schools—including one group focused on nanotechnology and one group focused on energy—represents a first attempt at using justice variables in the pre- and post-testing of a specific engagement activity. Although the sample sizes were small, participation in the citizens' school was associated with less perceived risk and more positive views about the interpersonal fairness of community-based scientists such as the experts with whom they interacted during the citizens' schools in both schools (Kramer & Besley, 2008). This investigation, however, also pointed to the need for continued work on developing reliable composite indices for measuring fairness perceptions in the context of science and risk.

Table 3.1 summarizes the results from the three projects described above.

An Agenda for Future Research

Most scholars hope that the theories and concepts they study will endure. The idea of fairness—which appears so central to how people interact with authority—has the potential to provide substantial insight into how people evaluate potential decision making around issues of health and environmental risk. If, however, it turns out that the main factor influencing judgments by individuals assessing hazards is the distribution of benefits and

Table 3.1 Summary of Findings and Areas for Future Improvement of Existing Science Communication Research on Justice as Fairness

Project	Results Relevant to Justice	Areas for Future Research
Local cancer cluster project Studies explored views of participants in public meetings, people from affected areas who had not attended meetings	• Initial support for consideration of distributive, procedural, and interpersonal justice as independent variables • Support for use of justice concepts in analyzing open-ended texts from surveys and media content	• Reliability of the measurement of fairness perceptions • No inclusion of informational justice • May be important to consider issues of competence, in addition to fairness perceptions
Views of local scientists project Studies explored communication variables as predictors of fairness perceptions along four dimensions of justice and used justice perceptions to predict outcomes such as satisfaction with local scientists conducting controversial research	• Attention to science news main media predictor of fairness perceptions • Distributive justice was the primary predictor of views about specific technology but all sub-dimensions of justice predict overall satisfaction with local research	• Reliability of the revised measurement of fairness perceptions continues to be a problem • Competence was not included in study
Citizens' School project Studies explored past participants' interpersonal discussion about experts involved in an outreach program and pre- and post-participant views about authority	• Participants used criteria consistent with procedural justice, in particular, to describe their Citizens' School experience • Post-engagement increases in perceptions that scientists are interpersonally fair, as well as changes in risk perceptions	• Reliability of a further revised measurement instrument still problematic • Post-test surveys did not assess competence • Small, self-selected sample

risks, then the proposed line of research will challenge the original work in social psychology that emphasizes the importance of non-outcome forms of justice. If the research, however, shows that factors such as fair process, fair interpersonal treatment, and fair provision of information also matter, then the proposed research will provide support for risk assessors and managers who want to engage citizens in meaningful deliberations about risk-related decisions. Evaluators of such engagement could also use risk perceptions to evaluate whether participants (or those who observe engagement via the media) who complete a decision-making process feel that it has been fair. Research in the areas of trust and credibility has convincingly shown that outcomes are not everything when it comes to managing risk. But the main argument of this chapter is that a focus on the full range of fairness perceptions, not just trust, would enhance future efforts.

Indeed, while there are many potential avenues for research, it is first necessary to establish reliable indices for each dimension of justice and ensure that these dimensions reflect the reality of how people assess issues of interest to science communication. Besley and colleagues have attempted to develop and refine such measures in the context of each new study, but what ultimately may be needed is a stand-alone project specifically devoted to question development. Attempts to use student samples for such measurement have not been successful, possibly because students have a relatively undeveloped sense of how they feel about hazard-related risk and public officials. Therefore, it seems necessary to use adult samples with the concomitant extra cost. Ideally, these measures need to be adaptable to different science-related decision-making contexts. As part of the process of scale development, it will also be important to determine how different fairness dimensions are correlated to previous measures of trust and competence. The need to develop a unique stand-alone measure of perceived competence of authority exists apart from any need to explore fairness, but correlating perceived competence and fairness will help build a more complete understanding of what matters to people when evaluating risk decisions.

One of the difficulties in adapting justice research for use by science communicators is how to conceptualize distributive justice. Much of the original justice research focuses on organizational contexts where conceptualizing outcome fairness, in terms of money or some other tangible reward, is relatively straightforward. Early discussions on distributive justice make it somewhat more complicated by suggesting that fair outcomes are thought about in terms of (1) distribution based on norms of equality (i.e., all receive equal benefits/costs), (2) equity (i.e., respondents receive benefits/costs relative to input), and (3) need (i.e., recipients receive benefits/costs based on what they need or can sustain) (Adams & Freedman, 1976). Whereas the initial Cancer Cluster project measured only general risk perceptions, the two later projects made the argument that the outcome of relevance to justice researchers is who potentially benefited or faced harm from risk-related decisions. More specifically, a focus on risk-related distributive justice should look at whether respondents perceive that decisions benefited or harmed one person more than another (equality), whether the benefit/harm was justified based on relative contribution to the benefit/harm (equity), and whether the benefit/harm was based on the unique needs of the participants. Consistent with past research on the dimensionality of risk (Slovic, 1987), future research needs to further investigate the relationship between risk distribution and classic measurement of risk, which focuses on issues such as dread and the novelty of risks. Further, evidence shows that traditionally marginalized groups tend to have higher risk perceptions (Slovic, 1999).

In addition to measurement issues, a justice-focused approach can also provide guidance to content analysis research, which may help us better understand the process of science and risk decision making. Developing a coding scheme that both draws on existing theory and is applicable to a range of projects would represent a significant advance for science communication research. For example, a coding scheme designed to study media coverage of emerging technology (Gamson & Modigliani, 1989) has been used effectively to study the emergence of biotechnology (Nisbet & Lewenstein, 2002) and nanotechnology (Gorss & Lewenstein, 2005) as issues of public concern. This coding scheme, however, focuses on the technology itself, rather than the decision makers involved. Given the importance placed on actors in science communication (e.g., trust in authority), an opportunity exists to develop a coding scheme based on justice that enables researchers to assess how often media stories or interview subjects frame science decision makers and their decisions. As noted in the studies described earlier, Besley and colleagues have begun to develop such a coding scheme, but as with the design of most survey measures, work remains.

Experiments aimed at testing the impact of news stories or other forms of media content would help support arguments about the impact of fairness perceptions. Such research could also support the development of efforts to advance the type of coding scheme described above. For example, it should be expected that a news story coded as being about interpersonal justice should influence readers' views about interpersonal justice or result in the increased use of interpersonal justice perceptions in evaluating decision makers. Much of the social psychological research on justice as fairness has used experimental methods to demonstrate the impact of treatment along the various sub-dimensions of justice.

Ultimately, only further research can determine whether a justice as fairness approach provides a lasting contribution to science communication research. Fairness, whether as part of trust or existing evaluation frameworks, is already a part of science communication. This chapter has further suggested, however, the use of concepts from the social psychological study of justice to further enhance our understanding of how people evaluate risk decisions and decision makers. In this regard, it is not only worth asking if individuals feel they receive a fair outcome from science but also whether they feel they have experienced fair treatment at the hands of authority. A great deal of work remains before it will be possible to say the justice as fairness approach is central to science communication. But, as has been argued, a number of paths seem open for productive future research.

Notes

1. Frewer and her colleagues used six questions related to whether respondents see the source as trustworthy, accurate, factual, knowledgeable, responsible, and in possession of a good track record for a trust dimension called "source expertise" while a second dimension called "source trustworthiness" includes questions about whether a respondents felt a source was likely to withhold evidence, distort information, provide information proven wrong in the past, and inaccurate information to protect their own interests. Interestingly, the trustworthiness question was included in the expertise dimension.
2. He also discusses the issue of conceptualizing trust in terms of value similarity (Earle & Cvetkovich, 1995), but this approach would seem to have less overlap with a discussion of fairness and so is not discussed here. It might be possible to make linkages between the social value similarity approach to trust and the role that social identity plays in fairness perceptions, but no such attempt will be made at present.
3. Percentages do not add up to 100% because respondents could be classified as providing up to three reasons, including multiple reasons under any one broad category.

References

Adams, J. S., & Freedman, S. (1976). Equity theory revisited: Comments and an annotated bibliography. *Advances in Experimental Social Psychology, 9,* 43–90.

Allum, N. C. (2007). An empirical test of competing theories of hazard-related trust: The case of GM food. *Risk Analysis, 27*(4), 935–946.

Besley, J. C., Kramer, V. L., Yao, Q., & Toumey, C. P. (2008). Interpersonal discussion following citizen engagement on emerging technology. *Science Communication, 30*(4), 209–235.

Besley, J. C., & McComas, K. A. (2005). Framing justice: Using the concept of procedural justice to advance political communication research. *Communication Theory, 15*(4), 414–436.

Besley, J. C., & McComas, K. A. (2007). Reporting on fairness in civic life: Interviews with journalists about writing on local political leaders. *Journalism Practice, 1*(3), 339–355.

Besley, J. C., McComas, K. A., & Trumbo, C. W. (2007). Local newspaper coverage of health authority fairness during cancer cluster investigations. *Science Communication, 29*(4), 498–521.

Besley, J. C., McComas, K. A., & Waks, L. (2006). Media use and the perceived justice of local science authorities. *Journalism & Mass Communication Quarterly, 83*(4), 801–818.

Bies, R. J., & Moag, J. S. (1986). Interactional justice: Communication criteria of fairness. In R. J. Lewicki, B. H. Sheppard, & M. H. Bazerman (Eds.), *Research on negotiations in organizations* (vol. 1, pp. 43–55). Greenwich, CT: JAI Press.

Chaffee, S. H., & Schleuder, J. (1986). Measurement and effects of attention to media news. *Human Communication Research, 13*(1), 76–107.

Chess, C., & Purcell, K. (1999). Public participation and the environment: Do we know what works? *Environmental Science & Technology, 33*(16), 2685–2692.

Colquitt, J. A. (2001). On the dimensionality of organizational justice: A construct validation of a measure. *Journal of Applied Psychology, 86*(3), 386–400.

Colquitt, J. A., Conlon, D. E., Wesson, M. J., Porter, C., & Ng, K. Y. (2001). Justice at the millennium: A meta-analytic review of 25 years of organizational justice research. *Journal of Applied Psychology, 86*(3), 425–445.

Colquitt, J. A., Greenberg, J., & Zapata-Phelan, C. P. (2005). What is organizational justice? A historical overview. In J. Greenberg & J. A. Colquitt (Eds.), *Handbook of organizational justice* (pp. 3–58). Mahwah, NJ: Lawrence Erlbaum Associates.

Colquitt, J. A., & Shaw, J. C. (2005). How should organizational justice be measured? In J. Greenberg & J. A. Colquitt (Eds.), *Handbook of organizational justice* (pp. 113–152). Mahwah, NJ: Lawrence Erlbaum Associates.

Creighton, J. L. (2005). *The public participation handbook: Making better decisions through citizen involvement* (1st ed.). San Francisco, CA: Jossey-Bass.

DeVellis, R. F. (2003). *Scale development: Theory and applications* (2nd ed.). Thousand Oaks, CA: Sage Publications.

de Waal, F. B. M. (2006). Joint ventures require joint payoffs: Fairness among primates. *Social Research, 73*(2), 349–364.

Earle, T. C., & Cvetkovich, G. (1995). *Social trust: Toward a cosmopolitan society*. Westport, CT: Praeger.

Fiorino, D. J. (1990). Citizen participation and environmental risk: A Survey of institutional mechanisms. *Science, Technology & Human Values, 15*(2), 226–243.

Folger, R. (1977). Distributive and procedural justice: Combined impact of "voice" and improvement on experience equity. *Journal of Personality and Social Psychology, 35*(1), 108–119.

Folger, R., Rosenfield, D., Grove, J., & Corkan, L. (1979). Effects of "voice" and peer opinions on responses to inequity. *Journal of Personality and Social Psychology, 37*(12), 2253–2261.

Frewer, L. J., Howard, C., Hedderley, D., & Shepherd, R. (1996). What determines trust in information about food-related risks? Underlying psychological constructs. *Risk Analysis, 16*(4), 473–486.

Frewer, L. J., Scholderer, J., & Bredahl, L. (2003). Communicating about the risks and benefits of genetically modified foods: The mediating role of trust. *Risk Analysis, 23*(6), 1117–1133.

Gamson, W. A., & Modigliani, A. (1989). Media discourse and public opinion on nuclear power: A constructionist approach. *American Journal of Sociology, 95*(1), 1–37.

Gangl, A. (2003). Procedural justice theory and evaluations of the lawmaking process. *Political Behavior, 25*(2), 119–149.

Gastil, J., & Levine, P. (2005). *The deliberative democracy handbook: Strategies for effective civic engagement in the twenty-first century* (1st ed.). San Francisco, CA: Jossey-Bass.

Gorss, J. B., & Lewenstein, B. V. (2005). *The salience of small: Nanotechnology coverage in the American press, 1986–2004.* Paper presented at the Annual Meeting of the International Communication Association.

Greenberg, J. (1993). The social side of fairness: Interpersonal and informational classes of organizational justice. In R. Cropanzano (Ed.), *Justice in the workplace: Approaching fairness in human resource management* (pp. 79–103). Hillsdale, NJ: Erlbaum.

Greenberg, M. R., & Williams, B. (1999). Geographical dimensions and correlates of trust. *Risk Analysis, 19*(2), 159–169.

Habermas, J. (1989). *The structural transformation of the public sphere: An inquiry into a category of bourgeois society.* Cambridge, MA: MIT Press.

Hibbing, J. R., & Theiss-Morse, E. (2002). *Stealth democracy: Americans' beliefs about how government should work.* New York: Cambridge University Press.

Humphrey, N. (2006). Introduction: Science looks at fairness. *Social Research, 73*(2), 345–347.

Huo, Y. J., Smith, H. J., Tyler, T. R., & Lind, E. A. (1996). Superordinate identification, subgroup identification, and justice concerns: Is separatism the problem; Is assimilation the answer? *Psychological Science, 7*(1), 40–45.

Johnson, B. B. (1999). Exploring dimensionality in the origins of hazard-related trust. *Journal of Risk Research, 2*(4), 325–354.

Joss, S., & Brownlea, A. (1999). Procedural justice: Considering the concept of procedural justice for public policy and decision-making in science and technology. *Science and Public Policy, 26*(5), 321–330.

Jungermann, H., Pfister, H. R., & Fischer, K. (1996). Credibility, information preferences, and information interests. *Risk Analysis, 16*(2), 251–261.

Kramer, V. L., & Besley, J. C. (2008). *Assessment of a university-based program of citizen engagement on emerging technologies.* Paper presented at the Annual Conference of the Association for Education in Journalism and Mass Communication, Chicago, IL.

Lang, J. T., & Hallman, W. K. (2005). Who does the public trust? The case of genetically modified food in the United States. *Risk Analysis, 25*(5), 1241–1252.

Leventhal, G. S. (1976). Fairness in social relationships. In J. W. Thibaut, J. T. Spence, & R. C. Carson (Eds.), *Contemporary topics in social psychology* (pp. 211–239). Morristown, NJ: General Learning Press.

Leventhal, G. S. (1980). What should be done with equity theory? New approaches to the study of fairness in social relationships. In K. Gergen, M. Greenberg, & R. Willis (Eds.), *Social exchange: Advances in theory and research.* New York: Plenum Press.

Lind, E. A., Kulik, C. T., Ambrose, M. L., & Deverapark, M. V. (1993). Individual and corporate dispute resolution: Using procedural fairness as a decision heuristic. *Administrative Science Quarterly, 38*(2), 224–251.

Lind, E. A., & Tyler, T. R. (1988). *The social psychology of procedural justice.* New York: Plenum Press.

McComas, K. A. (2001). Theory and practice of public meetings. *Communication Theory, 11*(1), 36–55.

McComas, K. A. (2003). Public meetings and risk amplification: A longitudinal study. *Risk Analysis, 23*(6), 1257–1270.

McComas, K. A., Besley, J. C., & Trumbo, C. W. (2006). Why citizens do and don't attend public meetings about possible local cancer clusters. *Policy Studies Journal, 34*(4), 671–698.

McComas, K. A., Besley, J. C., & Yang, Z. (2007). *The perceived justice of local scientists and community support for their research.* Paper presented at the Annual conference of the Association for Education in Journalism and Mass Communication.

McComas, K. A., Besley, J. C., & Yang, Z. (2008). Risky business: The perceived justice of local scientists and community support for their research. *Risk Analysis, 28*(6), 1539–1552.

McComas, K. A., & Trumbo, C. W. (2001). Source credibility in environmental health-risk controversies: Application of Meyer's credibility index. *Risk Analysis, 21*(3), 467–480.

McComas, K. A., Trumbo, C. W., & Besley, J. C. (2007). Public meetings about suspected cancer clusters: The impact of voice, interactional justice, and risk perception on attendees' attitudes in six communities. *Journal of Health Communication, 12,* 527–549.

Metlay, D. (1999). Institutional trust and confidence: A journey into a conceptual quagmire. In G. Cvetkovich & R. E. Lofstedt (Eds.), *Social trust and the management of risk* (pp. 100–161, 180–181). London: Earthscan Publishers.

Meyer, P. (1988). Defining and measuring credibility of newspapers. *Journalism Quarterly, 65,* 567–574, 588.

Nisbet, M. C., & Lewenstein, B. V. (2002). Biotechnology and the American media: The policy process and the elite press, 1970 to 1999. *Science Communication, 23*(4), 359–391.

Norris, P. (2000). *A virtuous circle: Political communications in postindustrial societies.* New York: Cambridge University Press.

Poortinga, W., & Pidgeon, N. F. (2003). Exploring the dimensionality of trust in risk regulation. *Risk Analysis, 23*(5), 961–972.

Rawls, J. (1971). *A theory of justice.* Cambridge, MA: Harvard University Press.

Rawls, J. (2001). *Justice as fairness: A restatement.* Cambridge, MA: Harvard University Press.

Renn, O., Webler, T., & Wiedemann, P. M. (1995). A need for objective discourse on citizen participation: Objectives and structure of the book. In O. Renn, T. Webler, & P. M. Wiedemann (Eds.), *Fairness and competence in citizen participation: Evaluating models for environmental discourse* (pp. 1–15). Boston, MA: Kluwer Academic.

Rosenstone, S. J., & Hansen, J. M. (1993). *Mobilization, participation, and democracy in America.* New York: Macmillan.

Rowe, G., & Frewer, L. J. (2000). Public participation methods: A framework for evaluation. *Science, Technology & Human Values, 25*(1), 3–29.

Rowe, G., & Frewer, L. J. (2004). Evaluating public-participation exercises: A research agenda. *Science Technology & Human Values, 29*(4), 512–557.

Ryan, A. (2006). Fairness and philosophy. *Social Research, 73*(2), 597–606.

Scheufele, D. A., & Nisbet, M. C. (2002). Being a citizen online: New opportunities and dead ends. *Harvard International Journal of Press-Politics, 7*(3), 55–75.

Siegrist, M., Cvetkovich, G., & Roth, C. (2000). Salient value similarity, social trust, and risk/benefit perception. *Risk Analysis, 20*(3), 353–362.

Sjoberg, L. (1999). Perceived competence and motivation in industry and government as factors in risk perception. In G. Cvetkovich & R. E. Lofstedt (Eds.), *Social trust and the management of risk* (pp. 89–99, 179–180). London: Earthscan Publishers.

Slovic, P. (1987). Perception of risk. *Science, 236*, 280–285.

Slovic, P. (1999). Trust, emotion, sex, politics, and science: Surveying the risk-assessment battlefield (Reprinted from *Environment, ethics, and behavior* (1997), pp. 277–313). *Risk Analysis, 19*(4), 689–701.

Stouffer, S. A., Schuman, E. A., DeVinney, L. C., Star, S. A., & Williams, R. M. (1949). *The American soldier: Adjustments during army life*. Princeton, NJ: Princeton University Press.

Thibaut, J. W., & Walker, L. (1975). *Procedural justice: A psychological analysis*. Mahwah, NJ: Lawrence Erlbaum Associates.

Toumey, C. (2007). Rules of engagement. *Nature Nanotechnology, 2*(7), 386–387.

Toumey, C., & Baird, D. (2006). Building nanoliteracy in the university and beyond. *Nature Biotechnology, 24*(6), 721–722.

Trumbo, C. W., & McComas, K. A. (2003). The function of credibility in information processing for risk perception. *Risk Analysis, 23*(2), 343–353.

Trumbo, C. W., McComas, K. A., & Besley, J. C. (2008, May 22–26). *A multilevel analysis of cancer risk perception*. Paper presented at the annual meeting of the International Communication Association, Montreal, QC.

Tyler, T. R. (2000). Social justice: Outcome and procedure. *International Journal of Psychology, 35*(2), 117–125.

Tyler, T. R., & Blader, S. L. (2003). The group engagement model: Procedural justice, social identity, and cooperative behavior. *Personality and Social Psychology Review, 7*(4), 349–361.

Tyler, T. R., Boeckmann, R. J., Smith, H. J., & Huo, Y. J. (1997). *Social justice in a diverse society*. Boulder, CO: Westview.

Tyler, T. R., & Lind, E. A. (1992). A relational model of authority in groups. In M. Zanna (Ed.), *Advances in experimental social psychology* (vol. 25, pp. 115–191). New York: Academic Press.

van den Bos, K. (2001). Uncertainty management: The influence of uncertainty salience on reactions to perceived procedural fairness. *Journal of Personality and Social Psychology, 80*(6), 931–941.

van den Bos, K., & Miedema, J. (2000). Toward understanding why fairness matters: The influence of mortality salience on reactions to procedural fairness. *Journal of Personality and Social Psychology, 79*(3), 355–366.

Verba, S., Schlozman, K. L., & Brady, H. E. (1995). *Voice and equality: Civic voluntarism in American politics*. Cambridge, MA: Harvard University Press.

Viklund, M. J. (2003). Trust and risk perception in Western Europe: A cross-national study. *Risk Analysis, 23*(4), 727–738.

Webler, T. (1995). "Right" discourse in citizen participation: An evaluative yardstick. In O. Renn, T. Webler, & P. M. Wiedemann (Eds.), *Fairness and competence in citizen participation: Evaluating models for environmental discourse* (pp. 35–86). Boston, MA: Kluwer Academic.

Chapter 4

Understanding Public Response to Technology Advocacy Campaigns

A Persuasion Knowledge Approach

Janas Sinclair and Barbara Miller

Imagine you are flipping through your favorite weekly news magazine and you notice an ad that shows a large locomotive juxtaposed with a single sunflower. The graphic image captures your attention, and you pause to read the copy of the ad for General Electric (GE):

> Can technology and the environment peacefully coexist? Ecomagination answers yes with the Evolution Series locomotive. Who would have dreamed that a 415,000 lb diesel locomotive could have an environmental conscience? The Evolution locomotive is designed to be more fuel efficient and more powerful while it exceeds stringent EPA emissions standards, making the air cleaner and clearer for all. No small technological feat. This is the little engine that could. And will. GE imagination at work.
>
> (GE, 2007)

Imagine you have no particular expertise in engineering, fuel efficiency, environmental science, or EPA emission standards. How do you respond to this message about technology? Perhaps you think about GE. Is this an advertiser to be trusted? You might consider the motives behind the ad and whether or not GE is being forthcoming about its "Ecomagination" activities. Beliefs about this industrial sector might also come to mind. You might think about whether GE and similar corporations are generally committed to "doing good"—or if it seems more likely they are up to no good. You also might consider whether or not the government is keeping this industry in check through agencies such as the Environmental Protection Agency (EPA), which is mentioned in this ad. These thoughts, most likely occurring in a split second, lead to an outcome. If you trust GE and feel the industry is accountable, then the ad could very well produce a favorable response. The message may seem informative, and you may be attracted to the promise of having it all: new technologies, a clean environment, and no worries. On the other hand, if you find the trustworthiness of GE and the accountability of the industry to be questionable, then this ad is unlikely to generate positive attitudes, and the ad message may have failed in its objective—for at least one audience member.

Theoretical Approach

This chapter shares a common goal with most of the agendas presented in this book, which is to understand how science is communicated with general or lay audiences. More specifically, this chapter is focused on audience perceptions and how the general public makes sense of scientific information, and a number of chapters similarly focus on the reception component of communication. For example, in Chapter 1, Brossard and Lewenstein explore models of audience understanding of science, while in Chapter 3, Besley employs social psychological frameworks to explore specific attitudes that audiences may form during the process of science communication. This chapter similarly adopts a social psychological approach. This chapter is distinguished, however, by its focus on science communication in an explicitly persuasive context. In this chapter, the focus is on public interpretation of science information that (a) is delivered via the mass media and (b) originates from a marketer or marketer-dominated source(s). Thus, while persuasion could certainly be a goal in an interpersonal, public engagement setting (as explored in the chapter by Besley), here the focus is mass-mediated science communication.

Advertising and public relations are two kinds of tools that organizations may use to communicate with audiences via the mass media. Advertising typically involves placing messages by purchasing time or space within a media vehicle (e.g., a specific magazine or episode of a television show), while public relations efforts involve generating unpaid coverage of a story, event, or issue. While advertising offers an organization the greatest control over the message, public relations often appears more credible and more objective to audiences because the message is not clearly sponsored by the organization itself. The disadvantage of public relations, of course, is that organizations lack control of the message (Guth & Marsh, 2006). Both tactics are attempts to promote ideas, goods, and/or services in the interest of the organization (O'Guinn, Allen, & Semenik, 2006). A prime reason for an organization to use advertising or public relations is to communicate with larger numbers of people than can be reached feasibly in an interpersonal setting. The current chapter argues that an important reason to study these types of persuasive messages is that they may constitute a sizable proportion of the relatively limited amount of scientific information received and consumed by members of the general public, the vast majority of whom have been described as lacking in understanding of basic scientific concepts and processes (Miller, 1998; Miller, 2002; Miller & Pardo, 2000).

In this chapter, the origins of technology advocacy as well as a definition of this type of science communication—in terms of message content and target audience—are discussed. How technology advocacy has been used by a number of corporate interests and the intended outcomes of these campaigns is then examined. Next we present a model of public response to technology advocacy, which is based theoretically on the Persuasion Knowledge Model (Friestad & Wright, 1994) and has been developed through qualitative and quantitative research on audience perceptions of technology advocacy campaigns. Finally, directions for future research and implications for science communication are discussed.

The Rise of Advocacy Campaigns

Advocacy campaigns have been defined as efforts to support organizational goals by promoting the sponsor's interests on a social, political, or marketplace issue with the goal of defending the sponsor's current and future activities (Bostdorff & Vibbert, 1994; Haley, 1996; Sethi, 1977). An examination of the history of advocacy campaigns illustrates how they have been used to market ideas and why they are closely associated with science communication. Advocacy campaigns have existed, in some form or another, since the initiation of corporate institutional advertising in the early 1900s (Sethi, 1977). One of the earliest examples involved efforts by German textile interests to recover property seized during World War I. Textile Mills Corporation was retained on behalf of German interests to gain public support for the return of property lost by Germans during the war. Initiated shortly after the war, the campaign included speeches, news items, and editorial comment regarding international relations, treaty rights, and issues of respect for alien property during times of war (*Textile Mills Corporation* v. *Commissioner*, 1941). In addition to shaping public sentiment, the campaign is also regarded as having been influential in shaping legislative policy matters, including the passage of the Settlement of War Claims Act of 1928 (Sethi, 1977). While other examples of issue advocacy can be traced back to the 1930s, the political and social changes of the 1970s—namely the growing concern about energy and environmental issues (Burgoon, Pfau, & Birk, 1995; Sethi, 1977)—are often credited with the rise of advocacy campaigns. As public and media criticism regarding issues such as the environment and energy gained a foothold in mainstream America, industries in particular began looking for ways to defend themselves. Subsequently, technology advocacy, as exemplified by the GE Ecomagination campaign described above, has become increasingly common as companies and industry associations seek to promote acceptance of technology-based industries through public relations and advertising.

Technology Advocacy

Here, we define technology advocacy as efforts to support an organiza-tion's interests on issues related to science and technology, particularly energy and the environment. Technology advocacy messages typically address (a) the positive effects of the sponsor's activities and (b) the associ-ation between those activities and commonly held societal values. For example, some campaigns may generally emphasize the role of business in society and its contribution to the health and prosperity of the community. The GE ad discussed at the beginning of this chapter cites the benefit of "cleaner and clearer air for all" and explicitly associates GE's program of innovation with values through *The Little Engine That Could*, the classic children's story about the value of determination in overcoming seemingly insurmountable challenges. The non-technical nature of the appeal can be explained in part by the target audience. While target audiences for tech-nology advocacy campaigns can include lawmakers, corporate customers, investors, consumers, and current and future employees (Cutler & Muehling, 1989), these audiences are typically characterized by lay-level knowledge of science and technology. GE's "Ecomagination" campaign, for example, was designed to reach a broad swath of stakeholders; all the groups listed above (with the exception of lawmakers) were identified as target audiences (EFFIE Awards, 2005). Arguably most consumers; many lawmakers, corporate customers, and investors; and even some of a tech-nology firms' current and future employees can be characterized as members of the non-scientist, lay public.

Technology Advocacy Spending

Spending on technology advocacy indicates these messages are an ever-present source of science-related information for the general public. In 2006 over $150 million was spent on media buys for the GE "Ecomagina-tion" campaign alone, making GE's efforts to bridge technology and the environment the 119th largest campaign of the year in terms of advertising spending (Ad Age, 2007). Of course, this was just a fraction of the $1.8 billion spent to advertise all GE companies and brands (Ad Age, 2007). Still, there is evidence that technology advocacy campaigns represent a sig-nificant subset of all advocacy campaigns. The Annenberg Public Policy Center's ongoing study involving print and television issue ads in the Washington, DC[1] area found that for the 108th Congress, campaigns focusing on energy or the environment ranked third in spending at $53.8 million, which placed these campaigns just behind advocacy for business or the economy and health care (Annenberg Public Policy Center, 2005). Of the total spending on legislative issue advertisements during this period ($404 million), 79% involved corporate interests rather than citizen-based/

cause advocacy groups. Despite the sizable amount spent on this form of advertising, relatively little research has investigated audiences' responses to these messages.

Campaign Sponsors

Available spending data indicate that corporate entities command the largest share of voice in technology advocacy; here, the types of sponsors that launch these campaigns are examined. Corporate campaigns may be launched by a single sponsor, such as GE, or they may be sponsored by an industry association that represents the collective interests of the sector. For example, the American Chemistry Council, representing over 100 chemical companies including BASF, DuPont, Eli Lilly, and Merck launched the "essential$_2$" advocacy campaign in 2005. The campaign "shares stories about the many ways that products of American chemistry make modern life possible" (American Chemistry Council, 2007) and includes television commercials, public relations, media relations, and employee grassroots efforts. Similarly, the Council for Biotechnology Information, founded in 2000, comprises the leading companies involved in development of biotechnology-derived crops (including BASF, Bayer, Dow, DuPont, Monsanto, and Syngenta). Its "Good Ideas Are Growing" campaign has focused on the benefits of biotech crops, including protecting crops from viruses, reducing need for pesticides, reducing soil erosion, providing new energy sources through biofuels, and providing nutritionally enhanced foods, such as "golden rice." The "Good Ideas Are Growing" campaign includes television and magazine advertising as well as a website with materials targeted to journalists, consumers, farmers, teachers, and students (Council for Biotechnology Information, 2007).

Campaign sponsors may be national or local in scope; the West Virginia Coal Association began the "Friends of Coal" (FOC) campaign in West Virginia in 2002 to promote and gain support for the coal industry and public policies that affect the industry. The association includes coal companies and other coal-related businesses, small-business owners operating in areas where the local economy is dependent on coal mining, and other interested citizens. In addition to statewide television, radio, and outdoor advertising, the organization has used direct mail, Internet, and word-of-mouth promotion (Friends of Coal, 2006). The FOC campaign is indicative of the recent emphasis the coal industry in general has placed on improving its public image via the media, especially in light of increased environmental awareness. The FOC campaign targets local and regional audiences, and it emphasizes the role of coal mining in both the employment and economic development of the region as well as the value of coal in meeting the constantly growing energy demands of an expanding nation without relying on foreign energy sources.

Sponsor identification

Associations that sponsor advocacy messages have sometimes been criticized for the use of vague or misleading pseudonyms that serve to conceal the identities of individual corporate sponsors, such as Americans for Balanced Energy Choices, which is a coalition of mining companies, coal transporters, and electricity producers (Annenberg Public Policy Center, 2005). The term "front group" describes the use of a seemingly independent third-party organization to gain credibility for a campaign (Cutlip, 1994; Pfau, Haigh, Sims, & Wigley, 2007). Further, the identity of a *stealth* front group is purposively crafted to deceive audiences as to the sponsor's actual intentions. Stealth front groups have been examined in political advocacy contexts; for example, the purpose of the National Wetlands Coalition is to *oppose* government restrictions on wetlands development (Pfau et al., 2007). In the case of many technology advocacy campaigns, however, the use of association names may not be particularly deceptive or misleading. Audiences are likely to conclude that the source of a message promoting an industry is the industry itself. Our research has indicated most people correctly identify the source of technology advocacy campaigns sponsored by crop biotechnology (Sinclair & Irani, 2005) and coal (Miller & Sinclair, 2009) industry associations. Nevertheless, it is important to consider how audiences react to association sponsors and how this affects their overall response to technology advocacy messages.

Campaign Objectives

As a review of campaign sponsors indicates, companies engage in technology advocacy to protect their position in the marketplace, specifically by building public support for the sponsor and its products. Specific campaign objectives include counteracting perceived media bias and influencing public opinion, policy debate, and legislation. Technology advocacy campaigns are launched in response to current or anticipated controversy, and are therefore designed to build trust while deflecting criticism of the organization, its policies, products, or services (Bostdorff & Vibbert, 1994). In that way, campaigns can indirectly reduce the potential for future government intervention in corporate activities that results from public calls for investigations of, or protection from, industry (Cutler & Muehling, 1989; Sethi, 1977). Advocacy campaigns may also lay the groundwork for counteracting future legal or policy arguments by increasing the potential for audience adherence to certain values that may contradict values that are likely to be invoked by the opposition.

For example, in the 1970s, American Electric Power (AEP) initiated a campaign to promote the use of coal mining and reduce the number of regulations imposed on mining, including strip mining and pollution codes. In reference to the United States' reliance on foreign sources of oil, the campaign was titled "We have more coal than they have oil—Let's use it" (Sethi, 1977). The campaign emphasized the national economy while avoiding litigious discussions related to the environment. Other campaigns have been used by Mobil Oil to challenge legislative passage of an excess profits tax directed at oil companies, by the Chrysler Corporation to slow down the implementation of automotive pollution controls, and by Bethlehem Steel to restrict steel imports (Cutler & Muehling, 1989).

Organizations have also initiated advocacy campaigns in response to a perceived lack of objectivity by the media and an anti-business media climate (Fox, 1986). According to Cutler and Muehling, "Extensive attacks by the media, unbalanced by recognition of business' contribution to the American standard of living, have contributed to what might be referred to as business' persecution complex" (1989, pp. 41–42). In particular, oil, gas, and other energy companies have used technology advocacy campaigns to respond to media criticism on issues such as the environment and energy conservation.

Sethi (1977), however, pointed out that many of these attempts downplay industry's adverse effects on the environment by exaggerating the often-minuscule efforts of industries to control pollution, while publicizing adverse effects to the economy that may result from various pollution control efforts. Corporate messages have also been criticized for suggesting individual action can help solve environmental problems, thereby absolving the industry of responsibility. Moreover, the campaigns depict industry's response as voluntary while, in fact, environmental changes in corporate policy may have been initiated under threat of governmental prosecution (Sethi, 1977).

In the next section, we lay the foundation for development of a model to explain public response to technology advocacy.

The Persuasion Knowledge Model

Science communication research indicates technical knowledge alone does not predict non-scientists' attitudes toward scientific topics (Dunwoody & Neuwirth, 1991; Friedman, 1991; Gaskell, Bauer, Duran, & Allum, 1999). The question, therefore, is what types of beliefs do people use to interpret messages about science—and technology advocacy messages in particular? The Persuasion Knowledge Model (PKM) provides a guide for identifying a variety of beliefs that audiences access in response to a persuasive situation, and focuses on audience members' knowledge of a persuasive agent's goals and tactics (Friestad & Wright, 1994; Campbell & Kirmani, 2000; Kirmani & Campbell, 2004). According to the PKM, three types of consumer knowledge affect the outcome of a persuasion attempt: (1) topic knowledge, (2) agent knowledge, and (3) persuasion knowledge. *Topic knowledge* encompasses beliefs about the merit of the information pre-sented in the persuasive message. People use topic knowledge to evaluate the supporting arguments in a message as strong or weak; in the context of technology advocacy, this may involve judgments about the perceived merit of claims related to science or technology. Topic knowledge has received a great deal of attention in the literature on persuasion; it has been the focus of research based on attitude change models such as the Elabora-tion Likelihood Model (Petty & Cacioppo, 1986) and Heuristic-Systematic Model (Chaiken, 1987).

The PKM adds to this body of research by emphasizing, in addition to topic knowledge, beliefs about the persuasion experience itself, including agent and persuasion knowledge. *Agent knowledge* encompasses beliefs about the goals and characteristics of the persuasive agent. In PKM terms, this would be the message source, whether that source is an individual such as a salesperson encountered face-to-face or the sponsoring organiza-tion of an advertising campaign. *Persuasion knowledge* consists of beliefs about the purpose of a particular type of persuasive tactic, an audience member's own goals related to the persuasion attempt, and the actions one can take to manage the persuasion attempt. Figure 4.1 presents the

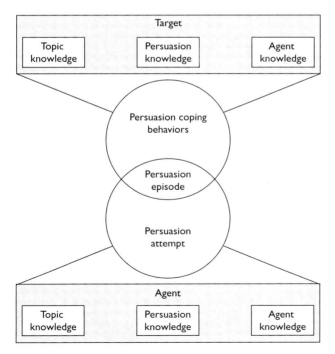

Figure 4.1 Friestad and Wright's Persuasion Knowledge Model (1994).

PKM as conceptualized by Friestad and Wright (1994). This model accounts for the topic, agent, and persuasion knowledge of both the target and agent of the persuasive attempt. Most research, however, has explored only the target's knowledge—specifically the audiences' focus on ulterior motives for persuasion. Findings indicate that a reduced focus on ulterior motives leads to more information gained from an advertising message (An, Jin, & Pfau, 2006).

A key element of the PKM is that audiences are conceptualized as actively "coping" with the persuasive attempt by pursuing their own desired goals. According to Friestad and Wright (1994) many different goals may drive responses to persuasion attempts. In some cases, people may pursue identity goals, such as managing other people's impressions or managing their own self-images. In other situations, people may primarily seek to manage the experiential benefits of the persuasion episode and enjoy the sensory, cognitive, or emotional stimulation it provides. Still another coping goal is managing one's long-term relationship with the marketer. Consumers may seek to manage this relationship, for example, by developing and maintaining accurate attitudes toward the marketer so they can better assess its motives and future behavior.

The PKM and Technology Advocacy

The PKM provides insight into some of the unique features of a technology advocacy campaign and supplies a framework for understanding audience beliefs and attitudes in response to these persuasive efforts. In corporate technology advocacy campaigns, the message source is typically a company or industry organization, and the message topic focuses on that company's (or industry's) actions. Corporate technology advocacy campaigns differ, therefore, from many persuasive attempts in that the message sponsor *is* the topic of the message. For example, in an advocacy campaign by Americans for Job Security, an association that promotes conservative candidates for national political races (Annenberg Public Policy Center, 2005), the message sponsor is not the focus of the message. On the other hand, in the case of the "Friends of Coal" technology advocacy campaign sponsored by the West Virginia Coal Association, the persuasive messages are focused on the coal industry, which is also the sponsor of the message.

While corporate technology advocacy campaigns do address matters related to science, technology, energy, and the environment, the real focus is on the sponsor's activities and the purported benefits of those activities. Distinctions can be made, however, among the relevant types of beliefs about the sponsor's activities. A key insight that can be drawn from the PKM is that audiences can interpret the persuasive agent's actions on multiple levels, both in terms of the immediate persuasive context and in terms of generalized knowledge about the agent's goals and characteristics. At an immediate level are beliefs about the sponsor in delivering a particular persuasive message. At a broader level are beliefs about the sponsor's actions as a member of an industry. Finally, the PKM indicates that audiences should be viewed as active participants in the persuasion experience, and that persuasion outcomes result from audience motives to engage with the message.

A Model of Public Response to Technology Advocacy Campaigns

The goal of the research agenda outlined in this chapter is to identify not only the types of perceptions that predict audience response to technology advocacy campaigns, such as topic, agent, and persuasion knowledge, but also to understand the specific content of those perceptions. We posit that two types of perceptions are central to audiences' responses to technology advocacy. These are (a) perceptions about the trustworthiness of the message sponsor and (b) perceptions about the past behavior and accountability of the sponsor and/or an entire industry. Figure 4.2 presents a model of public response to technology advocacy campaigns. According to this model, perceptions of sponsor trustworthiness and industry accountability lead audiences to evaluate a technology advocacy message favorably in terms of information content and also to identify with positive message themes. These responses, in turn, lead to positive attitudes toward the

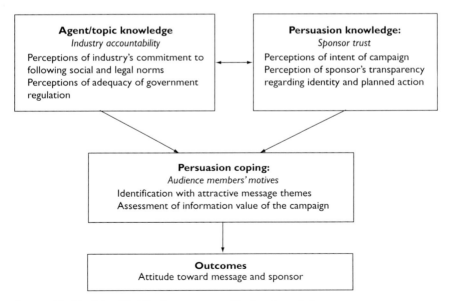

Figure 4.2 Model of Public Response to Technology Advocacy.

message and its sponsor. The model is based on findings from studies focusing on biotechnology (Sinclair & Irani, 2005) and coal advocacy campaigns (Miller, 2006; Miller & Sinclair, 2009), which are discussed below. There is also quantitative support for this model including the linkages among the accountability and trust constructs and their influence on audience attitudes (Sinclair & Miller, 2008).

Sponsor Trust

In the case of technology advocacy messages, the salient persuasion knowledge appears to focus on the sponsor's intentions in presenting the message and, more generally, the trustworthiness of the sponsor. Qualitative findings provide support for the relevance of trust in audience response to technology advocacy. In a study using focus group methodology, citizens in West Virginia were asked to respond to several ad concepts for the West Virginia Coal Association's Friends of Coal campaign (Miller & Sinclair, 2009). The ad concepts emphasized various attributes of the coal industry, including the following: (1) energy (e.g., meeting the demands for state and national electricity); (2) economy (e.g., building a strong economy through employment and coal tax revenues); (3) environmental responsibility (e.g., clean coal technologies and improved reclamation); and (4) the history and evolution of the industry (e.g., the industry's history in the region and new technologies for revitalizing the industry).

Four focus groups with nine to 11 participants per session, 40 total participants, were held in West Virginia in 2003. The focus group participants voiced questions and beliefs about the intentions behind the messages that were both negative and positive. Examples of negative responses included, "What are they up to?" and "What propaganda are they trying to shove down our throat now?" An example of a positive response included, "It's like they've really taken an interest, like they're really trying to help." Participants also expressed beliefs related to the advertiser's transparency in using a third-party organization name. For example, one respondent said, "There's a lot of coal companies who have a very bad image and, boy, do they need it cleaned up." Another offered, "Are they going to hide behind Friends of Coal? It needs to be opened up so you know exactly who you're dealing with." Similarly, participants voiced questions about the sponsor's activities mentioned in the ad concept. A typical response was "What did you really do? What are you really doing?" These thoughts about intentions and transparency are consistent with conceptual definitions of trust. Trust is strong when the organization's intentions are thought to be good and when the organization is perceived as transparent in communicating about its identity and activities.

In the field of psychology, researchers have noted that perceptions of trust are particularly important when individuals do not know other people's intentions and activities. Indeed, Kramer (1999) defined trust as "a state of perceived vulnerability or risk that is derived from individuals' uncertainty regarding the motives, intentions, and prospective actions of others on whom they depend" (p. 571). This definition is consistent with other research on advocacy advertising. In a qualitative study, Haley (1996) examined consumer responses to ads that associated advertisers with important health issues, including AIDS and drinking and driving, and found that perceptions of an advertiser's intent were a key aspect of organizational credibility. Intentions have traditionally been identified as a component of source credibility (Hovland, Janis, & Kelley, 1953), and research in speech communication has similarly focused on good will, or perceived caring of the source (McCroskey & Teven, 1999). Intent has specifically been defined as perceptions of whose interest will be served: only the good of the organization, or the good of the organization and of consumers and society (Haley, 1996; Javalgi, Traylor, Gross, & Lampman, 1994; Stafford & Hartman, 2000).

Additional literature has also identified information about the "prospective actions of others" as an important component of trust, as in Kramer's (1999) definition. Sharing information has been theorized to enhance trust. When an organization is perceived to be transparent in regard to its activities, it may be seen as open and honest, and access to this information empowers the public in dealing with the organization (Peters, Covello, & McCallum, 1997). Stafford and Hartman (2000) defined transparency as a component of the credibility of a "green alliance" between a marketer and an environmental NGO. According to these authors, in a transparent alliance all activities between a marketer and an environmental group are open to stakeholder scrutiny and feedback. Other researchers have similarly identified transparency as a factor in building trust in (a) partnerships between corporations and NGOs (Dutton, 1996; Fowler & Heap, 1998), (b) government- and NGO-led restoration efforts (Michaelidou, Decker, & Lassoie, 2002; Press, Doak, & Steinberg, 1996), and (c) communication with the public about potential environmental risks (Kasperson, Golding, & Tuler, 1992; Peters et al., 1997).

Industry Accountability

In the same qualitative study discussed above (Miller & Sinclair, 2009), focus group participants also expressed thoughts about the coal industry and its behavior beyond the immediate context of the persuasive message. Specifically, they discussed beliefs about the coal industry's commitment (or lack thereof) to community welfare. For example, one participant indicated, "They come and get what they want and they leave, and they leave you with a mess." Participants not only considered the degree to which the industry held itself accountable to the community, they also discussed the degree to which regulators held the industry accountable. In this case, regulation was often characterized as inadequate, or a mere "smack on the hand," and regulators were described as having "looked the other way" in the face of industry violations. These thoughts are consistent with definitions of public accountability.

Accountability has been defined in interpersonal contexts as an actor's answerability to audiences for fulfilling obligations, duties, and expectations (Schlenker, Britt, Pennington, Murphy, & Doherty, 1994; Schlenker & Weigold, 1989; Schlenker, Weigold, & Doherty, 1991). According to this perspective, when individuals in a society are held accountable for their actions, citizens can trust that those individuals will follow society's rules, and if the rules are broken, the offenders will be appropriately sanctioned. Accountability fosters trust because, as Schlenker and his colleagues state, "social control rests on a society's ability to hold people responsible for their conduct and to sanction violations of important prescriptions" (1994, p. 632). In other words, people can trust a system in which actors—or organizations—are bound by society's rules. An actor is held accountable to the extent that three conditions are met. These conditions are that (a) prescriptions apply to the particular event under scrutiny, (b) prescriptions apply to the actor by virtue of his or her characteristics and roles, and (c) the actor can be causally linked to the events in question (Schlenker et al., 1994).

This conceptualization of accountability was applied to the context of technology advocacy in a study of consumer response to advertisements from the Council for Biotechnology Information's "Good Ideas are Growing" campaign (Sinclair & Irani, 2005). Participants ($n = 258$) completed a survey questionnaire after reading one of four magazine ads from the campaign. Each ad depicted a different genetically modified crop on the market: cotton, corn, soybean, and papaya. The headline of each ad began with "Would it surprise you to know…?" and then described a benefit of the biotech crop. These benefits were less pesticide spraying, growing biofuels, reducing soil erosion, and protecting crops from viruses. The ads ended with an invitation to call or visit a website for additional information. Public accountability was defined in terms of the answerability of an industry (companies that produce biotech crops) for complying with social and legal norms. The elements of public accountability were operationalized as perceptions that (1) government regulation of biotechnology was adequate, (2) biotech companies were concerned with complying with regulation and protecting the public good, and (3) a particular company could be linked to potentially harmful effects of biotechnology.

Two elements of public accountability had a significant effect on attitudes toward the ad: perceptions of industry concern (measured as "companies that produce biotech crops are committed to protecting the public from possible risks of biotech crops/concerned about following U.S. government regulations/do not care about complying with U.S. government regulations," with the last item reverse-coded) and perceptions of the adequacy of government regulation (measured as "U.S. government agencies have regulations that specifically apply to the production of biotech crops/ have clear rules for the production of biotech crops/do not have policies related to the production of biotech crops," with the last item reverse-coded). The third element of public accountability did not impact attitudes in this study—and similarly failed to emerge as a theme in the qualitative study of the coal advocacy campaign. This may be because people assume corporations can be linked to how they treat their employees and the environment. The actions of companies may be seen as more public and perhaps more easily traceable than the actions of individuals.

Audience Motives and Outcomes

The quantitative study of the Council for Biotechnology Information campaign (Sinclair & Irani, 2005) found that perceptions of industry accountability and trust in the advertiser were both related to attitudes toward the ad. Findings from the qualitative study of the Friends of Coal campaign support this relationship and also provide more specific insight into the processes by which trust and accountability impact attitudes (Miller & Sinclair, 2009). These qualitative findings concerning motives that drive responses to a persuasion attempt are consistent with the conceptualization of audience coping strategies in the Persuasion Knowledge Model. Friestad and Wright (1994) outline a variety of coping strategies which audiences pursue, including holding valid attitudes toward the persuasive agent to better understand its motives and activities and to manage their ongoing interactions with the marketer. When sponsor trust and industry accountability are believed to be strong, audiences are expected to accept the information in the message and identify with message values. Conversely, low trust and accountability would hinder these outcomes.

In the Friends of Coal study many participants rejected message claims based on beliefs that the advertiser could not be trusted and that the industry was not accountable. As one participant stated, "It's not believable … Living here and seeing it, it's just that this is—it's just too good to be true." In the Friends of Coal study, participants had extensive knowledge of and experience with the coal industry to draw upon in considering advertiser trustworthiness and industry accountability. Even when audiences have less experience with an industry, however, it seems likely that perceptions of sponsor trust and industry accountability would impact their interpretation of the information value of the persuasive message. For example, audiences unfamiliar with the biotechnology industry based their attitudes toward the messages disseminated by the Council for Biotechnology Information on existing perceptions of trust and accountability in the campaign sponsors (Sinclair & Irani, 2005).

Despite rejecting message claims based on an inconsistency between knowledge of the industry and the message claims, the focus group participants also expressed motives to identify with the positive values in the ad concepts: "It reflects the pride that we have, and the miners have, in bringing that power to our country." In this case, citizens of West Virginia may have been particularly likely to identify with positive themes due to the close relationship between the industry, the community, and their own identity. It seems more generalized audiences, however, could also pursue identity benefits through technology advocacy by identifying with positive messages about being environmentally conscious and with commonly held values such as optimism, determination, and working to solve a problem. Other studies have similarly identified liking an advertiser and perceiving its values to be congruent with one's own values as key components of attitudes toward advocacy advertising (Haley, 1996).

Future Research Directions

Past research provides support for a conceptual model of audience response to technology advocacy. An important next stage of research involves quantitative assessment of the variables, which will allow for empirical tests of the proposed relationships among the variables. While past studies provide direction for measurement of most of the variables in the model, future work will need to establish measures for the persuasion coping variables. These measures need to isolate identification with the message themes (or values presented) and assessment of the information value of the campaign. In our research, the themes people identified with tended toward the values component of the advocacy message (e.g., the heritage of the coal industry, energy independence, etc.), while assessment of the value of the information focused on the benefits presented in the message. Future research could examine the connections between audience motives and message elements more explicitly. Additionally, an important issue to be addressed in future research is the conditions under which each motive is likely to drive responses to a technology advocacy campaign. In the case of the Friends of Coal campaign, the audience lived in a state that is closely associated with the coal industry. Research should examine how motives to identify with positive message themes operate when audiences are not as closely affiliated with the advocated industry. Indeed, further research is needed to explore the viability of the complete model across a variety of technology advocacy contexts.

We have focused on responses to corporate technology advocacy campaigns, but future qualitative and quantitative studies could examine the model in the context of citizen-based, non-profit, and/or environmental issue campaigns. Future research should also examine additional types of corporate campaigns. The proposed model of audience response was developed, in large part, in the context of the Friends of Coal campaign in West Virginia. This campaign deals with a relatively old and well-established industry, and targets an audience with direct, ongoing experience with that industry. This audience was certainly familiar with the risks associated with the coal industry, including damage to the environment, human illness, injury, and death. On the other hand, this familiarity means that participants most likely did not associate the coal industry with anxiety or the "dread" that is often associated with unknown risks. Exploring how the model operates across a variety of technology advocacy situations will not only address its generalizability but also enhance theoretical understanding of audience response to this type of persuasive science communication. Future qualitative and quantitative research should examine contexts in which audiences have varying levels of familiarity with the advocated industry and in which the industry is associated with varying levels of emotional risk. Below we propose specific effects of these perceptions on variables in the model.

The Effect of Industry Familiarity on Trust and Accountability

The audience's familiarity with the advocated industry may affect perceptions of trust in the technology advocacy sponsor and perceptions of the industry's accountability. We theorize, however, that trust and accountability are key factors in audiences' responses to technology advocacy campaigns across levels of familiarity. The general public, after all, will always be dependent on technical experts and organizations with the capital to fund technologies when it comes to understanding and utilizing technology. However, the cognitive richness of thoughts about trust and accountability and, potentially, the valence of these thoughts, could be expected to depend on familiarity with the industry. Specifically, as familiarity with the industry increases, people may generate more thoughts relative to the sponsor's trustworthiness and the industry's credibility. Conversely, as familiarity decreases, fewer thoughts may come to mind. Familiarity may also lead to more critical assessments of trust and accountability, both of which are likely fundamental in ultimately generating favorable attitudes toward an advocacy message and campaign (see Figure 4.2). This effect could be due to negative experiences with a sponsor or industry. It is also possible that familiarity over time could, in itself, lead to more critical assessments. The greater experience of older individuals, for example, is thought to lead to more critical views of organizations' intentions relative to younger individuals (Haley, 1996).

The Effect of Risk Judgment on Audience Motives

The research discussed here has not focused on the effects of risk perception on audience responses to technology advocacy. The Friends of Coal campaign can be characterized, however, as an advocacy situation where risks to people and the environment are significant, yet known and familiar. It seems cognitive dimensions may largely characterize audience members' judgment of this known risk, with emotion potentially tied to specific experiences with the industry. The "Good Things are Growing" campaign for the Council for Biotechnology Information, on the other hand, represents a scenario where the scope and nature of the potential risks are more likely seen as unknown. Risk judgment for crop biotechnology may be characterized by affective dimensions, including feelings of dread associated with a hazard that is new, unobservable, experienced involuntarily, and possibly dangerous for future generations (Fischoff, Slovic, Lichtenstein, Read, & Combs, 1978; Sjoberg, 2000, 2004; Slovic, 1987). Such unknown hazards are generally perceived as riskier than known hazards, according to the psychometric model of risk.

It seems risk judgment could also affect the saliency of motives to cope with the persuasion attempt by identifying with positive message themes and/or by assessing the information value of the message. When technologies are perceived to be high-risk, audiences might be especially motivated to identify with positive message themes. Many technology advocacy ads incorporate appeals to traditional American values involving an optimistic outlook and promise that problems can be solved. The underlying theme is that everything will be okay, a message that could be especially attractive when risk is judged to be high. At the same time, high risk could lead to a desire to avoid potentially anxiety-producing information in a message (Kahlor, Dunwoody, Griffin, & Neuwirth, 2006) and reduce motives to consider the information value of a campaign. In moderate-risk scenarios, motives to identify with positive message themes and motives to consider the information value of the campaign might both operate at moderate levels. In low-risk scenarios, audiences may identify with positive message themes as a heuristic and have low motivation to consider the information value of a message. Future research can test these assertions by including industry familiarity, risk perception, and more precise measures of processing strategies in the model. Future research may also examine how the saliency of each coping motive influences the model's dependent variable, attitude toward the message and its sponsor.

Implications for Designing Effective Campaigns

The proposed model of audience response to technology advocacy supports previous calls in science communication literature to examine effective communication as distinct from "educating" the public about science (Dunwoody & Neuwirth, 1991; Friedman, 1991). This research program indicates that effective corporate advocacy campaigns require trust in the sponsor. Sponsors can work toward this goal by demonstrating positive intent toward communities and the environment and by being transparent about their identity and activities. In addition, industries should foster accountability through a commitment to social and legal norms, and they should consider that effective government regulation is an aid to building accountability. NGOs and other non-corporate advocacy groups could benefit from considering that while science education is certainly vital, in an advertising and public relations context, persuasion knowledge may play a major role in communication outcomes. A media literacy approach may be useful in raising critical awareness of a sponsor's persuasion techniques and aiding audiences in evaluating the trustworthiness of a message sponsor. The target audience's familiarity with the industry should be assessed so that the campaign can provide appropriate information to help audiences appraise industry accountability. Both corporate and non-corporate campaigns are likely to benefit from knowledge of target audiences' risk perception, and campaigns may be designed to make risk more or less salient depending on the preferred persuasion coping motives.

For the GE Ecomagination ad discussed at the beginning of the chapter, effectiveness may very well depend on audience perceptions of GE's trustworthiness as a message sponsor, and on perceptions of GE's activities beyond the ad in terms of its public accountability. The message presents both an appeal to the values of *The Little Engine That Could* and information about GE technology as exemplified by the Evolution locomotive, thereby providing audiences an opportunity to pursue two types of identity coping motives. Understanding how audiences respond to technology advocacy, which may be one of the more commonly encountered forms of science communication, will contribute not only theoretical understanding but also practical knowledge about how best to communicate with audiences through an advocacy campaign—whether the purpose is to promote or counteract corporate interests. Designing effective campaigns, whether to protect a market, counter biased messages, or enhance science-related media literacy, requires first understanding public response to technology advocacy.

Note

1. The ads appeared in *Roll Call, National Journal, CQ Weekly, The Hill, Congress Daily AM, Washington Post, Washington Times,* and the Washington edition of the *New York Times.* Television ads were broadcast on Washington, DC television stations or run nationally on cable or the major networks.

References

Ad Age. (2007). *100 Leading National Advertisers; Top 200 Brands.* Retrieved November 17, 2007, from http://adage.com/datacenter/#100_leading_national_advertisers_global_marketers__other_ad_spending_data.

American Chemistry Council. (2007). *Chemistry is essential to living: The American Chemistry Council.* Retrieved November 19, 2007, from www.americanchemistry.com.

An, S., Jin, H. J., & Pfau, M. (2006). The effects of issue advocacy advertising on voters' candidate issue knowledge and turnout. *Journalism and Mass Communication Quarterly, 83*(1), 7–24.

Annenberg Public Policy Center. (2005, March). *Legislative issue advertising in the 108th Congress.* University of Pennsylvania, PA. Retrieved March 13, 2006, from www.annenbergpublicpolicycenter.org/issueads05/2003-2004/Source%20Files/APPC_IssueAds108thMM.pdf.

Bostdorff, D. M., & Vibbert, S. L. (1994). Values advocacy: Enhancing organizational images, deflecting public criticism, and grounding future arguments. *Public Relations Review, 20*(2), 141–158.

Burgoon, M., Pfau, M., & Birk, T. S. (1995). An inoculation theory explanation for the effects of corporate issue/advocacy advertising campaigns. *Communication Research, 22*(4), 485–495.

Campbell, M. C., & Kirmani, A. (2000). Consumers' use of persuasion knowledge: The effects of accessibility and cognitive capacity on perceptions of an influence agent. *Journal of Consumer Research, 27*(1), 69–83.

Chaiken, S. (1987). The heuristic processing model of persuasion. In Mark P. Zanna, James M. Olson, & C. Peter Herman (Eds.), *Social influence: The Ontario symposium, vol. 5* (pp. 3–39). Hillsdale, NJ: Erlbaum.

Council for Biotechnology Information. (2007). *Member companies and associations; Ads.* Retrieved November 19, 2007, from www.whybiotech.com.

Cutler, B. D., & Muehling, C. (1989). Advocacy advertising and the boundaries of commercial speech. *Journal of Advertising, 18*(3), 40–50.

Cutlip, S. M. (1994). *The unseen power: Public relations, a history.* Hillsdale, NJ: Lawrence Erlbaum Associates.

Dunwoody, S., & Neuwirth, K. (1991). Coming to terms with the impact of communication on scientific and technological risk judgments. In L. Wilkins & P. Patterson (Eds.), *Risky business: Communicating issues of science, risk, and public policy* (pp. 11–30). New York: Greenwood Press.

Dutton, G. (1996, January). Green partnerships. *Management Review, 85,* 24–28.

EFFIE Awards. (2005). *Brief of effectiveness (2005), GE: "imagination at work."* Retrieved April 12, 2006, from www.effie.org/award_winners/search_published_winners_list.html#2005%20Winners.

Fischoff, B., Slovic, P., Lichtenstein, S., Read, S., & Combs, B. (1978). How safe is safe enough? A psychometric study of attitudes towards technological risks. *Policy Sciences, 9,* 127–152.

Fowler, P., & Heap, S. (1998). Learning from the Marine Stewardship Council: A business–NGO partnership for sustainable marine fisheries. *Greener Management International, 24*(Winter), 77–90.

Fox, K. (1986). The measurement of issue/advocacy advertising effects. *Current Issues and Research in Advertising, 9*(1), 62–92.

Friedman, S. M. (1991). Risk management: The public versus the technical experts. In L. Wilkins & P. Patterson (Eds.), *Risky business: Communicating issues of science, risk, and public policy* (pp. 31–41). New York: Greenwood Press.

Friends of Coal. (2006). Retrieved February 9, 2006, from http:www.friendsofcoal.org.

Friestad, M., & Wright, P. (1994). The Persuasion Knowledge Model: How people cope with persuasion attempts. *Journal of Consumer Research, 21*(1), 1–31.

Gaskell, G. M., Bauer, M. W., Duran, J., & Allum, N. C. (1999, July 16). Worlds apart? The reception of genetically modified foods in Europe and the U.S. *Science, 2885*, 384–387.

GE. (2007). *GE's ecomagination series: "Evolution."* Retrieved November 17, 2007, from http://ge.ecomagination.com.

Guth, D. W., & Marsh, C. (2006). *Public relations: A values-driven approach* (3rd ed.). Boston, MA: Allyn & Bacon.

Haley, E. (1996). Exploring the construct of organization as source: Consumers' understandings of organizational sponsorship of advocacy advertising. *Journal of Advertising, 25*(2), 19–35.

Hovland, C. I., Janis, I. L., & Kelley, H. H. (1953). *Communication and persuasion: Psychological studies of opinion change.* New Haven, CT: Yale University Press.

Javalgi, R. G., Traylor, M. B., Gross, A. C., & Lampman, E. (1994). Awareness of sponsorship and corporate image: An empirical investigation. *Journal of Advertising, 23*(4), 47–58.

Kahlor, L., Dunwoody, S., Griffin, R. J., & Neuwirth, K. (2006). Seeking and processing information about impersonal risk. *Science Communication, 28*(2), 163–194.

Kasperson, R. E., Golding, D., & Tuler, S. (1992). Social trust as a factor in siting hazardous facilities and communicating risks. *Journal of Social Issues, 48*(4), 161–187.

Kirmani, A., & Campbell, M. C. (2004). Goal seeker and persuasion sentry: How consumer targets respond to interpersonal marketing persuasion. *Journal of Consumer Research, 31*(3), 573–582.

Kramer, R. (1999). Trust and distrust in organizations: Emerging perspectives, enduring questions, *Annual Review of Psychology, 50*, 569–598.

McCroskey, J. C., & Teven, J. J. (1999). Goodwill: A reexamination of the construct and its measurement. *Communication Monographs, 66*, 90–103.

Michaelidou, M., Decker, D. J., & Lassoie, J. P. (2002). The interdependence of ecosystem and community viability: A theoretical framework to guide research and application. *Society and Natural Resources, 15*, 599–616.

Miller, B. M. (2006). Issue advocacy to community stakeholders: A structural equation model of potential outcomes. *Dissertation Abstracts International, 67/02*, 384 (UMI No. AAT 3207312).

Miller, B., & Sinclair, J. (2009). Community stakeholder responses to advocacy advertising: Trust, accountability, and the Persuasion Knowledge Model (PKM). *Journal of Advertising, 38*(2), 37–52.

Miller, J. D. (1998). The measurement of civic scientific literacy. *Public Understanding of Science, 7*, 1–21.

Miller, J. D. (2002). Civic scientific literacy: A necessity in the 21st century. *Journal of the Federation of American Scientists: Public Interest Report, 55*(1), 3–10. Retrieved April 10, 2009, from www.fas.org/faspir/2002/v55n1/v55n1.pdf.

Miller, J. D., & Pardo, R. (2000). Civic scientific literacy and attitude to science and technology: A comparative analysis of the European Union, the United States, Japan, and Canada. In M. Dierkes & C. von Grote (Eds.), *Between understanding and trust: The public, science and technology* (pp. 81–129). Amsterdam: Harwood Academic Publishers.

O'Guinn, T. C., Allen, C. T., & Semenik, R. J. (2006). *Advertising and integrated brand promotion* (4th ed.). Mason, OH: Thomson South-Western.

Peters, R. G., Covello, V. T., & McCallum, D. B. (1997). The determinants of trust and credibility in environmental risk communication: An empirical study. *Risk Analysis, 17*(1), 43–54.

Petty, R. E., & Cacioppo, J. T. (1986). The elaboration likelihood model of persuasion. In Leonard Berkowitz (Ed.), *Advances in experimental social psychology* (vol. 19, pp. 123–205). New York: Academic Press.

Pfau, M., Haigh, M. M., Sims, J., & Wigley, S. (2007). The influence of corporate front-group stealth campaigns. *Communication Research, 34*(1), 73–99.

Press, D., Doak, D. F., & Steinberg, P. (1996). The role of local government in the conservation of rare species. *Conservation Biology, 10*(6), 1538–1548.

Schlenker, B. R., Britt, T. W., Pennington, J., Murphy, R., & Doherty, K. (1994). The triangle model of responsibility, *Psychological Review, 101*(4), 632–652.

Schlenker, B. R., & Weigold, M. F. (1989). Self-identification and accountability. In R. A. Giacalone & P. Rosenfeld (Eds.), *Impression management in the organization* (pp. 21–43). Hillsdale, NJ: Lawrence Erlbaum Associates.

Schlenker, B. R., Weigold, M. F., & Doherty, K. (1991). Coping with accountability: Self-identification and evaluative reckonings. In C. R. Snyder & D. R. Forsyth (Eds.), *Handbook of social and clinical psychology: The health perspective* (pp. 96–115). New York: Pergamon.

Sethi, S. P. (1977). *Advocacy advertising and large corporations*. Lexington, MA: Lexington Books.

Sinclair, J., & Irani, T. (2005). Advocacy advertising for biotechnology: The effect of public accountability on corporate trust and attitude toward the ad. *Journal of Advertising, 34*(3), 59–73.

Sinclair, J., & Miller, B. (2008, February). *Understanding public response to technology advocacy campaigns: A persuasion knowledge approach*. Paper presented at the New Agendas in Science Communication conference, Austin, TX.

Sjoberg, L. (2000). Factors in risk perceptions. *Risk Analysis, 20*(1), 1–12.

Sjoberg, L. (2004). Local acceptance of a high-level nuclear waste repository. *Risk Analysis, 24*(3), 737–749.

Slovic, P. (1987). Perception of risk. *Science, 236*, 280–286.

Stafford, E. R., & Hartman, C. L. (2000). Environmentalist: Business collaborations— Social responsibility, green alliances, and beyond. In G. Zinkan (Ed.), *Advertising research: The internet, consumer behavior and strategy*. Chicago, IL: American Marketing Association.

Textile Mills Corporation *v.* Commissioner, 314 U.S. 326 (1941).

Chapter 5

Using Temporally Oriented Social Science Models and Audience Segmentation to Influence Environmental Behaviors

Bret R. Shaw

There is widespread empirical evidence that human behaviors are having harmful effects on the environment (Gardner & Stern, 1996; Leiserowitz, Kates, & Parris, 2006; Manfredo & Dayer, 2004; Osborn & Anjan, 2006). Furthermore, many of the studies that link degradation of the environment to human activity also issue concrete recommendations about how that impact can be reduced (e.g., Dietz, 2007; Dietz & Clausen, 2005; Tornes, 2005). Still, many people continue their daily lives with what appears to be a "business as usual" approach, paying little heed to these ecological concerns. This state of affairs suggests that, while communicating the scientifically supported reasons why people should change their behaviors is important, simple education that invokes this information is often insufficient to move people to action (Finger, 1994; Stern, 2002). As some research has suggested, persuasive communication campaigns are likely needed to promote science-based practices (Biglan, Mrazek, Carnine, & Flay, 2003).

Many communicators focusing on environmental and conservation issues have been turning to social marketing for guidance in meeting behavior-change goals (McKenzie-Mohr & Smith, 1999; Monroe, 2003; Tyson, Broderick, & Snyder, 1998). Kotler and Roberto (1989) define social marketing as "a program planning process that promotes the voluntary behavior of target audiences by offering benefits they want, reducing barriers they are concerned about and using persuasion to motivate their participation in program activity" (p. 24). Social marketing has a growing list of anecdotal and empirical evidence related to environmental behavior change, all of which is driving continued interest in this approach (e.g., Marcell, Agyeman, & Rappaport, 2004; McKenzie-Mohr & Smith, 1999). A likely factor influencing interest in social marketing relative to other approaches is its focus on behavior versus softer outcomes such as increased knowledge or attitude change; at the end of the day, behavior is truly the only dependent variable that will produce positive, measurable effects on the environment.

While social marketing may be considered a useful approach to behavior-change campaigns, this chapter argues that studies on the use of social marketing to encourage environmental behavior change have not adequately leveraged the temporal dimensions of other social science theories. Specifically, the idea of influencing behavior change typically implies that phenomena occur over time. Yet, behavior change is often conceptualized as if it is a discrete event rather than a process (Andreasen, 2006; Prochaska & Velicier, 1997). Understanding "processes of change" may be particularly important constructs for the translation of an intention into a behavior because they represent the use of cognitive and behavioral strategies to enact a behavior over time (Rhodes & Plotnikoff, 2006). Such an approach may allow social marketing campaign planners to use evidence-based insights about when, on a temporal scale, to use different strategies that influence awareness, knowledge, and attitudes en route to achieving behavior-change goals.

To illustrate the potential value of this integration of communication theories as it relates to science communication, this chapter highlights potential intersections between social marketing and two temporally oriented social science models—Stages of Change and Diffusion of Innovations. In this chapter, the temporal aspect conceptualizes behavior change as a dynamic rather than a static process. The Stages of Change model capitalizes on this idea with the premise that people will be differentially ready to adopt a new behavior based on their respective knowledge, beliefs, and motivations relative to the specific behavior. As well, the model proposes that people must move through a natural progression of stages before adopting a new practice. In comparison, the Diffusion of Innovation model suggests that people can be classified into different segments relative to particular behavioral domains, starting with the early adopters who are most likely to enthusiastically adopt a new practice and ending with laggards who are least likely to adopt—and perhaps even antagonistic toward adopting—a specific new behavior (Rogers, 2003).

These models have achieved ample attention in the health communication literature related to influencing behavior change such as smoking cessation (Erol & Erdogan, 2008), weight loss (Logue et al., 2004), dental hygiene (Tillis et al., 2003), increased vegetable consumption (Di Noia, Contento, & Prochaska, 2008), and condom use (Wallace et al., 2007). However, these models have not received sufficient consideration by communication researchers and practitioners focused on changing behaviors to improve the environment. Therefore, the connections made in this chapter are intended to generate additional insights into how researchers, natural resource educators, and outreach professionals might more effectively promote sustainable environmental behaviors.

This chapter specifically directs attention to the potential role of the Stages of Change and Diffusion of Innovation models to assist in audience segmentation efforts. Simply stated, segmentation refers to dividing an audience into groups whose members are more like each other than the members of other segments (Grunig, 1989); the practice of segmenting audiences and developing unique marketing programs for each segment has long been considered fundamental to modern marketing (Bloom & Novelli, 1981) and is still considered an essential strategy in social marketing today (Perloff, 2008). While research indicates that multiple motivations attend any given behavior (DeYoung, 2000), and that these motivations will vary among audience segments (Angelina & Hull, 2005), the central argument made here is that knowing where a segment is on a temporal basis—relative to their understanding and adoption of a new behavior—has implications for effectively tailoring and evaluating interventions. For example, a key principle behind the social marketing approach is to focus on the customers, targeting them based on perceived barriers that prevent them from adopting behaviors that will lead to desired benefits (Kotler & Lee, 2008). A better understanding of where audiences are in the process or stages of change, then, may lend additional insights into the specific barriers they perceive and how those barriers are being weighed against the perceived benefits. The central assumption to this approach is that perceived barriers and benefits (and their relationship to one another) are likely to shift as the audience moves through the temporal behavior-change process.

The remainder of this chapter explicates the Stages of Change and Diffusion of Innovations models and integrates recent theoretical developments and research advances to highlight how these models can be used to more effectively promote behavior change to improve the environment.

Stages of Change

As touched on briefly above, the Stages of Change Model (also known as the Transtheoretical Model) asserts that health behavior change involves progress through six stages of change: precontemplation, contemplation, preparation, action, maintenance, and relapse. This model, rooted in explaining health behavior change, offers a potentially useful framework for understanding that people are not monolithically motivated toward adopting or maintaining any type of behavior, whether it relates to health, the environment, or any other domain. Using this model, behavior change is conceptualized as an ongoing process in which people progress through a series of stages from not considering making a behavioral change to actually adopting a new behavior and maintaining it (Kreuter, Farrell, Olevitch, & Brennan, 2000). A number of factors such as awareness, knowledge, attitudes, and social norms all influence who is in what stage and what factors are likely to move people along this trajectory. The section that follows delineates each of those stages, all the while making linkages to social marketing within the context of environmental behavior change. Again, the assumption made in this chapter is that specific audience segments reside within each stage. All references to the Stages of Change model are cited from Prochaska and Velicier (1997) unless otherwise noted.

Precontemplation

Precontemplation refers to the earliest stage, the stage in which people are not intending to take action in the foreseeable future related to the behavior in question. In the context of environmentally sustainable behaviors, this may be because members of this audience segment are unaware, uninformed, or under-informed about the consequences of their existing behaviors, and therefore do not see a need to investigate or otherwise pursue behavior change. Although information alone certainly cannot be expected to produce behavior change, providing relevant information may lead to increased awareness, which can precipitate behavior change, particularly when lack of knowledge is a notable barrier to action (Stern, 2002).

That is, contexts exist in which people simply have no idea about the negative consequences of their behavior. For example, many people are unaware that unused pharmaceuticals that are flushed down a toilet or poured down a sink drain are damaging to the bodies of water into which those drains eventually flow (Seehusen & Edwards, 2006). While there is a growing awareness in the scientific community that unused medications discarded in this way are harmful to the plants and animals that live downstream because waste-water treatment plants do not remove medications, recent estimates show that over one-third of all Americans believe it is acceptable to dispose of their unused medication this way (Seehusen & Edwards, 2006). In fact, over 50% admit to having followed this practice themselves (Seehusen & Edwards, 2006). In this example, particularly for the one-third who are unaware of the consequences of this behavior, this segment of the audience could be said to reside in the precontemplation stage. Yet, because it is easy *not* to flush unused pharmaceuticals down the toilet or sink, people in this stage might be moved along the motivational trajectory—to contemplation—simply as a result of being educated about the ramifications of this behavior. Of course, the barrier of what they *should* do with these products will accompany that movement.

In addition to awareness (or lack thereof), another factor likely related to the precontemplation phase is how personally involved the audience may be with the particular behavior and its likely outcomes. Involvement is said to be high when individuals perceive that an issue is personally relevant or bears directly on their own lives, and low when individuals perceive that an issue has little or no impact on their own lives (Perloff, 2008). Thus, if an audience segment in the precontemplation stage has low involvement with a given environmental issue—such as plants and animals that live downstream—motivation to move beyond precontemplation may also be low. Campaign sponsors might respond to this by tailoring a message that highlights an aspect of the behavior or its consequences that resonates more effectively with a specified audience segment. Research indicates that people engage in issue-relevant thinking (which relates to the next stage—contemplation) when they are highly involved with an issue. Conversely, when they have low involvement with an issue, they are more likely to focus on simple cues like the expertise, respectability, or attractiveness of the source delivering the message (Perloff, 2008). Thus, another approach for reaching this audience may be to focus on cues (such as a highly respected or admired source) that may at first seem peripheral to the argument, but may be exactly what is needed to move this segment beyond precontemplation.

Contemplation

Contemplation refers to the stage in which people are intending to change. The Stages of Change Model suggests that contemplators are acutely aware of the pros and cons of changing, but the cons may continue to outweigh the pros. According to Andreasen (2006), early contemplators are just beginning to think about adopting a new behavior, so it is particularly important to emphasize benefits to people in this group. This is strategically important because if target audience members do not think they will see significant personal benefits, they are unlikely to go further in the process. The balance between the costs and benefits of adopting a new behavior can produce ambivalence in contemplators that can keep members of this audience segment stuck in this stage for long periods of time (Andreasen, 2006).

One example of a segment in the contemplation phase might be people who know about and agree with the basic premise that there are environmental benefits to switching to compact fluorescent light bulbs to save energy and reduce carbon emissions to slow the advance of climate change. Indeed, research by Fahar (1993) suggests that the public consistently shows support for conservation and believes that energy use is something that could be better managed by consumers. However, even though contemplators are told that these bulbs have the above benefits and will save them money over time, when they go to the store to buy compact fluorescent bulbs for the first time, they may be struck by the fact that this more sustainable option is approximately eight times as expensive per unit as traditional bulbs (Barbaro, 2007). Therefore, price may become a significant barrier.

In this example, an effective message needs to address awareness of the benefits, but also of the barrier. Thus, people in the contemplation category who are influenced by economic motivations might relate to a message which highlights that, while the up-front per-unit costs of each bulb favor the incandescent bulbs, fluorescent bulbs use about two-thirds less energy and last up to 10 times longer than incandescent bulbs. In this way, communicators might do well to emphasize the long-term economic benefit in tandem with the benefit of reduced carbon needed to produce energy for fluorescent bulbs.

Furthermore, for those audience members who dislike the swirl shape of the fluorescent bulbs (another perceived barrier), environmental communicators may work with retail outlets to feature the bulbs in their lamps and hanging fans to illustrate the bulb's versatility and overcome aesthetic concerns about the shape or hue of light they produce (Sandahl, Gilbride, Ledbetter, Steward, & Calwell, 2006). Or, they could work with the media to emphasize the perception that compact fluorescent bulbs are in style and essential to an environmentally friendly lifestyle (Crosbie & Guy, 2008). In sum, when targeting contemplators, communicators should shift the decisional balance such that the pros of adopting a behavior clearly outweigh the cons.

Tapping into contemplators' emotions may also motivate this segment to move along the motivational trajectory toward adopting a new environmentally friendly behavior. For example, research has long indicated that incidental positive mood (induced by a small gift, for example) tends to increase the likelihood of people adopting pro-social behaviors (Cohen, Pham, & Andrade, 2008; Baumgartner & Pieters, 2008). Research also indicates that eliciting negative emotions such as guilt can motivate citizens to adopt pro-environmental behaviors (Bamberg & Moser, 2007). Guilt has been defined as a "painful feeling of regret that is aroused when the actor actually causes, anticipates causing, or is associated with an aversive event" (Ferguson & Stegge, 1998, p. 20). It has been argued that guilt is an important pro-social emotion because it results in a felt obligation to compensate for the caused damage (Baumeister, 1998). Strategically, if campaign managers can communicate a disconnect between contemplators' values (e.g., being supportive of clean air and energy conservation) and their behavior (e.g., ongoing use of less efficient, incandescent light bulbs), contemplators may be influenced via guilt or related cognitive dissonance as motivators for adopting recommended practices.

Preparation

Preparation is the stage in which people are intending to take action in the immediate future. Perhaps they have decided that when their traditional bulbs go out the next time, they will replace them with compact fluorescent bulbs. Members of this segment may already be sufficiently educated about the benefits of following through on their intended behavior, but they need a little extra push to trigger their adoption of the new behavior. This is where classic marketing tactics may be especially useful. For instance, in its drive to promote increased sales of compact fluorescent bulbs, Wal-Mart moved them from the bottom shelf of the lighting aisle, where shoppers had to bend down to see them, to shelves at shoppers' eye-level. As a result, sales increased markedly (Barbaro, 2007). Direct mailings, in-store and online promotions, and coupons for the environmentally friendly bulbs may also help people in the preparation stage to make their initial purchase.

Researchers have also found that when individuals are encouraged to publicly express commitment to a behavior, they will often adopt an identity that is consistent with that behavior, which often results in long-lasting attitude and behavior change (Bator & Cialdini, 2000). The process of making a public commitment may influence whether people adopt a new behavior because they fear looking bad in front of others (Perloff, 2008) or a desire to maintain good standing within a particular reference group (Prislin & Wood, 2008). These findings suggest that strategies such as asking people to sign written contracts to adopt a new practice and encouraging them to commit in public or online spaces, may motivate preparers who may otherwise slip backwards, rather than progressing toward adopting the targeted behavior (McKenzie-Mohr & Smith, 1999).

Action

Action refers to the stage in which people have made specific overt modifications in their lifestyles, though typically this stage has been operationalized as the stage at which people have made the change for 6 months or less (Prochaska et al., 1994). For most behaviors, people still need to work to keep up their new practice. For example, given the way that people typically change their light bulbs (as each goes out), professionals promoting the use of fluorescent bulbs should not expect those in the action group to take action all at once. Where monitoring of such actions is possible, social marketing campaigners focused on this issue might set up a website that keeps track of energy and money savings in real time along with reductions in carbon output as people continue to switch traditional bulbs out for the more energy efficient type. However, going to a website to monitor benefits may assume considerable motivation on the part of the target audience, so other, more proactive outreach techniques such as postcards, email, or phone calls may be helpful to remind people in the action stage about the immediate, short-term benefits that may have occurred (e.g., measurable cost savings or reductions of carbon dioxide in the atmosphere) from their adoption of the new behavior. In the future, centralized home control systems might indicate to residents how much energy savings and carbon prevention they have contributed to as they continue to replace old incandescent bulbs with the more energy-friendly fluorescent variety.

Maintenance

Maintenance is the stage in which people work to prevent relapse, but they are no longer actively involved in the deliberative processes associated with the contemplation or action phases, and they typically have been successful for 6 months or more (Prochaska et al., 1994). The behavior is believed to be relatively stable by this point because past behavior is a notable predictor of future behavior (Ajzen, 1991), though there still remain many opportunities for segments in this stage to revert to former behavior patterns. In past research, perceived barriers or disadvantages related to starting a new behavior appear to differentiate between successful and unsuccessful adopters (Rhodes & Plotnikoff, 2006). This suggests that social marketers might continue with communication strategies that reduce perceived and real barriers even after a target audience segment has adopted a new behavior.

Returning to the example invoked above, if people continue to be concerned by the significantly higher up-front costs of compact fluorescent bulbs, outreach materials may continue to remind target audience members about the long-term economic savings and environmental benefits resulting from their use. Additionally, where vestiges of doubt remain about the benefits of adopting compact fluorescent bulbs, reminders about the benefits that have accrued at both the individual and community levels from people committing to such behaviors should be highlighted. Where feedback is possible, promoting the concrete, cumulative benefits that have been achieved over time through adoption of a new behavior should reinforce positive perceptions of ability and control among people who have adopted a new behavior (Monroe, 2003). For example, the same ongoing website that may track the carbon footprint and the money that adopters have saved due to energy conservation could also offer sustained motivation to people who have switched to compact fluorescent bulbs. With a single bulb preventing 100 pounds of carbon per year being emitted into the atmosphere, the contributions of people adopting this behavior can add up over time to substantial contributions that people can readily understand and appreciate.

Reinforcement in the maintenance stage to promote lasting behavior change may include ongoing emotional appeals that strengthen or maintain associations between the attitude object and desired outcomes (Johnson, Maio, & Smith-McLallen, 2008). These may include associating compact fluorescent bulbs with positive imagery, such as healthy landscapes and clean air. Some of the strategies used in the maintenance stage are similar to those employed for people in the action stage, but distinguishing between the stages reminds researchers and communicators that influencing long-term behavior change may be enhanced by ongoing communication efforts.

Another strategy for addressing people in the maintenance phase is the use of social support. Borrowing from the health behavior-change literature, research indicates that lack of actual and perceived positive social support or the existence of social pressure is associated with a relapse or return to previous behaviors (Beattie & Longabaugh, 1999; Broome, Simpson, & Joe, 2002). Conversely, people in other behavior-change contexts who stay involved with self-help groups have superior outcomes in terms of not relapsing to previous behaviors (Dobkin, De, Paraherakis, & Gill, 2002; Ouimette et al., 2001; Ouimette, Moos, & Finney, 2003). Feasible tactics to provide people support to stay engaged in behavior-change efforts may include offering neighborhood support groups where individuals get together to exchange ideas or support for living a "green lifestyle." Using an email listserv of a social networking platform (e.g., Facebook) where people can participate in a virtual community that is committed to making behavioral choices to improve the environment is another tactic.

Relapse

The Stages of Change model also discusses relapse, in which people return from action or maintenance to an earlier stage. We might normally think of relapse in the context of addiction—the individual who smokes a cigarette after having successfully quit for a few months or has a drink after following a successful period of abstinence following addiction treatment. However, the idea that people might relapse following adoption of sustainable behaviors has numerous parallel examples in an environmental context. In the above examples of disposal of pharmaceuticals or use of compact florescent bulbs, people who have sustained behavior change for a time are not immune to the pull of old behaviors when those behaviors are again more convenient or less costly than the newer, more ecologically friendly behaviors. Similarly, people who have committed to taking public transportation or riding a bicycle to work to reduce their carbon footprint and reduce their individual contributions to global warming may fall back on driving a car to work because it is the most convenient thing to do.

Notably, in the case of health-related behaviors, relapse is now considered to be an integral part of the behavior-change process (Prochaska & Velicier, 1997). For example, despite numerous advances in the treatment of addiction, some relapse to previous substance-use behaviors remains common—sometimes as high as 80% (Dennis, Scott, & Funk, 2003; McKay & Weiss, 2001; McLellan, 2002; Witkiewitz & Marlatt, 2004). However, according to Prochaska and Velicier (1997), individuals very seldom regress all the way back to the precontemplation phase, and the majority return to contemplating or preparing for another serious attempt at action. Therefore, as described above, it is imperative that communicators seeking lasting behavior change among their target audiences should not rest on their laurels after an audience segment has adopted the desired behaviors.

Follow-up communication about re-engaging with a desired behavior change (e.g., using compact fluorescent bulbs or using public transportation or riding a bike rather than driving alone to work) may reinforce the incentives and reduce the perceived barriers of returning to the targeted behavior and help people get back on track in living more sustainably. For instance, people in the maintenance or relapse stage may still receive periodic coupons for a discounted bulb or a free bus ride that can aid in bringing the person back to practice of the desired behavior. Coming from the context of changing health behaviors with its related concepts such as relapse, the Stages of Change model may not be a perfect fit for informing how to change environmental behaviors but it does provide a useful heuristic for identifying audience segments and thinking about new ways to improve the effectiveness of social marketing campaigns designed to foster sustainable behavior.

Some researchers persuasively argue that human behavior-change processes do not work as simply as the model suggests (e.g., Davidson, 1992). Nevertheless, the framework still offers value to researchers and practitioners concerned with planning, implementing, and evaluating social marketing campaigns designed to influence environmentally sustainable behavior change. Specifically, it can offer insights about targeting audience segments depending on their relative motivation toward adopting a behavior and crafting different messages for reach, emphasizing different barriers and incentives and selecting outcome measures that are most relevant for the audience segment being targeted. Earlier work has shown that progressing from one stage of change to the next may be as important as actual behavior change (Prochaska, DiClemente, & Norcross, 1992). As such, progression through the stages of change may be an appropriate outcome measure in evaluating outreach programs (Kreuter et al., 2000).

The Stages of Change model relates primarily to changes that occur *within* people as they move along a behavior-change trajectory, though people can be classified in different segments depending on where they are in the process. The next section focuses on the Diffusion of Innovation model, which relates more to differences *between* people as it relates to communicating more effectively with audience-segment members to improve outcomes of environmental behavior-change campaigns.

Diffusion of Innovations

The Diffusion of Innovations model (Rogers, 2003) provides some insights about how to communicate barriers and incentives to members of a particular target audience depending on where they are in the adoption process, and can also be a valuable framework for conceptualizing behavior-change campaigns (Hubbard & Sandmann, 2007). The model suggests that in promoting most new practices, there are innovators, early adopters, early majority adopters, late majority adopters and "laggards." These five categories are often visually represented as a bell-shaped curve (Rogers, 2003) representing a normal distribution.

When promoting any behavior designed to protect the environment, there will typically be relatively few adopters at first. However, as the new practice is picked up by innovators and early adopters, their influence will have an impact on people who will adopt the behavior later on and who will ultimately make up a majority of potential adopters. Rogers (2003) uses the bell-shaped curve to graphically illustrate different categories of adopters (Rogers, 2003).

From a social marketing standpoint, the Diffusion of Innovations model has temporal implications for targeting specific audience segments and understanding how people move along this natural adoption trajectory. It can also inform how to craft messages for each of these adoption category segments because people in different categories may have different reasons for adopting the same behavior. While not referring specifically to the adoption of new environmentally friendly behaviors, important differences between adopter categories suggests that social marketers should use somewhat different communication approaches with each adopter category (Rogers, 2003). Below, insights from the Diffusion of Innovations model are highlighted along with insights from other communication and social science research as these studies relate to promoting the adoption of environmentally friendly behaviors within each adopter category. All descriptions of each segment in the Diffusions of Innovation typology are from Rogers (2003) unless otherwise noted.

Innovators

Innovators are characterized by their venturesome nature, and are highly interested in new trends and ideas. Their enthusiasm for new ideas drives them out of local peer networks and into more cosmopolitan social relationships with similar others who also are excited by novel practices and are receptive to new ways of doing things. In an environmental context, a person in the innovator segment is a highly motivated, interested, and committed individual who is typically "overtly" environmental, defining his or her lifestyle in many ways by his or her personal experiences and practices (Barr, 2008). One example of an environmental behavior is promoting residential storm-water management to reduce run off of pollution and excess nutrients (e.g., lawn fertilizer) into local water bodies. Social marketers may find that the innovator segment is already aware of or implementing best practices such as rain barrels or rain gardens or may simply need to be educated about the ecological benefits of adopting these behaviors. These individuals value their role as innovators and are driven to adopt new behaviors in part because they see themselves as mavericks and relish being ahead of what other people in their communities are doing. They likely pay attention to media that highlights innovative environmental practices and communicate with others who are deeply involved with these issues who may reside inside or outside their proximate community.

For those seeking to promote new practices to the innovator category, they may want to communicate directly with a few of its members to find out what events, publications, websites, and organizations environmental innovators pay attention to. For example, people who are most enthusiastic and influential related to a particular topic, such as environmental conservation, may be more likely to participate in social media such as blogs to communicate with others who care passionately about similar issues (Gillin, 2007). As such, posting interesting information about the benefits of adopting a new environmentally friendly behavior may facilitate the diffusion of such a practice among innovators and other early adopters.

Additionally, when adoption of a new practice is nearly non-existent, social marketers may want to emphasize the visionary nature of the new practice and how those adopting it may be starting a movement that could help make the world a better place. Innovators are driven by creativity and big ideas. Sometimes they adopt behaviors that make them appear prescient and ahead of the times while other practices they adopt may ultimately appear to be less well founded or useful (Rogers, 2003).

Early Adopters

The Diffusion of Innovations model asserts that the most important audience segment to win over in a campaign is the category of early adopters who tend to be more integrated into their local communities and serve as opinion leaders in their peer groups (Rogers, 2003). Opinion leaders are usually seen as persons of a social status that is similar to that of the persons they influence (Lam & Schaubroeck, 2000). They tend to want to do the "right thing" and are respected by others in their peer groups as a result of their judicious adoption of new ideas.

In communicating the science of adopting environmental behaviors, they might be more attracted to learning specifically how their changing a behavior might affect a specific local water body (e.g., that if everybody practiced a specific behavior, a specific lake or stream would be healthier). Furthermore, social marketers may remind this group about present and past experiences in nature—particularly those shared with family members and friends (Kals, Schumacher, & Montada, 1999). This tactic can serve to increase early adopters' emotional affinity toward specific places that may motivate them to adopt targeted ecologically friendly behaviors (Kals & Maes, 2002) that protect these valued locations in their community.

Early adopters are respected by their peers in part because of their selective, sensible use of new ideas. Their function in the diffusion process is to decrease uncertainty by others relative to a new practice and conveying subjective evaluations of the innovation to their peers via their interpersonal networks.

Early Majority

The early majority adopts new ideas just before the average member of their community. They may interact frequently with their peers but are seldom opinion leaders within their social networks. Since members of this segment do not take on an opinion leadership role themselves, it may be effective to recruit leaders in the early adopter segment to serve as models for the early majority who can follow their lead (Valente & Schuster, 2002). Similarly, social marketers can try to raise the visibility about the growing prevalence of others who have adopted the practice (Shultz, 2002). Communicating descriptive social norms involves influencing what target audience members believe others would do in a similar situation (Griskevicius, Cialdini, & Goldstein, 2008). Past research indicates that the use of social norms may be particularly powerful when people feel internally uncertain about whether to adopt a new behavior. When people are unsure about what to do, they are especially likely to look toward others for evidence of how to act (Cialdini & Goldstein, 2004; Griskevicius et al., 2008)

Research indicates that this segment may deliberate for some time before adopting a new idea, and they are more practical than both the innovators and early adopters (Rogers, 2003). Some in this category may be sufficiently inspired to adopt a new behavior merely because others they look up to in their communities have done so. However, others may want evidence that the efforts of early adopters are making a difference or may want to see results from scientific studies indicating that adopting a new behavior in a similar community elsewhere had produced the desired outcomes.

Approaches using respected block leaders in their neighborhoods, highlighting adoption of new behaviors by well-known opinion leaders in the community in media stories and other communications material (e.g., brochures, websites, newsletters) doing the same may be effective with early majority adopters. The key to communicating with the early majority is to promote the targeted behavior as being likely to impact personally relevant outcomes and to highlight that the behavior has become normative among opinion leaders in the community.

Late Majority

The late majority would be expected to adopt new behaviors just after the average member of a population. People in this category do not perceive themselves as leaders of innovation, whether environmentally focused or otherwise. Research by Rogers (2003) indicates that later adopters are less rational and have a less favorable attitude toward science. Therefore, as campaigners are targeting individuals later in the adoption curve, they should rely less on rational, scientific messages and more on messages that emphasize emotional appeals, testimonials, social norms, or regulatory threats. Education alone will almost certainly not suffice for late adopters who will want concrete evidence that it is personally worth their time and effort to adopt a new practice.

Additionally, when adoption of a new behavior may require a significant effort, technical assistance or cost-sharing programs may reduce barriers to this group. Addressing the role of social norms may be particularly important in promoting behavior change to this group. Using the example of residential storm-water management again, the late majority will want to see that many if not most other people in their respective neighborhoods have adopted a new behavior (Rogers, 2003). Promoting social norms can be a useful way to encourage people to adopt these norms as their own (Harland, Staats, & Wilke, 1999). One practical technique to leverage the power of social norms to raise the visibility about the prevalence of others who have adopted the behavior is to disseminate data on community rates of adopting a relevant sustainable behavior (Shultz, 2002). This tactic, however, is more effective in behavioral domains where the disseminated normative information is higher than the overall normative belief among segment members (McKenzie-Mohr & Smith, 1999). The use of models, case studies, and examples in a campaign can also help to create or redefine a social norm by communicating that the community accepts and applauds a newly adopted behavior to preserve or protect the environment (Monroe, 2003). For instance, highlighting that leaders of the neighborhood association have installed rain gardens or rain barrels as a storm-water management strategy implicitly communicates that these are respectable practices worth consideration by others in the community.

Laggards

Laggards are the last group of people to adopt a new behavioral practice in a community, and their decisions are made in terms of what has been done in the past. This decidedly non-environmentalist group rarely undertakes environmental action, which is mirrored by their generally negative attitudes toward conservation. Demographically, this group tends to be younger, more male than female, and has lower socioeconomic status combined with higher levels of political apathy (Barr, 2008).

Not surprisingly, this group is considered the most challenging from the perspective of influencing behavior change. This audience segment also tends to be suspicious of innovations and people who are promoting those changes. For people who are unmotivated or even antagonistic about changing their behaviors despite education and information from earlier adopters about the benefits from doing so, social marketers may choose to focus on regulatory strategies to pressure them into changing (Rothschild, 1999). Regulation may be an appropriate strategy if the campaign sponsors view the political climate as amendable and a sufficient environmental response has not been recognized by influencing earlier adopters toward desired behaviors deemed essential for the greater good.

Conclusion

This chapter has highlighted the potential value of two classic temporally oriented social science models, Stages of Change and Diffusion of Innovation, in the context of environmental behavior change campaigns. The two models can provide insights to social marketers about how to more effectively promote sustainable behaviors using audience segmentation in tandem with a social marketing approach. The potential role of these two models in communicating science behavior change has not received sufficient attention in prior research. In keeping with the theme of this volume of identifying new agendas for science communication in the 21st century, the suggestions in this chapter are based on theoretically informed, evidence-based insights and suggest potentially fruitful directions for enhancing and extending the impact of social marketing and positively influencing behaviors that affect the environment. At the same time, these suggestions are intentionally speculative, encouraging researchers to explore new hypotheses and research questions for addressing the increasingly important issue of promoting environmentally sustainable behaviors. Understanding that perceived barriers and benefits will vary depending on where audience segments are on a motivational and behavioral trajectory with temporal characteristics may offer high returns but whether this potential can be realized is still an open question. Future research should evaluate the value of the Stages of Change and Diffusion of Innovations models for informing audience segmentation efforts in social marketing campaigns focused on improving the environment.

The use of the models presented here need not be considered mutually exclusive. Campaigners may be likely to achieve more impactful campaigns by developing communication interventions that employ concepts from both of these models. For example, campaigners might examine the stages of change separately within each adopter category to better understand how to encourage a particular environmental behavior. Furthermore, these temporally oriented social science models are only highlighted to complement other useful frameworks and not to replace them. Future research should examine how various models might work together synergistically to plan and implement more effective social marketing campaigns and audience segmentation to preserve and protect the environment.

These models are also presented here primarily for the heuristic value they offer in thinking about behavior change on a temporal dimension and are not intended to be interpreted literally. Whether the process of behavior change is best viewed as occurring in a series of stages that are qualitatively different from one another or along adjacent segments of an underlying continuum (Marshall & Biddle, 2001) is less important for the purposes of this chapter than illustrating that people are variously motivated to adopt a new behavior. The key point is that these models may inform how an audience is segmented and evaluated in behavior-change campaigns. Different strategies might be needed for each segment, and so it might be necessary to initially prioritize some segments over others if resources are limited. Similarly, the adoption categories described by the Diffusion of Innovation perspective may not be mutually exclusive. For instance, we may not reasonably expect that there would be a dramatic shift in personal characteristics between the last person in the early majority to adopt a new behavior and the first in the late majority to do so. However, the model does offer the valuable insight that people who adopt new behaviors earlier tend to have different characteristics than those that adopt those behaviors later on, and behavior-change campaigns should address these differences. This model also has timing implications by suggesting that early adopters often need to be won over before late adopters as part of a natural diffusion process.

Communication scientists should also begin to document what theories work best to encourage short-term versus long-term sustainable behaviors. For instance, persuading a target audience to install low-flow shower heads to reduce home water consumption and reduce the amount of energy needed to heat that water is a one-time behavioral act. However, many other environmentally friendly behaviors like recycling, properly disposing of toxic household waste (e.g., batteries, motor oil, pharmaceuticals), or biking rather than driving require ongoing, even life-long commitment from citizens. These long-term behaviors may require campaigners to target unique sets of psychosocial variables to make a lasting impact on the environment (Montada, Kals, & Becker, 2007).

Earlier in this chapter, it was argued that social marketers could use the Stages of Change and Diffusion of Innovation models to segment audiences and prioritize where and when to allocate resources to gain maximum return on investment measured by achieving sustainable behavior change with associated environmental benefits for the amount of time and money spent. Considering the pressing issue of environmental justice, however, at least one caveat is required to qualify this argument. In many cases it is obvious that the most important distal goal of encouraging sustainable behaviors is to achieve measurable environmental effects (e.g., improvement in the quality of local lakes or rivers, reduced carbon output) rather than behavior change in and of itself being most important. However, it is also the case that people with lower socioeconomic status are less likely to be early adopters of new sustainable behaviors and they also tend to live in areas with greater environmental degradation than their counterparts with higher incomes and more education (Brulle & Pellow, 2006). (The topic of environmental justice is covered in more depth in Chapter 9.) These environmental differences in living environments may be largely explained by the association of people with lower incomes living in areas closer to facilities that generate industrial or agricultural waste. This issue is more likely to be addressed at the policy level than at the level of individual behavior change. However, situations like these underscore the need for social marketers to weigh the merits of efficiently achieving a measurable environmental response against the fact that sometimes the most efficient segmentation strategy for achieving ecological improvements may serve to increase—or at least not diminish—environmental disparities in the population.

Finally, in this author's experience, environmental educators tend to have been trained in various disciplines related to natural resources (e.g., water management, forestry, wildlife) with little or no training in the social sciences. It is hoped that this chapter will encourage greater multidisciplinary integration between the natural and social sciences to address the growing need to encourage environmentally friendly behaviors for a more sustainable future.

References

Ajzen, I. (1991). The theory of planned behavior. *Organizational Behavior and Human Decision Processes, 50*, 179–211.

Andreasen, A. R. (2006). *Social marketing in the 21st century*. Thousand Oaks, CA: Sage.

Angelina, K., & Hull, B. R. (2005). Motivations and behaviors of new forest owners in Virginia. *Forest Science, 51*, 142–154.

Bamberg, S., & Moser, G. (2007). Twenty years after Hines, Hungerford, and Tomera: A new meta-analysis of psycho-social determinants of pro-environmental behaviour. *Journal of Environmental Psychology, 27*, 14–25.

Barbaro, M. (2007, January 2). The energy challenge: Wal-Mart puts some muscle behind power-sipping bulbs. *New York Times*. Retrieved November 27, 2007, from www.nytimes.com/2007/01/02/business/02bulb.html?_r=1&oref=slogin.

Barr, S. (2008). *Environment and society: Sustainability, policy and the citizen*. Burlington, VT: Ashgate Publishing Company.

Bator, R. J., & Cialdini, R. B. (2000). The application of persuasion theory to the development of effective proenvironmental public service announcements. *Journal of Social Issues, 56*, 527–541.

Baumeister, R. F. (1998). The self. In D. T. Gilbert, S. T. Fiske, & G. Lindzey (Eds.), *The handbook of social psychology* (pp. 680–740). Boston, MA: MacGraw-Hill.

Baumgartner, H., & Pieters, R. (2008). Goal-directed consumer behavior: Motivation, volition and affect. In C. P. Haugtvedt, P. M. Herr, & F. R. Kardes (Eds.), *The handbook of social psychology* (pp. 367–392). New York: Lawrence Erlbaum Associates.

Beattie, M., & Longabaugh, R. (1999). General and alcohol-specific social support following treatment. *Addictive Behaviors, 24*, 593–606.

Biglan, A., Mrazek, P. J., Carnine, D., & Flay, B. R. (2003). The integration of research and practice in the prevention of youth problem behaviors. *American Psychologist, 58*, 433–440.

Bloom, P. N., & Novelli, W. D. (1981). Problems and challenges in social marketing. *Journal of Marketing, 45*, 79–88.

Broome, K., Simpson, D., & Joe, G. (2002). The role of social support following short-term inpatient treatment. *The American Journal on Addictions, 11*(1), 57–65.

Brulle, R. J., & Pellow, D. N. (2006). Environmental justice: Human health and environmental inequalities. *Annual Review of Public Health, 27*, 103–124.

Cialdini, R. B., & Goldstein, N. J. (2004). Social influence: Compliance and conformity. *Annual Review of Psychology, 55*, 591–621.

Cohen, J. B., Pham, M. T., & Andrade, E. B. (2008). The nature and role of affect in consumer behavior. In C. P. Haugtvedt, P. M. Herr, & F. R. Kardes (Eds.), *The handbook of social psychology* (pp. 297–348). New York: Lawrence Erlbaum Associates.

Crosbie, T., & Guy, S. (2008). En"lightening" energy use: The co-evolution of household lighting practices. *International Journal of Environmental Technology and Management, 9*, 220–235.

Davidson, R. (1992). Prochaska and DiClemente's model of change: A case study? *British Journal of Addiction, 87*, 821–822.

Dennis, M. L., Scott, C. K., & Funk, R. (2003). An experimental evaluation of recovery management check-ups (RMC) for people with chronic substance abuse disorders. *Evaluation and Program Planning, 26*, 339–352.

DeYoung, R. (2000). Expanding and evaluating motives for environmentally responsible behavior. *Journal of Social Issues, 56*, 509–526.

Dietz, M. E. (2007). Low impact development practices: A review of current research and recommendations for future directions. *Water, Air and Soil Pollution, 186*, 351–363.

Dietz, M. E., & Clausen, J. C. (2005). A field evaluation of rain garden flow and pollutant treatment. *Water, Air and Soil Pollution, 167*, 123–138.

Di Noia, J., Contento, I. R., & Prochaska, J. O. (2008). Computer-mediated intervention tailored on transtheoretical model stages and processes of change increases fruit and vegetable consumption among urban African-American adolescents. *American Journal of Health Promotion, 22*, 336–341.

Dobkin, P. L., De, C. M., Paraherakis, A., & Gill, K. (2002). The role of functional social support in treatment retention and outcomes among outpatient adult sub-stance abusers. *Addiction, 97*(3), 347–356.

Erol, S., & Erdogan, S. (2008). Application of a stage based motivational inter-viewing approach to adolescent smoking cessation: The Transtheoretical Model-based study. *Patient Education and Counseling, 72*, 42–48.

Fahar, B. (1993). *Trends in public perceptions and preferences on energy and envi-ronmental policy*. Report No. NREL/TP-461-4857. Washington, DC: National Renewable Energy Laboratory.

Ferguson, T. J., & Stegge, H. (1998). Measuring guilt in children. A rose by any other name has still thorns. In J. Bybee (Ed.), *Guilt and children* (pp. 19–74). San Diego, CA: Academic Press.

Finger, M. (1994). From knowledge to action? Exploring the relationship between environmental experiences, learning and behavior. *Journal of Social Issues, 50*, 141–160.

Gardner, G. T., & Stern, P. C. (1996). *Environmental problems and human behav-ior*. Boston, MA: Allyn Bacon.

Gillin, P. (2007). *The new influencers: A marketer's guide to the new social media*. Sanger, CA: Quill Driver Books.

Griskevicius, V., Cialdini, R. B., & Goldstein, N. J. (2008). Social norms: An underestimated and underemployed lever for managing climate change. *Interna-tional Journal of Sustainability Communication, 3*, 5–13.

Grunig, J. E. (1989). Publics, audiences and market segments: Segmentation princi-ples for campaigns. In C. T. Salmon (Ed.), *Information campaigns: Balancing social values and social change* (pp. 199–228). Newbury Park, CA: Sage.

Grunig, J. E., & Hunt, T. (1984). *Managing public relations*. New York: Holt, Rinehart and Winston.

Harland, P., Staats, H., & Wilke, H. A. (1999). Explaining pro-environmental intention and behavior by personal norms and the theory of planned behavior. *Journal of Applied Social Psychology, 29*, 2505–2528.

Hubbard, W. G., & Sandmann, L. R. (2007). Using diffusion of innovation con-cepts for improved program evaluation. *Journal of Extension, 45*(5), 5FEA1.

Johnson, B. T., Maio, G. R., & Smith-McLallen, A. (2008). Communication and attitude change: Causes, processes and effects. In D. Albarracin, B. T. Johnson, & M. P. Zanna (Eds.), *The handbook of attitudes* (pp. 617–669). Mahwah, NJ: Lawrence Erlbaum Associates.

Kals, E., & Maes, J. (2002). Sustainable development and emotions. In P. Schmuck & W. P. Schultz (Eds.), *Psychology of sustainable development* (pp. 97–122). Norwell, MA: Kluwer Academic Publishers.

Kals, E., Schumacher, D., & Montada, L. (1999). Emotional affinity toward nature as a motivational basis to protect nature. *Environment & Behavior, 31*(2), 178–202.

Kotler, P., & Lee, N. R. (2008). *Social marketing: Influencing behaviors for good* (3rd ed.). Los Angeles, CA: Sage.

Kotler, P., & Roberto, E. (1989). *Social marketing: Strategies for changing public behavior*. New York: Free Press.

Kreuter, M., Farrell, D., Olevitch, L., & Brennan, L. (2000) *Tailoring health mes-sages: Customizing communication with computer technology*. Mahwah, NJ: Lawrence Erlbaum Associates.

Lam, S. S. K., & Schaubroeck, J. (2000). A field experiment testing frontline opinion leaders as change agents. *Journal of Applied Psychology, 85*, 987–995.

Leiserowitz, A. A., Kates, R. W., & Parris, T. M. (2006). Sustainability values, attitudes, and behaviors: A review of multinational and global trends. *Annual Review of Environment and Resources, 31*, 413–444.

Logue, E. E., Jarjoura, D. G., Sutton, K. S., Smucker, W. D., Baughman, K. R., & Capers, C. F. (2004). Longitudinal relationship between elapsed time in the action stages of change and weight loss. *Obesity Research, 12*, 1499–508.

Manfredo, M. J., & Dayer, A. A. (2004). Concepts for exploring the social aspects of human–wildlife conflict in a global context. *Human Dimensions of Wildlife, 9*, 1–20.

Marcell, K., Agyeman, J., & Rappaport, A. (2004). Cooling the campus. Experiences from a pilot study to reduce electricity use at Tufts University, USA, using social marketing methods. *International Journal of Sustainability in Higher Education, 5*, 169–189.

Marshall, S. J., & Biddle, S. J. H. (2001). The Transtheoretical Model of behavior change: A meta-analysis of applications to physical activity and exercise. *Annals of Behavioral Medicine, 23*, 229–246.

Massy, W. F., & Weitz, B. A. (1977). A normative theory of market segmentation. In F. M. Nicosia & Y. Wind (Eds.), *Behavioral models for market analysis: Foundations for marketing action* (pp. 121–144). Hinsdale, IL: Dryden.

McKay, J. R., & Weiss, R. V. (2001). A review of temporal effects and outcome predictors in substance abuse treatment studies with long-term follow-ups: Preliminary results and methodological issues. *Evaluation Review, 25*, 113–161.

McKenzie-Mohr, D., & Smith, W. (1999). *Fostering sustainable behavior: An introduction to community-based social marketing.* British Columbia, Canada: New Society Publishers.

McLellan, A. T. (2002). The outcomes movement in substance abuse treatment: Comments, concerns and criticisms. In J. Sorenson & R. Rawson (Eds.), *Drug abuse treatment through collaboration: Practice and research partnerships that work* (pp. 119–134). Washington, DC: American Psychological Association Press.

Monroe, M. C. (2003). Two avenues for encouraging conservation behaviors. *Human Ecology Review, 10*, 113–125.

Montada, L., Kals, E., & Becker, R. (2007). Willingness for continued commitment: A new concept in environmental research. *Environment and Behavior, 39*(3), 287–316.

Osborn, D., & Anjan, D. (2006). Institutional and policy cocktails for protecting coastal and marine environments from land-based sources of pollution. *Ocean & Coastal Management, 49*, 576–596.

Ouimette, P., Humphreys, K., Moos, R. H., Finney, J. W., Cronkite, R., & Federman, B. (2001). Self-help group participation among substance use disorder patients with posttraumatic stress disorder. *Journal of Substance Abuse Treatment, 20*(1), 25–32.

Ouimette, P., Moos, R. H., & Finney, J. W. (2003). PTSD treatment and 5-year remission among patients with substance use and posttraumatic stress disorders. *Journal of Consulting and Clinical Psychology, 71*(2), 410–414.

Perloff, R. (2008). The dynamics of persuasion: Communication and attitudes in the 21st century (3rd ed.). New York: Lawrence Erlbaum Associates.

Prislin, R., & Wood, W. (2008). Social influence in attitudes and attitude change. In D. Albarracin, B. T. Johnson, & M. P. Zanna (Eds.), *The handbook of attitudes* (pp. 671–706). Mahwah, NJ: Lawrence Erlbaum Associates.

Prochaska, J. O., DiClemente, C. C., & Norcross, J. C. (1992). In search of how people change: Applications to addictive behaviors. *American Psychologist, 47,* 1102–1114.

Prochaska, J. O. & Velicier, W. F. (1997). The Transtheoretical Model of health behavior change. *The American Journal of Health Promotion, 12,* 38–48.

Prochaska, J. O., Velicer, W. F., Rossi, J. S., Goldstein, M. G., Marcus, B. H., Rakowski, W., et al. (1994). Stages of change and decisional balance for 12 problem behaviors. *Health Psychology, 13,* 39–46.

Rhodes, R. E., & Plotnikoff, R. C. (2006). Understanding action control: Predicting physical activity intention-behavior profiles across 6 months in a Canadian sample. *Health Psychology, 25,* 292–299.

Rogers, E. M. (2003). *Diffusion of innovations* (5th ed.). New York: The Free Press.

Rothschild, M. L. (1999). Carrots, sticks and promises: A conceptual framework for the management of public health and social issue behaviors. *Journal of Marketing, 63,* 24–37.

Sandahl, L. J., Gilbride, T. L., Ledbetter, M. R., Steward, M. E., & Calwell, C. (2006). *Compact fluorescent lighting in America: Lessons learned on the way to the market.* Report prepared for U.S. Department of Energy. Retrieved January 8, 2009, from www.netl.doe.gov/ssl/PDFs/CFL%20Lessons%20Learned%20 -%20web.pdf.

Seehusen, D. A., & Edwards, J. (2006). Patient practices and beliefs concerning disposal of medications. *Journal of the American Board for Family Medicine, 19,* 542–547

Shultz, P. W. (2002). Knowledge, information, and household recycling: Examining the knowledge deficit model of behavior change. In T. Dietz & P. Stern (Eds.), *New tools for environmental education* (pp. 67–82). Washington, DC: National Academy Press.

Stern, P. C. (2002). Changing behavior in households and communities: What have we learned? In T. Dietz & P. Stern (Eds.), *New tools for environmental education* (pp. 201–211). Washington, DC: National Academy Press.

Tillis, T. S., Stach, D. J., Cross-Poline, G. N., Annan, S. D., Astroth, D. B., & Wolfe, P. (2003). The transtheoretical model applied to an oral self-care behavioral change: Development and testing of instruments for stages of change and decisional balance. *Journal of Dental Hygiene, 77,* 16–25.

Tornes, L. H. (2005). *Effects of rain gardens on the quality of water in the Minneapolis-St. Paul metropolitan area of Minnesota, 2002–04.* Scientific Investigations Report, United States Geological Survey.

Tyson, C. B., Broderick, S. H., & Snyder, L. (1998). A social marketing approach to landowner education. *Journal of Forestry, 96,* 34–40.

Valente, T. W., & Schuster, D. V. (2002). The public health perspective for communicating environmental issues. In T. Dietz & P. Stern (Eds.), *New tools for environmental education* (pp. 105–124). Washington, DC: National Academy Press.

Wallace, L. M., Evers, K. E., Wareing, H., Dunn, O. M., Newby, K., Paiva, A., & Johnson, J. L. (2007). Informing school sex education using the stages of change construct: Sexual behaviour and attitudes towards sexual activity and condom use of children aged 13–16 in England. *Journal of Health Psychology*, *12*, 179–183.

Witkiewitz, K., & Marlatt, G. (2004). Relapse prevention for alcohol and drug problems. That was Zen, this is Tao. *American Psychologist*, *59*, 224–235.

Part II

Characterization and Meaning-Making

Chapter 6

Competing Characters in Science-Based Controversy
A Framework for Analysis

Lisa Keränen

In 1994, Dr. Bernard Fisher, eminent American surgical oncologist and celebrated "pioneer" of breast cancer research, tumbled from dazzling heights. The award-winning physician and former member of the President's Cancer Advisory Panel came under intense scrutiny following allegations that one of his principal investigators had altered data used in the nation's leading breast cancer research. The research in question was conducted under Fisher's direction and had informed the treatment decisions of tens of thousands of North American women (Altman, 1996). Hailed as a major victory for women's health care, the research had demonstrated that breast conservation and radiation were as effective as breast removal for early-stage cancers (Fisher et al., 1985, 1989). As news of the tainted data spread, Fisher was forced to resign from a position he had held for over 35 years, he was called to testify before Congress, and 150 of his scientific articles were summarily marked with the tag "scientific misconduct" in electronic medical journal databases (Pascal, 1996). However, when the controversy subsided, Fisher was cleared of all wrongdoing. Moreover, reanalysis of the data had reaffirmed the value of breast conservation. Yet, throughout this complex, politically laden controversy—a time in which character assassinations were lodged, defended, and shot down—Fisher's character was defined, redefined, circulated, and contested by ensemble. As a result, *ethos* and *episteme*, character and knowledge were inextricably bound up in life and death decisions about biomedical knowledge. Trust, truth, hope, and healing—the pillars of scientific and medical knowledge and communication—were, for a time, shaken to their cores.

By exploring how rhetorical constructions of Fisher's character made a difference to the contours, meanings, and progression of the controversy during its initial months, this chapter advances a novel qualitative approach to understanding the dynamics of science-based controversies, which occur at the nexus of technical and public concerns.[1] More specifically, it employs three concepts from the rhetorical and literary lexicon—*ethos*, *persona*, and voice—as a method for tracking character construction. Although rhetoricians of science have often studied scientific *ethos* (see, e.g., Constantinides,

2001; Miller & Halloran, 1993; Prelli, 1989), the terms *ethos, persona,* and voice are often conflated (Brookey, 2001; Corder, 1989). Yet, each derives from a distinct intellectual tradition and accentuates a different dimension of character in science-based controversy. This chapter demonstrates how collective assumptions about normative behavior of scientists—the scientific *ethos* (Hyde, 2004; Merton, 1973)—coalesce into relatively stable and recurrent characterizations of individual types of scientists—scientific *personae* (Bordogna, 2005; Campbell, 1975)—which, in concert with the scientist's voice, or personal language choices (Elbow, 1994), shade the appropriate policy responses to science-based controversy.

In the case of Dr. Fisher specifically, this chapter argues that three *personae*—the scientific revolutionary, the beleaguered administrator, and the reluctant apologist—vied for acceptance and legitimacy in the initial months as the controversy unfolded. Considered together, these *personae* encouraged policy outcomes focused on purging science of individual transgressions, while obscuring systemic reforms that could have addressed patient and advocate concerns more directly. Further it is argued here that in public science-related controversies, credibility does not adhere to individuals. Rather, it affixes to constructed *personae* that are produced in interaction between cultural stereotypes and personal voice, and these *personae* shape what stakeholders to the controversy regard as acceptable outcomes and solutions.

On a theoretical level, the chapter demonstrates how disentangling disparate parts of character can enrich our understanding of the dynamics of science-based controversies (Brante, 1993; Lyne & Howe, 1986). Thus, it turns our attention squarely to the rhetoric of science, that is, the language scientists and stakeholders use to persuade one another about scientific information and processes (for an introduction to the field, see Harris, 1997). On a methodological level, it offers students of scientific discourse a means of chronicling how competing characterizations of scientists can influence the contours and policy outcomes of science-based controversies. Practically, it demonstrates how language strategies potentially help or hinder the public and professional face of scientists. The chapter ultimately maintains that sustained reconsideration of the interrelatedness of character and knowledge, of trust and truth, can augment studies of science-based controversies wherein scientists and members of various publics deliberate together about consequential decisions. To that end, the chapter begins by outlining the importance of character to science-based controversy and posing a three-part framework for analyzing the characters of such controversies. It then reviews salient features of the Fisher controversy as an entrée into a discussion of how *ethos, personae,* and voice made a difference to its resolution. The chapter concludes by considering what this case and framework suggest about the role of rhetorically constituted characters in controversies that bridge technical and public concerns.

Trust and Character in Science-Based Controversies: The Interaction of *Ethos, Persona,* and Voice

Trust is a necessary component of science. Citizens, politicians, scientists, policy makers, and health-care providers increasingly rely on the testimony of scientists—often strangers—to reach policy, funding, public health, and treatment decisions. As Zuckerman (1977) asserted, "mutual trust is central for the system of science" (p. 127). Yet, despite trust's pivotal role in the conduct of science, the Fisher controversy, and controversies like it (see, e.g., Dean, 2007; Schwartz, 2007), generate a relentless supply of allegations, disputes, and character assassinations that potentially trouble the delicate balance of trust that underwrites science. When science-based controversies unfold across the public sphere, they implicate a host of technical and political issues, and thus incur participation by diverse sets of publics who may or may not be well-versed in scientific reasoning. When knowledge claims become uncertain or challenged, many citizens, including the scientifically savvy, look to the character of knowledge generators as a proxy for the validity of the claims. Accordingly, science-based controversies teem with debates about character.

The idea that trust is related to perceptions of character dates back at least to Aristotle in whose *Rhetoric* we find an "art" of character (Garver, 1994). For Aristotle (1984), our perceptions of the moral character or the goodness, trustworthiness, and reliability of the speaker are cultivated through rhetoric—through the strategic use of language as a way of coordinating social action. During science-based controversies such as the one involving Fisher, when the credibility of scientists is on the line, participants look to communal understandings of science—to the scientific *ethos*—as a means of assessing if their faith is misplaced. Rhetorical scholars generally associate the term "character" with *ethos*. However, as is argued here, a more robust understanding of how characters are forged during science-based controversies will also involve *persona* and voice. Because a full exposition of these multifaceted and polysemic concepts could fill an entire book, this chapter's discussion of the varied and often contradictory meanings of the terms is truncated, focusing mostly on the definitions as they are employed in the ensuing analysis.

The term *ethos* derives from the rhetorical tradition and has a long and complex history (Amossy, 2001; Baumlin & Baumlin, 1994; Chamberlain, 1984; Constantinides, 2001; Hyde, 2004). While precise meanings are contested, the term generally conveys two senses. The first concerns the character of the individual speaker, as in Bernard Fisher's personal *ethos*, the view of his character as determined by others. Prelli (1989) defines this sense of *ethos* in science as "how an audience perceives the professional character of a scientific rhetor or a group of rhetors" (p. 105). The second sense of *ethos* relates to "the spirit or group character of a broader community of speakers," as in the *ethos* of scientists as a collective (Miller & Halloran, 1993, p. 121). These two senses are linked because communal values supply the means to assess an individual's character and credibility.

Thinking along these lines, rhetorician Michael Hyde (2004) has recently rehabilitated an older sense of *ethos* as communal dwelling place that binds community members to shared rituals and norms. In his introduction to *The Ethos of Rhetoric*, Hyde highlights the "architectural" function of *ethos*, describing this function as the use of language to "build a habitat, a dwelling place, where in moments of moral responsibility people can deliberate and 'know-together' (*con-scientia*) what is, arguably, the 'truth' of some contested matter and what actions should follow in light of the decision needed here" (p. xxiv). In the science studies and sociology of science communities, the idea of scientific *ethos*, the dwelling place of science—the communal values that encompass what have come to be known as the Mertonian norms of science—supply the underlying values that characterize the underlying "spirit or group" character of science. These include communality, universalism, organized skepticism, and disinterestedness (Merton, 1942).[2] Scientific *ethos*, then, evokes the shared sense of what science is, and what it can and should be; *ethos* also captures those same shared conceptualizations as they relate to scientists.

Drawing together this disparate literature suggests that *ethos* allows us to measure individual performance against collective values, since our assessment of the character of a scientist-rhetor is linked to the values of science he or she performs as a member of the scientific community. However, a second concept from the literary or dramatic tradition helps to flesh out our understanding of how group norms can coalesce into recognizable character types: *persona*. Derived from the Latin term for "mask" or "theatrical mask," *personae*, or *fictio personae* in Roman rhetorical education, were woven into narratives with students role-playing their particular character. Students produced "a kind of ritualized composition where stereotypes are called out for new service or renewed service in a conflict which itself is a remanifestation of a familiar problem" (Bloomer, 1997, pp. 57–58).[3] This connection between *persona* and stereotype suggests that *personae* may be viewed as symbolic condensations of role types that, when invoked, imply a host of pre-existing narrative elements and character traits that develop from shared cultural knowledge. That is, they are firmly rooted in communally held norms or *ethoi*.[4] In terms of stock roles in science, Francesca Bordogna (2005) called scientific *personae* both "the normative images of the man of science" and "collective images of the scientist" (p. 96). Bordogna (2005) linked these *personae* to late-19th-century scientific literature that discussed "the virtues, the moral sentiments, the temper, and the emotional constitution of the man of science" (p. 96).

Drawing from these works, *persona* is herein treated as a constructed public role, an image emanating from broader cultural values. Further, a *persona* carries potentiality for engendering trust or mistrust, faith or disbelief in audiences in order to induce persuasion or identification. *Personae* therefore correspond to recurrent cultural types. These types exist within widely recognizable narrative frameworks that encourage certain responses over others, but which also entail different possibilities in terms of assessing character for a particular case.

The third and final concept, voice, emanates from the rhetorical and literary traditions. Like *ethos* and *persona*, definitions of voice are multiple and contested; they range from tonal quality to the idea of voice as agency (see Elbow, 1994; Watts, 2001). In this chapter, voice refers to the particular inflections, diction, style, and tone that a historical person employs as he or she performs his or her role. It encompasses matters of syntax and style. If *ethos* and *persona* derive, in large part, from cultural mores, voice emerges during and through individual rhetorical performance. As Walter Ong (1962) noted, "voice is the foundation for rôle-playing among men" (p. 54). Voice therefore derives from particular linguistic choices made from among the universe of possible words. In performing the *persona* of scientific revolutionary, for example, a particular scientist can infuse the role with a unique register, a personal patois that further shapes others' assessments of that *persona*; that register results from the specific language choices that scientist makes.

Zagacki and Keith (1992) note that direct challenges to an existing scientific paradigm can be met with revolutionary, conciliatory, and/or conservative *personae* or stances; the stance(s) and accompanying language choice subsequently influence the reception of that challenge. In certain contexts, language that is peppered with revolutionary statements yet maintains a conciliatory tonal quality may be more readily accepted than revolutionary statements that are conservatively or angrily expressed. The words and tone scientists employ as they go about defending themselves and others in the public sphere—that is, the specific voice employed as they do so—modulate their *personae*. In Fisher's case, we may see evidence of not just a revolutionary *persona*, but one who was bold and challenging— a swashbuckling revolutionary.

In sum, in the study of rhetorical character in science-based controversy, this chapter suggests that scholars move away from conflating characteriological concepts toward a fuller understanding of the interrelations between *ethos*, *persona* and voice. In the remainder of this chapter, these concepts are defined as follows. *Ethos* refers to identifiable communal characteristics, the available norms of a culture or group. The values that inform *ethos* circulate the broader culture, are malleable through language, and largely pre-exist a rhetor's speech. *Personae*, or recurrent stereotyped role performances, emerge from the particular features of this shared, communal sense of *ethos*. Yet, *personae* also constrain identity, establishing potentialities for evaluating the credibility of individual scientists by how much they live up to shared ideals. In this way, we may say that a *persona* embodies a set of activated norms—it is "the mask that is there before any person turns up to fill it" (Ware & Linkugel, 1982, p. 50)—and therefore it mediates between collective ideals and the individual performance. Voice, by contrast, refers to the individual performance of role, to the particular language choices of a speaker, including diction, inflection, syntax, and tone. In the Fisher controversy, voice is refracted through mass-mediated forms, thus providing opportunities for collective modulation of a *persona* and for challenging or affirming communal norms.

By disentangling *ethos*, *persona*, and voice—and by demonstrating their complicated links to both group norms and individual performance—we come to see how distinct but competing *personae* emerge during a science-based controversy. These *personae* not only draw from the inventional wellspring of the scientific *ethos*, they also shade audience assessments of scientists' credibility. These assessments are, in turn, modified by the voice of the individual scientist as he or she attempts to bolster or repair his or her reputation, and by the voices of others who weigh in on the debate and who represent or attempt to recharacterize a particular scientist-speaker. Although this process of character construction is not limited to science-based controversies, widespread stereotypes and commonsense beliefs about science and scientists affect the available argumentative resources for those working to restore their character in the face of a science-based controversy.

In what follows, the construction of Bernard Fisher's character is chronicled following a controversy over his research oversight to illuminate how scholars might use this three-part framework to track the dynamics of a particular case. Although Fisher himself was not accused of falsifying data, the media became preoccupied with his management of the NSABP. On April 3, 1994, for example, the *New York Times* announced the "Fall of a Man Pivotal in Breast Cancer Research" (Altman, 1994, p. B10), while the *Pittsburgh Post-Gazette* offered the relatively more prudent "3 Weeks Shake Cancer Pioneer's 30 Year Record" (Twedt, 1994, p. A1). These headlines index the growing concentration on the actions of Fisher as both a scientist and as a person as the controversy surrounding data collected by an investigator under Fisher's direction mounted. Thus, the name "Fisher" controversy is used throughout the remainder of this chapter to reference the parts of the imbroglio that focused on Fisher's actions and character before his eventual exoneration.

The preoccupation with Fisher raises several questions for those who want to understand the rhetorical dynamics of science-based controversies. What factors encourage the focus on a particular scientist's character? What are the dominant scientific *personae* that emerge across technical and public texts and rhetorical performances? How are they scripted and by whom? And finally, how do these characterizations influence the progression of the controversy and attendant policy outcomes? In its subsequent sections, this chapter explores these questions by charting three *personae* of Bernard Fisher that competed for legitimacy across professional, political, and public spheres in the early months of the controversy. It will also consider what these *personae* mean for science as an institution and for the breast cancer patients who weighed in on the controversy. But first, some understanding of the facts of the case is in order.

Origins of the Fisher Controversy

The first glimmer of the controversy occurred in June of 1990, when a routine audit conducted by staff working on Fisher's federally funded National Surgical Adjuvant Breast and Bowel Project (NSABP) found anomalies in data submitted by an investigator from Montreal.[5] These anomalies spurred allegations that one of Dr. Fisher's principal investigators, Dr. Roger Poisson, who then headed cancer research at Montreal's Hôpital St. Luc, had falsified data used in the NSABP's highly influential B-06 Protocol. As published in 1985 and 1989 in the *New England Journal of Medicine*, the B-06 protocol had shown that breast-conserving lumpectomy with irradiation was as effective as mastectomy for early-stage cancers (Fisher et al., 1985, 1989). That landmark research informed the scientific consensus statement issued by the National Institutes of Health (1990) endorsing lumpectomy with radiation for the treatment of early-stage cancers.

The discovery of Poisson's discrepant figures eventually triggered an investigation headed by the U.S. Office of Research Integrity (ORI, which was then the Office of Scientific Integrity or OSI).[6] By 1994, the internal "controversy" surrounding Poisson's violations had faded. Although the ORI had officially found Poisson to have engaged in research misconduct when he confessed to falsifying or fabricating more than 100 separate instances of data in over 14 NSABP clinical trials over a 10-year period, that finding was reported, along with over a dozen others, on page 33,831 of the *Federal Register* (Sawyer, 1994a). Because Poisson's case was ninth in a list of 14 incidents of scientific misconduct, and because there was no mention of his link to a major clinical trial (Sawyer, 1994a, p.A1), ORI's finding passed without more than the merest of murmurs in the public sphere or even in the biomedical community until March 13, 1994. On this day, science reporter John Crewdson (1994) first broke the story to the public with his front page *Chicago Tribune* headline, "Fraud in Breast Cancer Study: Doctor Lied on Data for Decade."

The swirl of media attention following Crewdson's announcement pressured oversight officials at the NIH, NCI, and the University of Pittsburgh to maintain the image that they were responding appropriately to mounting perceptions of problems at NSABP. Since Poisson had confessed to research misconduct and been sanctioned, attention quickly centered on Fisher's management of his research enterprise. Subsequently, NCI investigative officials discovered problems with data from a second Montreal hospital, problems they believed NSABP officials had previously identified, and they demanded Fisher's removal from NSABP. Under pressure, Fisher requested administrative leave on March 29, 1994. Meanwhile, the NCI placed the NSABP on probation and ordered them to suspend new patient accruals and conduct extensive internal audits. Responding quickly to the dizzying turn of events, Congressman John Dingell of Michigan convened the House Subcommittee on Oversight and Investigations for hearings in April and June 1994 (U.S. House of Representatives, 1994). These followed on the heels of his previous hearings involving scientific luminaries like David Baltimore.

Somewhere along the way, Bernard Fisher's sincerity, reliability, and very character formed a powerful focus for scientific, political, and public media attention. Competing assessments of Fisher abounded as he, his spokespeople, his colleagues, critics, friends, journalists, congressional staffers, and investigators scrambled to define and redefine his character. Was he, for example, an overworked researcher unfairly caught in the limelight? Was he an arrogant administrator who thought himself above scrutiny? Was he a "hero" as representatives from the pharmaceutical firm Zeneca later suggested (Zeneca Pharmaceuticals, 1998)? The barrage of incidents, allegations, and explanations about Fisher's role in the controversy cohered into narrative form starring the character of science in general and competing *personae* of Bernard Fisher in particular. Understanding how these characterizations affected the contours of the controversy requires a return to the issue of trust and its relation to character and to an examination of how various rhetorically constituted images of Fisher animated the unfolding drama.

Fisher's Three *Personae* in the Early Months of the Controversy

Fisher as Swashbuckling Scientific Revolutionary

The *persona* of the scientific revolutionary remains firmly lodged in contemporary Western imagination. Popularized, if not challenged, in academic and popular culture by the success of Thomas Kuhn's (1962) radically influential *Structure of Scientific Revolutions*, this figure bears the residue of the Enlightenment ideals of science; it conjures notions of a perspicacious genius overthrowing entrenched but outmoded scientific theories. The popular image of Galileo Galilei is often considered to symbolize the scientific revolutionary because his vision of a heliocentric solar system stood in sharp contrast to Catholic dogma of geocentrism. Yet, by contrast to the revolutionary, the stereotypical man of science, according to social science researchers who study lay impressions of scientists, is often idealized "as an almost mythological figure" who is "viewed as the 'paragon of reason and objectivity, an impartial genius whose visions and insights are matched only by his quiet humility'" (Mahoney, 1976 p. 3, as cited in Petkova & Boyadjieva, 1994 p. 215). But in Fisher's case, instead of quiet humility, the *persona* of scientific revolutionary reigned as the dominant characterization both prior to the controversy and in its early stages.

Fisher's revolutionary characterization was readily invoked because of historical events in which he assumed a commanding role. Indeed, long before he was called to testify before Congress in 1994, Fisher took on the surgical establishment. Starting in the 1970s, Fisher challenged the prevailing theory of the spread of cancer. Moreover, he called into question one of the most enduring surgeries in U.S. medicine, the Halsted radical mastectomy, and by implication, the surgical establishment who stood behind its efficacy. The battles were fierce, and Fisher became, in medical historian Barron Lerner's (2001) words, the "bane of breast surgeons" (p. 139). As a result of this past, the dominant media frame to emerge early in the controversy positioned Fisher as a scientific revolutionary who challenged the surgical orthodoxy but whose renegade status also made him vulnerable; he appeared as the lone challenger to the status quo. Additionally, Fisher's performance in the role of scientific revolutionary was tinged with a brash voice, modulating it to that of arrogant revolutionary.

Some of Fisher's specific language choices that occur at the nexus of the revolutionary *persona* and his brash voice stem from the fact that over the years, Fisher would increasingly employ a Kuhnian rhetoric of "paradigm shifts" and "revolutions" when describing the change from the Halsted approach to the alternative hypothesis that he, among others, posited. He could have adopted the rhetoric of an accretion model of science in which scientific progress gradually builds up over time. Such an accretion model was posited by Kuhn's (1962) *Structure of Scientific Revolutions*. In 1992, just two years before the controversy fully erupted in the media, Fisher published an essay titled "The Evolution of Paradigms for the Management of Breast Cancer: A Personal Perspective" in the journal *Cancer Research*. A year later he maintained that "during the past two decades a revolution has occurred in the surgical treatment of primary breast cancer" (Fisher & Ore, 1993, p. 96). The rhetorical efficacy of this strategy was that it presented his alternative hypothesis as a radical rupture instead of a gradual change over the course of a century. Fisher opted to present his ideas as revolutionary, but there were other accounts that could have been made and other stances that could have been adopted, especially in light of the historical debates over breast cancer surgeries. Thus, although there was a competing rhetoric of gradualism—dozens of studies and physicians arguing for systemic theories of cancer—and although women's refusal to submit to breast removal in the 1970s ultimately helped dislodge the Halsted practice, these factors could only be accentuated as a response to Fisher's rhetoric of paradigm-changing revolution. In many ways, Fisher's revolutionary *persona* reinforces the "myth of the lone genius" (Charney, 2003, p. 215), whose vision of science is based on contest and overthrow rather than cooperation and communalism.

One of Fisher's persistent rhetorical strategies was to contrast the science of randomized clinical trials with the anecdotal happenstance of the past, further positioning himself as the revolutionary. For Fisher, the "anecdotal" explanations of Halstedian surgeons "had little enduring impact because they contained no special concept or scientific principle that could be subject to further testing and future investigation" (Fisher, 1985, p. 656). Note here his specific language choices of "little enduring impact" and "no special concept." They evince an air of judgment, a voice that positions Fisher as superior to his predecessors. Despite the fact that Halsted had prided himself on his laboratory techniques, the anecdotal explanations that followed from his studies and others like it "were each nothing more than a cul-de-sac!," Fisher (1985, p. 656) opined. With this statement, Fisher drew a dramatic contrast between the worthy practices of a man of science and the detours of the anecdotalist. Zagacki and Keith (1992) identified the strategy of naming oneself as "scientific" in contrast to one's "non-scientific" predecessors as a hallmark of the revolutionary *persona*. This strategy is evident in Fisher's rhetoric, extending from his 1985 *World Journal of Surgery* article, "The Revolution in Breast Cancer Surgery: Science or Anecdotalism?" to his 1991 essay "The Importance of Clinical Trials." Here, the so-called anecdotal approach is deemed unworthy for the new science represented by clinical trials. "By replacing anecdotal information (which has influenced therapeutic decision making in the past) with more credible and substantive data, clinical trials play a major role in transforming the practice of medicine from an art to a science" (n.p.). While others were "merely" providing retrospective studies, Fisher (1985) was engaged in something loftier, the pursuit of real science in the laboratory. Fisher explained, "during the time that the anecdotal clinical information was accumulating, we were carrying out a series of laboratory and clinical investigations. Our efforts were directed toward obtaining a better comprehension of the biology of metastases" (Fisher, 1985, p. 657). Fisher thus positioned himself as a scientist *par excellence*. His voice registered a superior tone.

However, this construction of self within the technical sphere of argument found in medical journals and academic conferences could have been incompatible with the dominant political frame that emerged in the media during the controversy. Instead, reports of his status as an arrogant and brash revolutionary were amplified through the media, thereby consolidating that unsavory perception of Fisher and fueling criticisms that he with-held critical information from American women in order to further his own agenda. The implication was that by not sharing news of Poisson's falsifications with the public when they occurred, he felt he knew what was best for patients, and thus displayed paternalistic arrogance. This *persona* thus undermined public trust in the integrity of the objective pursuit of science for a number of his audience members.

As news of the controversy evolved, the dominant construction of Fisher as a bold scientific revolutionary circulated widely. The April 3, 1994 *New York Times* article, "Fall of a Man Pivotal in Breast Cancer Research," confirmed Fisher's giant stature at the same time it shored up a picture of arrogance (Altman, 1994). Fisher was described as having "his own agenda." He "might not have accepted every piece of advice that was offered to him" and had a "refusal to take advice or heed instructions from his bureaucratic masters." Moreover, he exhibited a "manner that is often perceived as arrogant and abrasive," and had "a great deal of character" (Altman, 1994, p. B10). The terms *strong* or *forceful* appeared nine times in describing Fisher's personality in the *Times*. The *Pittsburgh Post-Gazette*'s local coverage was somewhat more sympathetic. For instance, the dominant theme to emerge of Fisher in Twedt's (1994) article, "3 Weeks Shake Cancer Pioneer's 30-Year Record," was Fisher's pioneering status. Indeed, the terms *pioneer* or *pioneering* appear more than four times. Fisher was moreover dubbed a "giant" and a "hero." He was a "straight shooter" with "intellectual integrity." Yet, he was also "arro-gant," "abrupt," "disdainful of non-scientists," and "abrupt with those who take opposing views to his" (p. A1). Here, we see testimony about Fisher's character that reveals a mixture of characterizations concerning his *voice* (arrogant, abrupt, disdainful) and a set of interrelated *personae* (hero, pioneer, giant).

Fisher's eminence and pioneering presence clearly emerge in these por-trayals. That he made important strides in breast cancer research is obvious, but combined with descriptions such as abrasive, abrupt, and "not to be pushed around" (Altman, 1994, p. B10) a verbal portrait of arrogance continued to develop. Fisher was not just a revolutionary, he was a swashbuckling one, and these perceived traits undermined efforts to restore his reputation and provided fodder for his critics. They undermined trust in his judgment, and by extension, in his scientific publications. Further, as reports of his brash voice and former arrogance grew, Fisher's critics were able to marshal his previous construction of self as "revolu-tionary" as evidence of his unfitness to manage the NSABP. It is important to emphasize here that it was not necessarily the *persona* of revolutionary itself that provided fodder for attacks against Fisher. Rather, it was amplified and perhaps distorted traces of his brash voice circulating the mediated infosphere that caused concern. This *persona* confirmed widespread stereotypes about the *ethos* of science as entailing a distance from everyday concerns. However, although it was dominant and early to emerge, this *persona* was not the only image of Fisher to circulate.

Fisher as Reluctant Apologist

A second *persona* emerged through Fisher's own voice as it interacted in concert with the voices of other scientist-administrators: that of the reluctant apologist. Fisher performed the role of reluctant apologist in two senses. On the surface, his silence during crucial moments of the controversy did not satisfy the public's or Congressman Dingell's demands for contrition. In a deeper sense, he refused to apologize for the scientific method. Part of Fisher's perceived reluctance to apologize can be explained by understanding the tough political climate participants in "big science" found themselves in the mid-1990s. Indeed, Fisher was not the first big-name scientist to be called to testify before Dingell's subcommittee.

Dingell's pursuit of fraud and corruption spanned the 14 years up to 1994, when reorganization of the house took him off chairmanship of the House Committee on Energy and Oversight (which oversaw the subcommittee before which Fisher and other scientists appeared). When he appeared before the House Subcommittee on Oversight and Investigations, Fisher was following on the heels of Nobel Prize-winning biologist and president of Rockefeller University David Baltimore, Stanford's president Donald Kennedy, and former NIH director Bernadine Healy. None of the hearings had gone particularly well for those three scientists. As Wade Roush of the Massachusetts Institute of Technology put it in 1992, "All three crossed Dingell in hearings conducted by his subcommittee —and all three are still licking their wounds" (p. 56). One unnamed researcher told *Science* magazine in 1991, "people are absolutely terrified of this Dingell business. They're afraid to make a mistake" (p. 510). Yet, in other quarters, Dingell, a second-generation career politician, earned praise for many of his investigative efforts. Some members of the general citizenry and patient advocacy groups lauded Dingell as a champion of patients' rights. In fact, in late 1994, just months after the Fisher hearings, Dingell and wife Debbie Dingell received the Betty Ford Award from the Susan G. Komen Breast Cancer Foundation for their work on breast cancer health issues at an annual awards luncheon in Dallas, Texas. Moreover, Dingell enjoyed a number of credits for ferreting out waste and fraud. A persecutor to some, an advocate to others—views of Dingell's public service were mixed. If Fisher developed the *persona* of a reluctant apologist before Dingell, then Dingell himself enacted the *persona* of inquisitor—at least in the view of some members of the scientific community.

The *persona* of reluctant apologist forged in Fisher's interaction with Dingell emerges from stock characterizations of political controversy, as opposed to technical or scientific controversy. However, given that the Fisher controversy was a science-based controversy—and given that publics can often lack the capacity to make informed judgments about the technical details of scientific research—Fisher's reluctant apologetic stance proved nearly insurmountable. Hints of Fisher's rhetorical quandary were evident when Fisher's Washington-based attorney, Joseph Onek, telephoned Fisher to inform him of a problem with his prepared testimony. Consistent with congressional practice, Fisher's testimony had been circulated to Dingell staffers in advance of scheduled hearings (Twedt & Carpenter, 1994b). Onek relayed to Fisher, "They said there isn't enough groveling" (Twedt & Carpenter, 1994b, p. A1). Dingell staffers expected a man in Fisher's position to express humility when called to appear before a House Oversight and Investigation Subcommittee hearing; yet Fisher, at least in the opinion of his auditors, was far from contrite. Still, in his public statement before the subcommittee, Fisher (as cited in U.S. House of Representatives, 1994) declared that he accepted his "share of the responsibility for those administrative deficiencies that occurred," and further explained that "perhaps my passionate attention to science overshadowed my administrative insight, and this was a mistake" (pp. 171–172). Elsewhere in his testimony, Fisher affirmed that he "sincerely share[d] the subcommittee's concern regarding fraud in science" and expressed deep regret at the "data falsification by a physician at one of the hospitals participating in the NSABP" (p. 169). His regret apparently fell on deaf ears. As Onek relayed to Fisher, the scientist's prepared testimony had not convinced the panel of Fisher's sincerity—in the mind of a powerful auditor, Fisher did not apologize enough, was not humble enough, and did not show audiences the humility they were due.

On the advice of his attorney, Fisher, citing "illness," did not attend the first Congressional subcommittee hearing in April. Fisher's absence from that hearing provided an opportunity for other scientists representing the NCI to point their fingers in Fisher's direction. Sam Broder, then Director of the NCI, testified in April that Fisher "did not respond to constructive criticism by NCI staff" and that he had not published a reanalysis of data when ordered to do so (Goldberg & Goldberg, 1994a, p. 1). According to accounts published in *The Cancer Letter*, one of the most widely circulated professional oncology newsletters, Broder repeatedly apologized, "we are very sorry," and assured the subcommittee that "errors will not happen again" (Goldberg & Goldberg, 1994a, p. 2). When Dingell noted that "top NCI officials have complained to the subcommittee staff that they could not even get Fisher to return their phone calls, let alone take any direction from the NCI," Broder did not correct his comment (Goldberg & Goldberg, 1994a, p. 3). "NCI Apologizes for Mismanagement of NSABP, Says Fisher Resisted Criticism," announced *The Cancer Letter* (Goldberg & Goldberg, 1994a, p. 1). *In absentia*, Fisher had unwittingly sent a powerful message of arrogant apathy that gelled with previous constructions of his *personae*. Other rhetors, sensing his demise, and acting under institutional shields, further cordoned him off: "Univ. of Pittsburgh Distances Itself From Fisher," "NSABP's Pink Sheet: Fisher's Control Had a Downside" (Goldberg & Goldberg, 1994a, p. 1). The reality was likely that Fisher was reeling from this devastating turn of events that marred a meteoric career; however, his withdrawal from this crucial moment allowed others the chance to define his character in ways that helped their own standing.

Although he did not attend the Dingell hearings, Fisher did appear at an annual American Society for Clinical Oncology (ASCO) meeting where he received a standing ovation.[7] In his address before the ASCO, Fisher noted that his review of data showed that Poisson's falsification did not alter the findings. However, "he did not apologize for the snafu that allowed falsified data from 99 patients to be entered into the studies, and he did not directly address the delays in making the problems public" (Sorelle, 1994, p. 2A). Such reports solidified the reluctant apologist *persona*.

Fisher did appear at the second Congressional hearing in June. However, despite his scientific eminence, Fisher's rhetorical performance in this political arena fell short. The June 24, 1994 issue of *The Cancer Letter* described the second hearing as "tragic for Bernard Fisher" and announced, "Fisher Unable to Answer Key Questions, Blames NCI" (Goldberg & Goldberg, 1994c, p. 1). In the words of one Dingell staff member who refused to be named in newspaper accounts of the hearing, "the real problem with Fisher's testimony" was that he "really couldn't come to grips with admitting the warts and wrinkles of the project" (Twedt & Carpenter, 1994b, p. A11).

Fisher had attempted to persuade the Dingell subcommittee of his integrity and dogged devotion to research. He began his 41-paragraph testimony with a six-paragraph attempt to use his own *ethos* to persuade the subcommittee of his good intentions and commitment to science. Unlike the other scientists who testified that day, most of whom merely mentioned their current positions, Fisher began his testimony with a catalog of his scientific accomplishments. He explained his 35-year, passionate devotion to the study and treatment of breast cancer, and pointed out that as a result of NSABP research, which he chaired for 35 years, women have a choice to avoid disfiguring surgery. Fisher's decision to begin his testimony in this way may have contributed to perceptions that he was arrogant (Altman, 1994) because it focused first on his own standing. Furthermore, he devoted two paragraphs to cataloging the harms that befell him and others from the controversy. "The events arising out of the data falsification in Canada have been tragic for me, my colleagues, our families, and for all the women in this country," he observed, concluding his introduction with the statement that "women must not become victims of these events" (U.S. House of Representatives, 1994, p. 169).

Fisher's efforts to address Dingell's charges against him reveal a mix of appeals to policy and character. He relied on three primary strategies in responding to Dingell's attack: denial, suggestion of injury, and ignorance of foreseeable consequences. First, Fisher repeatedly denied both action and motive:

> There was never any intent to hide information regarding the discovery of falsified data at St. Luc Hospital in Montreal, and I emphasize that. There was never any attempt by me or my associates to hide any information regarding the discovery of that information.
>
> (U.S. House of Representatives, 1994, p. 169)

Second, he suggested that he was injured from the allegations, an argument that was coupled with a denial of action and motive:

> For 30 years, the goal of the NSABP was to provide better information to patients and their physicians. The suggestion that we suppressed information is painful. We never attempted to hide any information. There could have been no conceivable reason to do so.
>
> (U.S. House of Representatives, 1994, p. 170)

Finally, he argued that he did not foresee the consequences of his actions:

> We didn't realize that the failure to publish our findings immediately would be misinterpreted by the public as an indication that we were concealing information. Such a perception resulted in the unjustified concern that women with breast cancer were receiving inappropriate therapy.
>
> (U.S. House of Representatives, 1994, p. 170)

Moreover, "let me emphasize this firmly," he argued,

> if our reanalyses had produced evidence that the conclusions of our studies were affected by the data alterations, we would have reported our findings immediately. Neither we, the NCI, the NIH, nor the OSI perceived that the Poisson falsifications had resulted in a public health problem.
>
> (U.S. House of Representatives, 1994, p. 170)

With this statement, Fisher explained his actions using scientific grounds. We can hear the dispassionate voice of science arguing that the data, even if slightly tainted, did not warrant public notification because the overall findings of the trial held. However, because he was debating within the constraints of public argument, which meant that the audience did not necessarily share his belief that the science was unaffected by Poisson's actions, some felt this argument was unpersuasive.

Indeed, a major rhetorical constraint that hampered Fisher's efforts at character rehabilitation pivoted on the gap between perceptions of technical reasoners and public-sphere reasoners. Despite their efforts, Fisher and others were unable to persuade broader audiences of the view held by statisticians and clinical investigators that Poisson's falsifications did not impact the outcome of the clinical trial in which Poisson was involved. Aside from Fisher's testimony, in 1997, 20 highly regarded European statistician-researchers, including Richard Doll, who is considered one of the founders of the modern clinical trial, weighed in on the imbroglio in an essay entitled "The Trials of Dr. Bernard Fisher: A European Perspective on an American Episode." They offered imaginary testimony that they would have given before Dingell's subcommittee in bold-faced text:

> It needs to be understood that randomization of a few slightly ineligible patients into a large clinical trial is a type of change that *cannot* introduce any material bias into the main results of that trial. What this means ... is that the main types of alteration that Dr. Poisson made could not have introduced any material bias into any NSABP trial. So, even before the trials were re-analyzed with and without his data and the results were submitted to the NCI, both NSABP and NCI officials knew that such changes couldn't make any material difference either way—and, of course, they didn't.
>
> (Peto et al., 1997, p. 7)

Viewed from this vantage point, it might seem as though the matter was straightforward. Poisson's falsifications, though wrong, were hardly damning of the entire study. Yet, interpretations of the seriousness of Poisson's actions and their implications for trust in science were anything but predetermined. In Fisher's view, the facts of the case meant that the trial's conclusions still held. Despite however many physician-investigators agreed with him, the struggle over the integrity of the research had moved to the public sphere where concerns about falsification undermined the integrity of the entire scientific enterprise. A different standard of proof and different type of assurance typified this discourse. Thus, for large numbers of both technical and public audiences, Fisher's *persona* of the reluctant apologist—who did not fully take responsibility for how NSABP action had harmed others—generated outcry.

Fisher as Beleaguered Administrator

The third *persona* competing for legitimacy and acceptance during the controversy was that of Bernard Fisher as a beleaguered administrator of science. At the height of the controversy, Fisher observed that the years prior had become especially busy. "The number of patients being followed in NSABP studies," he wrote in an April 13, 1994, statement to the House Oversight Subcommittee, "increased from 25,000 in 1991 to 41,000 in 1993, and the number of data forms processed expanded from 225,000 in 1991 to 413,000 in 1993." During its 35-year history, the growth and trajectory of the NSABP reflected the directions clinical biomedical research was taking on a national scale. Increased bureaucratization and professionalization of medicine, the rise of the randomized clinical trial as the gold standard of proof for medical therapy, and intensified demarcation of behaviors that were acceptable and unacceptable in clinical research all occurred during this period. Given the complexity and broad reach of the NSABP, its relationships with multiple governing agencies, and its rapid expansion, it is little surprise that for Fisher, the "man in charge" of the enterprise, the *persona* of beleaguered administrator would eventually emerge. While it was Fisher himself who first offered administrative duties as a reason for his delay in publishing a reanalysis of the data, Dingell and other critics would seize on this information to craft a picture of Fisher as a man overwhelmed by the day-to-day operations of the NSABP. Amplified in the media, this *persona* functioned to make Fisher seem negligent. However, the biomedical community was being forced to confront the fact that they lacked precedent for how to handle a situation like the one presently before them.

Fisher's appearance before Dingell's Oversight Subcommittee further encouraged a view of a man overwhelmed by the operations of the now sprawling NSABP which oversaw research at some 500 sites across North America. As the following dialogue reveals, even Fisher's ability to keep watch over the day-to-day operations of the organization was challenged:

MR. DINGELL: Doctor ... there were some fairly significant eligibility questions. For example, one site had three-quarters of the participants ineligible.

MR. FISHER: I am certainly unaware of that, sir. I really am not aware of it.

MR. DINGELL: But it was in audit reports that came to you, though.

MR. FISHER: I don't, I really don't remember seeing that report at all.

MR. DINGELL: Well, here they are, and I am just going to lay them out. South Nassau Hospital, Rush Presbyterian Hospital, St. Joseph in Lancaster, and in the University of Pittsburgh. Now, the University of California Davis had three quarters of the participants in the study ineligible.

MR. FISHER: I have never seen these.

MR. DINGELL: These were audits, these were audits in your project.

The discussion continues with Fisher commenting on the nature of eligibility requirements:

MR. FISHER: I certainly am not aware of any institution where there were three quarters of the patients ineligible. I should like to have more information about that than I have.

MR. DINGELL: Well, we will give it to you. It is, however, I would observe, Doctor, in your own audit reports. Now, here are other examples. Auditors turned up instances where patients were randomized twice. What is the result of randomizing a patient twice in a study of this kind? What does it do to the statistical validity of the study?

MR. FISHER: I can't answer that question.

. . .

MR. FISHER: Sir, I cannot answer these questions unless I know the specific cases and so on. I am sorry. We continue to try to educate these people.

MR. DINGELL: It is my impression that you were the man that ran this whole thing.

(U.S. House of Representatives, 1994, p. 173)

Viewed from a political or public-sphere frame, Fisher's inability to appear in command of his organization worked to construct the *persona* of a beleaguered administrator. Rather than crafting a voice of contrition, supplication, or apology, he appeared, on the one hand, defiant and on the other, defeated and besieged. Michael Friedman, who directed the NCI's cancer therapy evaluation program, observed, "It was clear that Dr. Fisher was being overwhelmed by the workload," said (Twedt & Carpenter, 1994a, p. A1). In a *Washington Post* report with the headline "Researcher Accused of 'Lavish Parties'," the newspaper summarized yet another line of questioning at the hearing during which, after nearly two hours at the witness table, Dingell told Fisher, "It does appear to me that you are more expansive with your expenditures for parties than you are for auditing" (Sawyer, 1994b, p. A10). Fisher slumped, shrugged, and replied, "After a lifetime of dedication to science, I find that absolutely devastating" (Sawyer, 1994b, p. A10). Slumping, shrugging, unable to answer questions, Fisher's appearance and specific language choices served as a powerful, visual rhetoric that reinforced his beleaguered administrator *persona* during his testimony.

In light of the administrative pressures that accompanied the flourishing NSABP—duties that increased further following the discovery of Poisson's falsifications—it is not surprising that it was Fisher himself who first raised the issue of multiplying administrative tasks as a reason for his slowness in publishing a reanalysis of the data from B-06. Although he did not appear in person at the first Dingell Subcommittee hearing on April 13, 1994, he did send a written statement. And while it was excluded from the published hearing transcripts, the statement was reprinted in full in *The Cancer Letter* on April 22. Fisher's 20-paragraph statement began, "having directed the National Surgical Adjuvant Breast & Bowel Project for over 25 years, I am now engaged in a comprehensive evaluation of the issues raised by recent disclosures" (Fisher in Goldberg & Goldberg, 1994b, p. 11). We can imagine that with this sentence, he sought to convey command of the operations, to take responsibility for uncovering what went wrong. Fisher then commented on the significance of NSABP breast cancer research, making an explicit appeal to the revolutionary nature of NSABP findings: "the findings from our trials have revolutionized the treatment of this dreaded disease by demonstrating that lumpectomy followed by radiation therapy, rather than a disfiguring radical mastectomy, is the preferable treatment for most women with breast cancer." After reviewing some of the other key findings of NSABP research, Fisher recounted events leading up to the present day in a dry, matter-of-fact voice. He recounted that in 1991, "We found that an investigator from St. Luc Hospital in Montreal had deliberately altered data relating to patient eligibility for clinical trials." Moreover, "we immediately informed the NCI," and "promptly reanalyzed the studies in which patients from St. Luc hospital had participated" (Fisher in Goldberg & Goldberg, 1994b, p. 11). These words sought to convey to his auditors that he had followed appropriate courses of action.

Later in the statement, Fisher offered a rationale for his delay in publishing a reanalysis of the B-06 data, one without Poisson's numbers. This rationale further solidified the *persona* of the beleaguered administrator. Specifically, Fisher maintained that he had not published a reanalysis of the data because he deemed other NSABP projects to be of higher priority and because auditing procedures were underfunded. More than that, his workload had multiplied since the initiation of the much-celebrated breast cancer prevention trial. Fisher noted, "In the past 18 months, our work has expanded enormously. A newly-initiated breast cancer prevention trial recruited more patients in one year than were recruited in any year in all of the treatment trials combined" (Goldberg & Goldberg, 1994b, p. 12). With now more than 500 sites participating in the data collection and processing, the triumph of the NSABP—its size, scope, and influence—would also be its weakness. For, how could one person ensure that 500 data-collection sites were all conforming to the protocol?

There is a tension inherent in the *persona* of beleaguered scientific administrator that reveals the dilemmas of the present *ethos* of science. This scientific administrator *persona* could evoke either sympathy for Fisher's deluge of work (accompanied by a belief that no single human could have been able to oversee such a sprawling operation) or confirmation that Fisher was derelict in his duties because he misjudged the seriousness of threats to the credibility of the data. Those sympathetic to Fisher as the beleaguered administrator might have been swayed by noting that "Fisher, renown for his self-assurance, said he had fallen into a deep depression after being forced to step down in late March as head of the project" (Carpenter, 1994b, p. B1). Fisher himself recounted that,

> after being and doing what I did for so many years, and then suddenly one day (to be) called and told I was no longer going to be chairman of this thing, and there was no due process or anything else, that was a devastating thing for me.
>
> (Carpenter, 1994b, p. B1)

These statements are consistent with the perception that Fisher was overwhelmed, regardless of which side of the tension one sided with. Ultimately, both undermined his credibility, for they made it appear that the situation at the NBABP was improperly managed.

Regrettably for Fisher, newspapers spread this perception further. Less than one week after his April 13, 1994 statement and his absence from the Dingell Subcommittee hearings, the *New York Times* ran a profile of Fisher featuring his administrative backlog. NCI's Dr. Bruce A. Chabner was quoted as saying that Fisher had "failed to respond to 'five or six' written requests to publish his reanalysis of the lumpectomy study without the Poisson data" (Altman, 1994, p. B10). Moreover, "Dr. Fisher's team was a year behind in visits to cooperating hospitals to audit their data and was extremely slow to report to the cancer institute serious deficiencies found in the audits" (p. B10). Chabner opined, "The fact that they were so far behind was not tolerable," and "Bernie just was not responding" (p. B10). Here, we see the *persona* of the reluctant apologist overlap with that of the beleaguered administrator to cement a picture of an overwhelmed, negligent scientist unable to oversee the now-sprawling organization. The credibility contest now pivoted on which *personae*, with its accompanying narrative of responsibility and attendant moral judgments, would reign. Surely, the NCI's motive in scapegoating Fisher for what might have been seen as their own administrative incapacities bears pointing out, but Fisher's voice in pointing the finger back at them was drowned out in a swirl of statements such as "respect for Dr. Fisher's contributions as a scientist does not mean he is up to running this project" (p. B10). That NCI officials were so ready to share the blame also gave them more rhetorical license to scapegoat Fisher.

Considered together, the three overlapping but competing *personae* that characterized Fisher in the initial months of the controversy coalesced into a narrative that rendered Fisher a convenient scapegoat for what was arguably a systemic failure. The focus on Fisher's character and the degree to which he lived up to the scientific *ethos*—as revolutionary, as beleaguered administrator, and as reluctant apologist—proved incompatible with the broader public framing(s) of the problem. His initial reluctance to speak also provided the opportunity for others to control the narrative and make him the agent responsible for lapses. Moreover, his voice, and characterizations of it offered by others, interacted with his *personae* in ways that further hampered his efforts at reputational restoration. Lingering perceptions of his brashness, his alleged reluctance to apologize, and his initial silence proved formidable obstacles.

By May 17, 1994, Fisher was portrayed as an "embattled doctor" who defended himself for the first time (Sorelle, 1994). An editorial that appeared in the *Pittsburgh Post-Gazette* on May 20, 1994 demonstrates the interaction of the *personae* of beleaguered administrator with that of the reluctant apologist: "There's blood in the water and the sharks are coming out to feed. That's not a very attractive way to look at the altruistic world of medical research, but it appears to be the case" (p. C2). The editorial further posited:

> the fact that Dr. Bernard Fisher, who headed the project at Pitt, was slow in publishing the new results and was perceived as arrogant and thus was not as compliant as he should have been has led to a firestorm of criticism.
>
> (p. C2)

By December, the *Pittsburgh Post-Gazette* announced that "Fisher's Years of Achievement Crumble[d] Overnight" (Carpenter, 1994a, p. A7). That same month, an editorial in the *Post-Gazette* noted that Fisher's "international acclaim" made his fall "all the more precipitous" ("Editorial," 1994, p. D2). Similarly, Fisher is said to have undergone a "staggering reversal of fortunes," and was "the victim of nearly hysterical overreaction and political gamesmanship at its worst" (p. D2).

Unraveling the *personae* that animated the controversy in the immediate months after it circulated in the public sphere helps to explain why the controversy progressed as it did. The swashbuckling revolutionary, the reluctant apologist, and the beleaguered administrator kept the focus squarely on Fisher's actions, rather than on the broader systemic challenges that surfaced throughout the controversy. Moreover, an exploration of these *personae* reveals how certain policy options—options that targeted individual transgressions, versus systemic failures—prevailed. Although a sliver of the public discourse focused on solutions that would address stakeholder concerns about the controversy, the majority of the public discourse appears to have scripted stakeholders out of participation in the public sphere. Fisher's *persona* as the scientific revolutionary retained the *mythos* of science as a sacred space reserved for cultural elites who could properly discern the meaning of clinical trials without public input. The reluctant apologist brought this view into even sharper relief. The beleaguered scientific administrator, by contrast, revealed the crushing weight of large-scale scientific projects in terms of staffing and management, but also did not provide room for lay participants to have a place at the table. Thus, it is no surprise that the most loudly trumpeted resolutions and policy outcomes of the controversy focused not on institutionalizing public participation in science or enhanced public communication policies—improvements many stakeholders clamored for—but on enacting tighter data monitoring and increased audits. The scientific *persona* shaped perceptions of appropriate policy responses by embedding characters of science controversy into story-lines emphasizing certain features of the case over others; namely, those that emphasized transgression from a system whose underlying assumptions were not fully ventilated.

As emotions began to settle, Fisher's public suffering provided a rhetorical opening for recasting him as vindicated scientific revolutionary. Following 3 years of legal battles, Fisher announced on August 27, 1997 the withdrawal of a lawsuit against the University of Pittsburgh and the U.S. federal government. The University of Pittsburgh agreed to pay a nearly $3 million settlement, of which the NCI would pay $300,000. According to the terms of the settlement, both institutions would issue apologies. In a formal statement, the University of Pittsburgh (1997, p. 1) expressed "sincere regret at any harm or public embarrassment that Dr. Fisher sustained," affirming that "at no time was Dr. Fisher found to have engaged in any scientific or ethical misconduct." These words formally marked the conclusion of this protracted biomedical controversy that had, for a time, tarnished the career and reputation of one of the most eminent breast cancer researchers of the 20th century, and nearly destroyed the organization to which he had devoted 35 years. Despite the controversy, the lumpectomies Fisher advocated gained widespread acceptance, the NSABP went on to resume its vigorous research agenda, and Fisher was named a "Legacy Laureate" at the University of Pittsburgh. A 20-year follow-up on his lumpectomy study—purged of Poisson's data—confirmed its original findings (Srikameswaran, 2002).

Yet, throughout this dark episode, the interacting constructions of Fisher as swashbuckling scientific revolutionary, as reluctant apologist, and as beleaguered administrator undercut his efforts to persuade his audience of his integrity. They also shook public faith in the outcomes of his science even as they supported visions of science that scripted publics out of meaningful participation in research that directly affected them. In each case, Fisher's voice modulated these *personae* in ways that potentially undercut his personal *ethos*—or, that provided resources for its rehabilitation. In each case, the underlying *personae* revealed the dilemmas of the *ethos* of science writ large. The scientific revolutionary underscored the difficulties of going it alone. The reluctant apologist demonstrated the problems that incur when a chasm exists between technical expertise and public concerns. The beleaguered administrator brought into high relief the pressures facing scientists as their profession becomes increasingly bureaucratized, dispersed, and accountable to varied publics. Each of these characterizations therefore reveals as much about the contest over Fisher's character as they do about broader understandings and collective longings about science itself.

Conclusion: Analyzing the Role of Characters in Science-Based Controversy

This analysis turned attention to the character struggles facing scientists who find themselves called to account for their actions during science-based controversies. The chapter tracked how, in the early months of such a controversy, rhetorical constructions of the principal player can transform the relationship between knowledge and character, and encourage particular policy outcomes. In high-flying, science-based controversies such as the one outlined in this chapter, perceptions of character act as yardsticks for whether or not, or to what degree, stakeholders accept particular scientific truths or claims. This exploration of rhetorical constructions of character also demonstrated the complicated link between character and reason, and the capacity for character modification during contests of credibility. From this perspective, science-based controversies are deeply influenced by the outcomes of a collective process of character contest. Accordingly, analyzing the interrelation of *ethos*, *persona*, and voice in science-based controversy allows us to discover that *personae*, in fact, reflect shared visions of the scientific endeavor. In the responses of scientists and advocates in this controversy, we are confronted with not just self-representation but a collective process of identity formation that evokes normative considerations of what a scientist ought to be, and of what science ought to be. The characterizations that enlivened this controversy were, therefore, screens onto which participants projected hopes and fantasies for the scientific endeavor in contemporary society. These characterizations are, in short, as much a reflection of collective wishes and anxieties about biomedical science, as they are about particular scientists and other key players.

By highlighting the rhetorical work of character construction in science-based controversies and by disentangling *ethos*, *persona*, and voice, this chapter offers a fresh but nuanced framework for understanding such controversies. This method demands detailed analysis of the interactions between the three concepts and what they mean as they relate to characterization, and entails consideration of what *personae* reveal about the underlying *ethos* of science. It also requires that attention be paid to both the technical and public texts that are likely to emerge during a science-based controversy. Moreover, since scientific *personae* emerge from the key communal concerns of an epoch, tracking the emerging *personae* that animate a particular case, and uncovering how *personae* are modulated by voice, may reveal normative assumptions about science and its relationships to (and broader conflicts with) publics and stakeholders. Indeed, as evidenced in the case of Bernard Fisher, scientists are not the only players who participate in science-based controversies. Therefore, future studies should consider the *personae* of the politicians and other actors who weighed into the controversy, track the implications of voice for specific characterizations, and chart the rhetorical dilemmas participants face in challenging the scientific orthodoxy. By analyzing the contentious constellation of characters to emerge from a controversy, the complex interconnection between character and knowledge can become clearer, which in turn allows for a better understanding of the rhetorical processes involved in public communication about science. Ultimately, this chapter maintains that investigating the rhetorically constituted characters that populate science-based controversies is both a fundamental task for understanding the influence of biomedical science in contemporary life and for tracking the contested relationship between the norms of the public sphere and the forms of specialized knowledge found in science.

Theoretically, this chapter made the case that trust and character should be considered at the core of contemporary science and that analyzing the interaction between *ethos*, *persona*, and voice can provide nuanced interpretations of how characterizations may influence science-based controversies. Methodologically, it demonstrated how this method can be used to limn out the dynamics of a particular case. A key tenet of the field of rhetoric, and of rhetoric of science, is that scholars must attend to the unique particularities and peculiarities of a particular case. *Ethos*, *persona*, and voice provide a framework for parsing out the particularities of characterizations for a given case. The Fisher case therefore illuminated the dilemmas of contesting characters that scientists may face when challenged in public, as opposed to technical, arenas. Practically speaking, this case should encourage reflection about how scientists can best forge partnerships with active publics to shore up trusting relationships so that they may withstand the heat of controversy.

Future investigations should continue to track the evolving *personae* of science-based controversies and interrogate what recurrent *personae* reveal about the *mythos* of science in the present day, what these constructions expose about our own collective expectations of scientists, and what they suggest about the overall place of science in a world increasingly dependent on scientific information. Some questions to consider include: Are scientific *personae* relatively stable across similar cases? Can quantitative analysis of *personae* provide generalizations that extend this initial qualitative heuristic? Future studies should address how the scientific *ethos* provides norms for the construction of scientific characters and how the resultant *personae* of a science-based controversy enable and constrain certain perspectives, policy outcomes, and preferred solutions to the controversy (Keränen, 2005). Such studies will no doubt enrich our under-standing of the interrelations between character and knowledge in public lives increasingly awash with technical information. Ideally, they will lay a foundation for understanding the rhetorical operations of trust in cases where public needs and technical information converge.

Notes

1. A fuller accounting of this method and its application to a number of other participants in this controversy is forthcoming in Keränen's *Scientific Characters: Rhetoric, Politics, and Trust in Breast Cancer Research*, which is under contract with the University of Alabama Press.
2. Most readers first encounter the reprint of this essay, entitled "The Normative Structure of Science," in *The Sociology of Science: Theoretical and Empirical Investigations*, edited by Norman Storer (Chicago, IL: University of Chicago Press, 1973), pp. 254–266. Turner (2007) offers an excellent review of the international scientific and political climate in which Merton produced his ideas. His essay is but one of a series of articles on Merton's norms that appear in volume 7 of the *Journal of Classical Sociology*, published in 2007.
3. Sociologist Marcel Mauss (1939/1979) speculated that the term "persona" may have Etruscan origins (*porsenna*) in *Une Catégorie de L'espirit Humain: La Notion de Personne, celle de "Moi."*
4. Mauss illuminates the cultural role of *personae* by tracing the shift from *personnage* or role in Greek, Roman, Indian, and indigenous cultures to the emergence of self, "*moi,*" in eighteenth-century European Christian cultures
5. The NSABP is a clinical trials cooperative supported by the National Cancer Institute and headquartered in Pittsburgh. Since its creation, the NSABP has enrolled more than 110,000 people in clinical trials related to breast and color-ectal cancers (see NSABP, 2008).
6. When the controversy began, the Office of Science Integrity (OSI) was respons-ible for investigation. In 1993, OSI underwent a structural reorganization resulting in the combining of two offices into the Office of Research Integrity (ORI). See U.S. Department of Health and Human Services (1993).
7. However, according to Sorelle (1994), the audience seems to have been divided. Dr. George Peters of Baylor-Sammons Cancer Center in Dallas also received loud applause when he demanded Fisher resign until the ORI's investigation was complete.

References

Altman, L. K. (1994, April 4). Fall of a man pivotal in breast cancer research. *New York Times*, p. B10.

Altman, R. (1996). *Waking up, fighting back: The politics of breast cancer*. New York: Little, Brown.

Amossy, R. (2001). *Ethos* at the crossroads of disciplines: Rhetoric, pragmatics, sociology. *Poetics Today, 22*, 1–23.

Aristotle. (1984). *The rhetoric and the poetics of Aristotle*. Translated by W. R. Roberts and I. Bywater. New York: The Modern Library.

Baumlin, J. S., & Baumlin, T. F. (1994). *Ethos: New essays in rhetorical and critical theory*. Dallas, TX: Southern Methodist University Press.

Bloomer, W. M. (1997). Schooling in *persona*: Imagination and subordination in roman education. *Classical Antiquity, 16*, 57–78.

Bordogna, F. (2005). Scientific *personae* in American psychology: Three case studies. *Studies in the History and Philosophy of Biology and the Biomedical Sciences, 36*, 95–134.

Brante, T. (1993). Reasons for studying scientific and scientific-based controversies. In T. Brante, S. Fuller, & W. Lynch (Eds.), *Controversial science: From content to contention* (pp. 177–192). Albany, NY: State University of New York.

Brookey, R. A. (2001). *Persona*. In T. O. Sloan (Ed.), *Encyclopedia of rhetoric* (p. 569). New York: Oxford University Press.

Campbell, P. N. (1975). The *personae* of scientific discourse. *Quarterly Journal of Speech, 61*, 391–405.

Chamberlain, C. (1984). From "haunts" to "character": The meaning of *ethos* and its relation to ethics. *Helios, 11*, 97–107.

Charney, D. (2003). Lone geniuses in popular science. *Written Communication, 20*, 215–241.

Carpenter, M. (1994a, December 26). Fisher's years of achievement crumble overnight. *Pittsburgh Post-Gazette*, p. A7.

Carpenter, M. (1994b, July 13). Scientist launches public offensive, makes case researcher appeals for reinstatement, restating of projects. *Pittsburgh Post-Gazette*, p. B1.

Carpenter, M., & Twedt, S. (1994, December 28). Anatomy of a scandal: Fisher feared Dingell inquiry. *Pittsburgh Post-Gazette*, p. A11.

Constantinides, H. (2001). The duality of scientific *ethos*: Deep and surface structures. *Quarterly Journal of Speech, 87*, 61–72.

Corder, J. W. (1989). Hunting for *ethos* where they say it can't be found. *Rhetoric Review, 7*, 299–316.

Crewdson, J. (1994, March 13). Fraud in breast cancer study: Doctor lied on data for decade. *Chicago Tribune*, p. A1.

Dean, C. (2007, October 26). James Watson quits post after remarks on races. *New York Times* online. Retrieved December 1, 2008, from www.nytimes.com.

Editorial. (1994, December 29). *Pittsburgh Post-Gazette*, p. D2.

Elbow, P. (1994). Introduction: About voice and writing. In P. Elbow (Ed.), *Landmark essays on voice and writing* (pp. i–xxxix). Mahwah, NJ: Hermagoras.

Fisher, B. (1985). The revolution in breast cancer surgery: science or anecdotalism? *World Journal of Surgery, 9*, 655–666.

Fisher, B. (1991). The importance of clinical trials. *News from the Commission on Cancer of the American College of Surgeons, 2*. Retrieved December 8, 2002, from www.asri.edu/bfisher/clinical_ trials.html

Fisher, B., Bauer, M., Margolese, R., Poisson, R., Pilch, Y., Redmond, C., et al. (1985). Five-year results of a randomized clinical trial comparing total mastectomy with or without radiation in the treatment of breast cancer. *New England Journal of Medicine, 312*, 665–681.

Fisher, B., & Ore, L. (1993). On the underutilization of breast-conserving surgery for the treatment of breast cancer. *Annals of Oncology, 4*, 96–98.

Fisher, B., Redmond, C., Poisson, R., Margolese, R., Wolmark, N., Wickerham, L., et al. (1989). Eight-year results of a randomized clinical trial comparing total mastectomy and lumpectomy with or without irradiation in the treatment of breast cancer. *New England Journal of Medicine, 320,* 822–828.

Garver, E. (1994). *Aristotle's rhetoric as an "art of character."* Chicago, IL: University of Chicago Press.

Goldberg, K. B., & Goldberg, P. (Eds.). (1994a, April 22). NCI apologizes for mismanagement of NSABP, says Fisher resisted criticism. *The Cancer Letter, 20*(16), 1–7.

Goldberg, K. B., & Goldberg, P. (Eds.). (1994b, April 22). Hearing highlights: "Science does not exist in a vacuum." *The Cancer Letter, 20*(16), 7–12.

Goldberg, K. B., & Goldberg, P. (Eds.). (1994c, June 24). Fisher unable to answer key questions, blames NCI at second hearing on NSABP. *The Cancer Letter, 20*(25), 1–5.

Harris, R. A. (Ed.). (1997). *Landmark essays on rhetoric of science: Case studies.* Mahwah, NJ: Lawrence Erlbaum.

Hyde, M. J. (2004). Rhetorically, we dwell. In M. J. Hyde (Ed.), *The ethos of rhetoric* (pp. i–xxviii). Columbia, SC: University of South Carolina Press.

Keränen, L. (2005). Mapping misconduct: Demarcating legitimate science from "fraud" in the B-06 lumpectomy study. *Argumentation & Advocacy, 42,* 94–113.

Keränen, L. (Forthcoming). *Scientific Characters: Rhetoric, politics, and trust in breast cancer research.* Tuscaloosa, AL: University of Alabama Press.

Kuhn, T. S. (1962). *The structure of scientific revolutions.* Chicago, IL: University of Chicago Press.

Lerner, B. H. (2001). *The breast cancer wars: Hope, fear, and the pursuit of a cure in twentieth-century America.* New York: Oxford University Press.

Lyne, J., & Howe, H. F. (1986). "Punctuated equilibrium": Rhetorical dynamics of a scientific controversy. *Quarterly Journal of Speech, 72,* 132–147.

Mahoney, M. (1976). *Scientists as subjects.* Cambridge, MA: Bellinger.

Mauss, M. (1939/1979). *Une catégorie de l'espirit humain: La notion de personne, celle de "moi."* London: Huxley.

Merton, R. K. (1942). A note on science and democracy. *Journal of Legal and Political Sociology, 1,* 115–126.

Merton, R. K. (1973). The normative structure of science. In N. Storer (Ed.), *The sociology of science: Theoretical and empirical investigations* (pp. 254–266). Chicago, IL: University of Chicago Press.

Miller, C. R., & Halloran, S. M. (1993). Reading Darwin, reading nature; Or, on the *ethos* of historical science. In J. Selzer (Ed.), *Understanding scientific prose* (pp. 106–126). Madison, WI: University of Wisconsin Press.

National Institutes of Health. (1990). *Treatment of early-stage breast cancer: NIH consensus statement online.* Retrieved September 30, 2007, from http://consensus.nih.gov/1990/1990 EarlyStageBreastCancer081html.htm.

National Surgical Adjuvant Breast and Bowel Project. (2008). *NSABP: Nearly 50 years of clinical trial history.* Retrieved December 1, 2008, from www.nsabp.pitt.edu.

Ong, W. J. (1962). Voice as summons of belief. In *The barbarian within and other fugitive essays* (pp. 68–87). New York, Macmillan.

Pascal, C. B. (1996). Misconduct annotations. *Science, 274,* 1065–1069.

Petkova, K., & Boyadjieva, P. (1994). The image of the scientist and its functions. *Public Understanding of Science, 3,* 215–224.

Peto, R., Collins, R., Sackett, D., Darbyshire, J., Babiker, A., Buyse, M., et al. (1997). The trials of Dr. Bernard Fisher: A European perspective on an American episode. *Controlled Clinical Trials, 18,* 1–13.

Prelli, L. (1989). *A rhetoric of science: Inventing scientific discourse.* Columbia, SC: University of South Carolina Press.

Roush, W. (1992, January). John Dingell: Dark knight of science. *Technology Review,* 56–62.

Sawyer, K. (1994a, April 13). Cancer researcher's credibility ailing; Exposure of surgeon's 13-year deception has heavy public impact. *Washington Post,* p. A1.

Sawyer, K. (1994b, June 16). Researcher accused of "lavish parties"; Dingell says Pittsburgh cancer program suffered as a result of "garden spot" meetings. *Washington Post,* p. A10.

Schwartz, J. (2007, January 25). Of gay sheep, modern science and bad publicity. *New York Times* online. Retrieved December 1, 2008, from www.nytimes.com.

Sorelle, R. (1994, May 17). Fisher defends study results at conference. *Pittsburgh Post-Gazette,* p. A2.

Srikameswaran, A. (2002, October 17). 20-year study shows lumpectomies work. *Pittsburgh Post-Gazette.* Retrieved October 29, 2002, from www.post-gazette.com/healthscience/20021017breast1017P2.asp.

Taking advantage: The completion begins for Pitt's prestigious cancer study. (1994, May 20). *Pittsburgh Post-Gazette,* p. C2.

Turner, S. (2007). Merton's norms in political and intellectual context. *Journal of Classical Sociology, 7,* 161–178.

Twedt, S. (1994, April 3). 3 weeks shake cancer pioneer's 30-year record. *Pittsburgh Post-Gazette,* p. A1.

Twedt, S., & Carpenter, M. (1994a, December 27). Fisher describes ordeal as "reign of terror." *Pittsburgh Post-Gazette,* p. A1.

Twedt, S., & Carpenter, M. (1994b, December 28). Fisher feared Dingell inquiry. *Pittsburgh Post-Gazette,* p. A1.

University of Pittsburgh. (1997, September 11). Fisher drops suit in exchange for apology, $2.75 million; University administrators credited with bringing about settlement. *University Times.* Retrieved February 7, 2009, from www.pitt.edu/utimes/ issues/091197/12.html.

U.S. Department of Health and Human Services. (1993). *Investigation report: St. Luc Hospital NSABP project.* Copy on file with author.

U.S. House of Representatives. (1994, April 13 and June 15). Bernard Fisher's testimony U.S. House of Representatives, subcommittee on oversight and investigations of the committee on energy and commerce. *Scientific misconduct in breast cancer research* (103rd Congress, 2nd session). Washington, DC: Government Printing Office.

Ware, B. L., & Linkugel, W. A. (1982). The rhetorical *persona*: Marcus Garvey as black Moses. *Communication Monographs, 49,* 50–62.

Watts, E. K. (2001). "Voice" and "voicelessness" in rhetorical studies. *Quarterly Journal of Speech, 87,* 179–196.

Zagacki, K., & Keith, W. (1992). Rhetoric, *topoi,* and scientific revolutions. *Philosophy & Rhetoric, 25,* 59–78.

Zeneca Pharmaceuticals. (1998). *Heroes among us. Solutions-business news and commentary for Zeneca pharmaceuticals U.S. employees.* Retrieved December 8, 2002, from www.asri.edu/bfisher/ heroes/html.

Zuckerman, H. (1977). Deviant behavior and social control in science. In E. Sagarin (Ed.), *Deviance and social change* (pp. 87–138). Beverly Hills, CA: Sage.

Chapter 7

Exemplary Objects

The Role of Materiality, Sociality, and Rhetoric in Articulating Science through Model Organisms

John Lynch

Although science communication scholars tend to focus primarily on the challenges faced when communicating science and scientific discoveries to the larger public, there is much to be learned from a closer look at the challenges faced by scientists when communicating among themselves. For example, scientists are frequently challenged by the need to adapt already existing language to new concepts and objects for which no descriptions yet exist (Keller, 2002). In that way, scientists must articulate a connection between words and the novel "things" found in experimental practice. In doing so, they must also endeavor to coordinate their rhetorical and material work with the larger social and economic components of the scientific enterprise. It is through these coordinating efforts that discoveries are able to move from the individual lab to the larger scientific arena.

One of the most common scientific methods for extending previous forms of speech to new scientific discoveries is the use of model organisms. Briefly, models are animals, plants, or single-celled organisms meant to stand in for an entire class of organisms. Model organisms do three things. First, they provide a locus for experimental activity. Scientists can easily adapt model organisms for experimental purposes, and the model's biological similarity to other creatures justifies scientists' conclusion about entire classes of life. Second, these organisms provide a locus for the organization of disparate disciplines, scientists, tools, and socioeconomic resources. Third, these organisms provide the initial starting point for subsequent rhetorical presentation through argument from example (as described by Perelman & Olbrechts-Tyteca, 1969). That is, argument generated by research employing a specific model organism provides a shared conceptualization of entire arenas of biological investigation for those who accept the model's use as valid. In the case of stem-cell research, which will be the focus of this chapter, two model organisms perform these varied functions. Those model organisms are the embryonic stem (ES) cells found in mice and the hematopoietic (blood-forming) stem cells (HSCs) found in adult humans.

Each of these models embodies different qualities that define a "stem cell." Use of the mouse model creates a stringent definition that discounts the possibility of adult stem cells, while the hematopoietic model provides an expansive definition that justifies arguments stating all organs of the adult body have stem cells that are similar to ES cells. Of course, given their differences, tensions exist within and between these competing models. These tensions arise, in part, through interference and cooperation among three key components of science—the material, the social, and the rhetorical (Shapin & Schaffer, 1985). Among these three components, which will be detailed in the following section, tension is especially present between the social and rhetorical components. That is, while arguments generated through the use of model organisms can serve to justify universalizing conclusions and shared knowledge, the economic self-interest of science requires scientists to develop and protect resources devoted to their specific model organism.

Through examples such as this, this chapter will argue that the use of model organisms in stem-cell research highlights the coordination of the material, social, and rhetorical components of science and, ultimately, illustrates how scientists engage in a continuous process of connecting words with things. Articulation theory further aids this endeavor by offering an explanation for how the three components of science relate and interact within this context. In exploring these relationships, this chapter will also recommend these components of science (as interpreted through articulation theory) as a framework for a robust rhetoric of science research program that justifies looking at all facets of science—from grant writing to hypothesis formation and experimental practice to science–public interactions.

Articulating Rhetoric and Science

In the field of rhetoric, some argue that science's focus on material reality renders it unfathomable to a scholarly tradition associated with symbols and words (Bokeno, 1987; Cherwitz & Hikins, 2000; McGuire & Melia, 1989). Rhetoricians of science have countered these criticisms with the claim that science is fundamentally rhetorical (Gross, 1991) and with arguments for a "Ciceronian" view of words and things that would "explicitly recognize the way in which linguistic and material factors cooperate" (Ceccarelli, 2001a, p. 317).

The perception of words and symbols as somehow derivative in relation to the material reality of science represents one of the main challenges to studies of science grounded in communication and rhetoric. Such a vision of the symbolic and the material elements of human existence (with the symbolic growing from the material) stems from a specific perspective—the "logic of representation" (Greene, 1998).[1] This chapter, however, eschews that representation for a view of materiality and symbols that is more solidly grounded in Articulation Theory and Shapin and Schaffer's (1985) tripartite vision of science.

Representation and Articulation

Greene (1998) discusses the logic of representation within the context of materialist rhetoric, a project that aims to reshape rhetorical theory into a critical enterprise that examines everyday practices of power and domination. According to Greene, much of the early work in this area recapitulated a logic of representation, where words and discourse were tools reflecting and mediating the economic, military, and material power of already existing ruling classes. This logic created a vision of the world bifurcated into the practice of material power and the derivative representation of it. Such logic also appears in popular understandings of science and symbols: Science, so the story goes, consists of a body of facts and experimental findings, which then are represented in the derivative and imperfect medium of words.

While scholars have repeatedly challenged this simplistic vision of science and symbols, it still has power. Furthermore, many of the arguments made *against* this vision often recapitulate its components and perpetuate the logic of representation undergirding it. Two brief examples illustrate this point. Ceccarelli argues that criticism of science's communication must trace "the ways in which professional assumptions, linguistic resources, *the constraints of the material world*, cultural beliefs, and reasoned arguments are woven together by scientists when they seek to persuade others" (Ceccarelli, 2001b, p. x; emphasis added). While recognizing that words and things exist in a complex interrelationship, Ceccarelli defines the material world as a constraint. In this interpretation, material things resist and limit the reach of words and symbols; materiality is the primary force in science that is then accompanied by a secondary order of words.

The work of Gross (1991, 1995) reverses this relationship, while still maintaining its primary components. He argues that the material components of the laboratory are "not primarily *sub specie materiae* but *sub specie intellectus*—a system equivalent to a hypothetical syllogism" (1995, p. 59). That is, words and ideas have greater power than material things, and persuasive, rhetorical structures play a greater role in shaping science than experiments. However, this view still maintains the a priori power difference between words and things established in the logic of representation. Views of scientific communication and materiality that assume power differences exist between words and things cannot account for the interaction of words and things in scientific practice that produces and distributes power and meaning between them.

An alternative that avoids determining a priori the relative power of words or things exists in the logic of articulation as developed in the work of Greene (1998) and Stormer (2004). Greene (1998) argues for viewing communication and rhetoric as a human tool that helps articulate elements of a situation (whatever those elements may be) and makes those elements available for judgment and subsequent action. Stormer (2004) develops this sense of articulation further in relation to words and things: "The emergence of distinctions between things and discourses, in which some bodies are seen as things and others as discourses (likewise, where some languages become things and some discourses) is a function of articulate performativities" (Stormer, 2004, p. 261). That is, neither words nor things must restrict or precede the other; rather, the logic of articulation suggests understanding both words and things as the products of a set of practices that provide the basis for future judgment and action. It also suggests that science represents a form of human practice and performance that generates facts from which future actions can be justified.

Science as Interrelated Technologies

The practice of science is described by Shapin and Schaffer (1985) as technologies within a tripartite schema. According to Shapin and Schaffer, the practices of laboratory science, established in the early modern era, produce "objects" and "matters of fact" (1985, pp. 22–23). Shapin and Schaffer propose that the laboratory employs three technologies. The authors describe these technologies in relation to the air pump experiments of Robert Boyle, a 17th-century scientist whose work was, in part, an attempt to establish norms for generating knowledge through laboratory experiments:

> The establishment of matters of fact in Boyle's experimental programme utilized three *technologies*: a *material technology* embedded in the construction and operation of the air-pump; a *literary technology* by means of which the phenomena produced by the pump were made known to those who were not direct witnesses; and a *social technology* that incorporated the conventions of experimental philosophers should use in dealing with each other and considering knowledge claims.
>
> (Shapin & Schaffer, 1985, p. 25)

These three technologies—the material, social, and rhetorical—work in unison. In a broader context, material technologies consist of the instruments found in the laboratory along with the protocols of observation and calculation used with those instruments. As Shapin and Schaffer note, the power of material technology is the "capacity to enhance perception and to constitute new perceptual objects" (1985, p. 36). In addition to providing new methods of observation and new objects to observe, the material technology of the laboratory provides for the possibility of manipulating objects and organisms through the creation of experimental handles: "they [handles] can be manipulated in such a way as to induce definite and reproducible effects" (Keller, 2000, p. 141).

Social technology refers to the ways that scientists organize themselves. Shapin and Schaffer (1985) only discuss the systems put in place by early scientists to adjudicate disputes; however, this technology could be extended to capture socialization, norms, and shared knowledge.

Rhetorical technology in a broader context can be defined as any language device or strategy. Shapin and Schaffer (1985) limited their discussion of rhetorical technology to the use of narratives describing an experiment, but contemporary rhetorical theorists have highlighted the almost limitless range of language devices that have been used in scientific discourse (e.g., Ceccarelli, 2001b; Fahnestock, 1999; Gross, 1995; Keller, 1995).

While powerful, this tripartite model also has some problematic aspects. Given the focus of this chapter, which is to investigate the link between existing language and new scientific discoveries, the most important shortcoming is raised by Latour (1993, 2003). Latour argues that Shapin and Schaffer's discussion treats the social as a stable point of explanation that ultimately controls the distribution of the material and literary/rhetorical technologies. Such a relationship has parallels with the a priori power differences found in the logic of representation, especially as it appears in Marxist-inspired rhetorical and communication criticism.[2] The goal for critics then is "to learn how to become sensitive to the contrary requirements, to the exigencies, to the pressures of conflicting agencies where none of them is really in command" (Latour, 2003, p. 33).

This sensitivity can be brought to Shapin and Schaffer's schema via Articulation Theory. Interpreting the typology through the lens of articulation means that, in principle, no category of technology precedes the other in logical priority. As a result, all three categories are required to realize the end goal of science, which is the establishment of new facts. While some cases might evidence the simultaneous emergence/presence of all three technologies, in other cases situation-dependent shifts in temporal priority for one or two of these technologies may emerge. Thus, in some cases, material technology might develop which then requires rhetorical explanation. In other cases, a group of already organized researchers might develop a new set of material equipment and new terminology as part of their research program. This latter situation is evidenced in the creation of rapid-processing DNA and gene-sequencing technology developed in the labs of 454 Life Sciences (454 Life Sciences, 2007). The lab was founded in 2000, the technology was developed in 2005, and the program was described in *Nature* magazine and applied to the example of the Neanderthal genome in 2006 (454 Life Sciences, 2008). In still other cases, the rhetorical technology will precede the material or social technologies, as was the case with the development of genetics in the 1960s. History suggests that the language of genes as a "program" evolved prior to the organization of dedicated research groups or the technology that enables genetic research (Keller, 1995, 2000, 2002).

In addition to overemphasizing the role of the social, which was the criticism levied by Latour (1993, 2003), another shortfall of Shapin and Schaffer's original formulation is that their test case (Boyle's experimental program) assumed the temporal priority of material technology, especially over the rhetorical/literary technology, and it did not highlight sufficiently the equal importance of all three technologies. The use of model organisms in modern biology offers a test case that allows us to highlight the simultaneous articulation and value of those technologies while also describing them in more detail.

Articulating Model Organisms and Scientific Technologies

This section begins with a definition of model organisms and how these organisms fit within the tripartite schematic. According to Keller (2002), a model organism is "an organism that can be taken to represent (that is, stand in for) a class of organisms ... its primary function is to provide simply a stable target of explanation" (p. 115).[3] For example, mice have been used in genetic research as a representative of all mammals. Scientists could take what was known about an animal upon which it was easy to perform experiments (i.e., mice) and through a set of material, social, and rhetorical strategies claim that the knowledge developed there applied to all animals within the group (i.e., all mammals, including humans). It is in this way that model organisms provide scientists a way of answering questions about entire groups of organisms. Furthermore, answering these questions ultimately produces new questions, all of which results in an increased understanding of the model organism and its relation to the broader class it represents.

According to Davis (2004), models became a prevalent means of organizing and explaining the diversity of biological functions with the rediscovery of Mendelian genetics.[4] "By 1940, many geneticists thought about their research organisms as representatives of living things in general" (Davis, 2004, p. 69). Ultimately, the use of model organisms led to an increased focus on mapping an organism's genome (Davis, 2003).

Model organisms provide for the simultaneous coordination of the scientific technologies identified by Shapin and Schaffer. It is argued here that the effective use of model organisms requires that all three technologies be present at the same time and, therefore, these organisms serve to highlight how all three technologies interpenetrate and depend on each other: no single technology predominates. The remainder of this section will highlight how model organisms incorporate the material, social, and rhetorical technologies.

Material Technology

Model organisms perform the perceptual functions of material technology because they allow researchers to perceive a specific biological problem. For example, scientists were able to use the *E. coli* bacteria in order to perceive and study the process by which genes were regulated (Davis, 2003). The manipulation of the conditions where the organism exists—for instance, the addition or subtraction of various amino acids to a petri dish containing *E. coli*—produces experimental handles. Manipulating the organisms' environment and observing the resulting effects allows researchers to draw conclusions about the biological problem under consideration.

The genetic similarities between the model organism and related species allows for conclusions about the model's biology to be extended to other species. For example, the mouse can stand in for all mammals, and corn can stand in for all crops (Davis, 2004). This use of model organisms became feasible as genetics developed. At the level of the individual elements of DNA, early geneticists saw more similarity between the various types of organisms than they saw differences. A handful of model organisms could, they felt, cover life in all its variety and explain how life developed. Indeed, much of this early research proved to be generalizable across a number of different organisms. While the number of other species a model organism represents can vary—mammals outnumber cereal crops, for example—some models became substitutes for all living organisms, or "supermodels" (Davis, 2003). This is most apparent in geneticist Jacques Monod's assertion that "whatever is true for *E. coli* is true for an elephant" (Ullmann, 2003, p. 181).

Model organisms can only become model organisms because they are—or can be—made amenable to experimental manipulation. This is both a productive and a limiting aspect of the material technology of model organisms. Davis uses the term "domestication" to describe the nomination of an organism to model status. This implies a high degree of control over the organism, a degree of control that experimental manipulation requires (Davis, 2003, 2004). Jorgensen and Mango (2002) explicitly recognize the important role that ease of manipulation plays in deciding what creatures become model organisms. They also add the criterion of rapid reproduction to the list of necessary qualities for a model organism: In order to carry out large numbers of experiments on large numbers of animals, animals that reproduce rapidly have become the ideal for scientific practice.

While rapid reproduction and ease of manipulation have allowed scientists to do studies and produce results in a relatively rapid fashion, these requirements limit research in two ways. First, they restrict the number of species with which geneticists and biologists can work. Organisms that do not reproduce quickly are not viable model organisms because they cannot help scientists produce experimental results for publication in a timely fashion. Second, the choice of model organism can also limit the types of questions that can be asked. Monod and Jacob's choice of the bacteria *E. coli* as a model organism for all animals exemplifies this limitation. While Monod and Jacob's work produced a great deal of information about the regulation of genes, the work could not address facets of the lives of more complex organisms. The most obvious of these limitations is that bacteria cannot provide a model for embryology and development: a single-celled bacterium does not go through the stages of birth and growth that verte-brates do (Keller, 2002). In addition to development, Monod and Jacob's work does not fully explain the regulation of genes in more complex organisms, which include mechanisms for altering the structure of chromo-somes and the "editing" of the genetic "message" by RNA. As Keller notes, not only did the original research not address this, but their tena-cious advocacy of *E. coli* as the ideal model for gene regulation also hin-dered research into other forms of gene regulation for the better part of 20 years (Keller, 1995, 2002). As described here, the material component of model organisms has proven to be a simultaneous driver of, and impedi-ment to, biological research.

Social Technology

The social technology of model organisms performs a number of functions. Model organisms serve a socializing function: they help unify groups of scientists. In addition to the models mentioned above (e.g., *E. Coli*), scien-tists have organized themselves around numerous other model organisms such as *Arabidopsis thaliana* (a small flowering plant) and *Caenorhabditis elegans* (a transparent roundworm) (Davis, 2003). Scientists who work on the same model organism develop a shared vocabulary and a shared set of experimental questions. As Davis notes, "The research community that works on a model organism becomes bound by shared interests, tech-niques, mutants, genetic maps and compendia, newsletters, terms of dis-course and focused meetings" (2004, p. 70).

In addition to fostering a system for sharing materials and communi-cating information, the social technology of model organisms—or the capacity to create forms of community—also has an economic dimension. Growing, maintaining, and manipulating model organisms is expensive and resource-intensive; it requires scientists to continually seek new sources of funding to maintain their research and to protect this invest-ment by maintaining the priority of their model over others. In order to balance the ideal of scientific openness and the economic self-interests of researchers, the National Institutes of Health implemented a policy about the sharing of model organisms (NIH, 2004). The policy offers guidelines for managing and sharing the money, time, and effort that go into the creation and maintenance of the material and social technologies of model organisms.

Rhetorical Technology

In addition to their material and social technologies, model organisms also incorporate a set of rhetorical technologies. Model organisms articulate a two-fold rhetorical technology that combines the argument from example and the use of illustrations. According to Perelman and Olbrechts-Tyteca (1969), argument from example is a means of developing generalizations and definitions, which then provide the foundation for moving through a variety of specific cases or illustrations (p. 361). In that way, examples help generate explicit and/or implicit links between multiple phenomena.

Usually, individuals resort to example when a prior rule does not exist to understand a phenomenon, but the individuals assume the possibility of creating a generalization about, or definition of, a phenomenon. *The New Rhetoric* turns to the sciences in order to describe how examples work: "In the sciences, particular cases are treated either as examples that are to lead to the formulation of a law or the definition of a structure or else as specimens or illustrations of a recognized law or structure" (p. 351). While Perelman and Olbrechts-Tyteca assert that one requires multiple examples to develop a general rule (p. 355), scientists often use a single example for creating generalizable rules. In cases where a single example is used to create a rule, as is the case with model organisms, the example is supplemented with the use of illustrations. Illustrations clarify and provide support for an existing generalization:

> Whereas an example is designed to establish a rule, the role of illustration is to strengthen adherence to a known and accepted rule, by providing particular instances which clarify the general statement, show the import of this statement by calling attention to its various possible applications, and increase its presence to the consciousness.
> (Perelman & Olbrechts-Tyteca, 1969, p. 357)

In this way, illustrations supplement an exemplar or example. Usually when examples and illustrations appear together in the same discourse, the examples will appear first in order to clearly establish the rule or generalization used throughout (Perelman & Olbrechts-Tyteca, 1969, p. 359).

To this point, this chapter has examined the tripartite technologies of science and begun to articulate the relationships among those technologies particularly in the case of model organisms. It is argued here that the combination of articulation theory and the tripartite schema offer a framework for examining the development of concepts and establishing "facts" in scientific practice, which are the two primary ways that scientists connect words and things. Out of this framework, two main points should be kept in mind. First, articulation theory places communication on an equal footing with the material and social components of science. In principle, all three are equally necessary and important. Any conclusion that words or things have greater power than the other is the result of a particular case study representing the dynamics of a unique situation. It is not a claim one can generalize to all scientific practices. Second, the equal value of all three technologies can be seen in the use of model organisms. The material technology provides perceptual tools for scientists, but specific material technologies—specific organisms—can limit scientific practice. The social technology provides resources in the form of shared vocabularies, tools, and economic funding sources. The rhetorical technology combines the use of argument from example and the use of illustrations to create general rules and definitions linked to the material and social technologies of the model organism. Like the material technology, the social and rhetorical technologies can inhibit and enhance the scientific practice.

The power of this framework for studying communication among scientists can be further evidenced by a closer study of stem-cell models. The next section, therefore, will examine the use of two different models in stem-cell research: embryonic stem (ES) cells from mice and hematopoietic, or blood-forming, stem cells (HSC). Each model defines stem cells differently. These definitions have different elements that come into conflict, and each model has internal elements that produce tension within the definition they provide.

Stem-Cell Models

As argued above, model organisms provide the point of intersection and articulation between the material technology (that allows scientists to perceive and manipulate biological processes), the social technology (that coordinates their vocabulary, tools, and financial resources), and the rhetorical technology (that allows scientists to create general rules covering entire classes of organisms). The model organism and the articulation it makes possible allows scientists to connect words and concepts to a material object and through that connection link those concepts to whole classes of objects and organisms. While multiple models exist in genetics, none of those models purports to describe the exact same category of organisms. The aforementioned mouse ES cells and HSCs represent two models or exemplars used in research on stem cells. While not organisms per se, these model cell types perform the same function as model organisms. They provide the basis for generalizing results, for unifying results from differing research programs, and for providing the justification for researchers to pool their techniques and resources and form social groups. This examination of models in stem-cell research highlights a number of qualities of scientific technologies and model organisms. While these models do overlap in terms of the general characteristics they define as necessary for stem cells, significant differences also exist and those differences lead to notable conflicts—primarily between the research communities that form around these models.

Mouse Embryonic Stem (ES) Cells

The embryonic stem cells found in mice often act as a model for research on all stem cells. The mouse ES cell model coordinates all three scientific technologies, but it also derives some of its power from the long history that mice themselves have as model organisms. And there is overlap in the qualities of mice as models and mouse ES cells as models.

The material technology of mouse ES cells develops from the genetic similarity between mice and humans.[5] The genetic *differences* between mice and humans account for only 1% of their DNA (Peters et al., 2007). This, in addition to the mouse's size, rapid reproduction and minimal cost of upkeep, make them an ideal model organism (Davis, 2004; Peters et al., 2007). Similar qualities inhere in mouse ES cells. Several varieties have been developed that reproduce rapidly in cell culture (Downing & Battey, 2004; NIH, 2001). They also can produce cells from most of the organs in the mouse's body, and they can be used to create mutant and genetically altered mice that mimic certain disease conditions (Downing & Battey, 2004; NIH, 2001). The status of mouse ES cells as a model has led to intense efforts to characterize them, but instead of trying to identify their genome (which has already been accomplished), characterization aims to identify the unique chemicals the cells produce and the exact set of genes that are activated in these cells (Downing & Battey, 2004; NIH, 2001).

The social technology of mouse ES cells also derives in part from that of mice. Research on mouse ES cells has been incorporated into the organizations that support research on the mouse model. Varieties of mouse ES cells have been available since 1999 through regional resource centers devoted to distributing mice, disseminating the research findings related to the mouse model, and providing training for researchers (Mutant Mouse Regional Resource Centers, 2007). National resources have been dedicated to making model organisms available to researchers and providing a shared platform of research questions and research tools (Battey & Peterson, 2004). Mouse ES cells have been incorporated into the larger mouse model research initiative. Not only does the ES cell research interact and contribute to those other agendas, these links with other mouse researchers also increase the access mouse ES cell researchers have to resources. Such resources include financing to support their work, low-cost services for maintaining and testing mouse ES cells, and connections to a larger community of researchers with similar interests.

For example, Vanderbilt University established in 1993 a resource center for mouse ES cells. The center provides basic research services, maintains and distributes mouse ES cell lines, and organizes conferences to bring together researchers interested in mouse ES cells and stem-cell research (Vanderbilt Center for Stem Cell Biology, 2004). The creation of centers that collect and disseminate material (and rhetorical) technology, and provide services for researchers, embodies the social technology of mouse ES cells.

The rhetorical technology of mouse ES cells consists of argument from example and illustrations. The example and attendant illustrations establish the general qualities that define what stem cells are, but the coordination of the rhetorical technology with the social and material technology produces caveats and exceptions to the general definitional rule that examples provide.

Many articles follow the pattern described by Perelman and Olbrechts-Tyteca (1969), where the example, the strongest case, is argued first and with great detail. Austin Smith's (2001) review of stem-cell research spends 13 of its 20 pages addressing mouse ES cells. Likewise, in two research articles announcing the isolation of human embryonic stem cells, the introductory paragraph uses a discussion of mouse ES cells to identify the qualities that define the category "embryonic stem cell" (Shamblott et al., 1998; Thomson et al., 1998). An article announcing the isolation of ES cells from rhesus monkeys also follows this pattern, but almost all the sentences specifically use the term "mouse ES cells" for emphasis (Thomson et al., 1995). These introductions establish mouse ES cells as the primary example from which scientists draw the qualities used to define the category of "stem cell."

Typically, a list of illustrations follows in summary fashion. After establishing the characteristics of mouse ES cells, researchers then shift those characteristics to other species. For example, one group of researchers noted, "Pluripotent stem cell lines that share most of these [mouse ES cell] characteristics also have been reported for chicken, mink, hamster, pig, rhesus monkey, and common marmoset" (Shamblott et al., 1998, p. 13726).[6] Another article similarly notes, "Reports have described the derivation of pluripotent, embryonic stem cells from multiple vertebrate species, including fish, chicken, rabbit, pigs, cows, sheep, non-human primates, and most recently humans" (Gorba & Allsopp, 2003, p. 269).

Some articles explicitly note that mouse ES cells provide the general rule defining the category of stem cells. Thomson and Odorico (2000) note, "Given the properties of mouse ES and EG cells, the essential criteria required for applying the term 'ES cell' or 'EG cell' line to human cell lines should include…" (p. 53).[7] The authors then go on to list the details of that general rule. In a similar vein, Smith (2001) claims that discussion of stem-cell research requires a definition of stem cells; he provides a list of 12 criteria "that are functionally important and/or unique to mouse ES (and EG) cells" to provide that definition (p. 448).[8] Indeed, most researchers base criteria for defining a group of cells as ES cells on a generalization from the ES cells found in mice.

As suggested earlier, and as evidenced here, model organisms—be they stem cell or other—offer a coordination of all three scientific technologies. This coordination of the three technologies links words (in this case, definitions of ES cells) to a specific object. That linkage allows scientists to further connect their definitions to other objects and also provides a locus around which scientists can organize themselves. Indeed, without all three technologies working in unison, a model organism would not be possible. Yet, along with this coordination, the interaction of the three technologies also can result in a level of "interference." For example, the material and social technologies can interact with the rhetorical technology to alter the potential scope (and effectiveness) of the argument from example.

Consider the stringent requirements that exist for determining what counts as a mouse ES cell. When using mouse ES cells as a model, those stringent requirements become the basis for defining all stem cells. This definition establishes an almost impossibly high standard for establishing that any group of cells is, in fact, stem cells. When researchers use the discovery of stem cells in other species as illustrations of the mouse model, they simultaneously undercut the value of those other stem cells (and the value of the discovery). For example, Thomson et al. (1995) note, "Well-characterized ES and EG cells have been derived only from rodents. Pluripotent cell lines have been derived from ... several non-rodent species, but the developmental potentials of these cell lines remain poorly characterized" (p. 7844). While these researchers use non-mouse ES cells as illustrations to reinforce the model, they simultaneously call the nature of these cells into question. Because of their poor characterization, they cannot be unequivocally defined as "stem cells." As a result, some researchers have renamed embryonic stem cells from other species as "ES-like." Gorba and Allsopp (2003) explain, "As only the established mouse lines have been so far shown to fulfill all the stringent criteria that define bona fide ES cells, we describe these lines, particularly human lines as ES cell-like" (p. 269).[9]

Researchers who use this model hold out hope that humans might have embryonic stem cells. A recent review has emphasized the validity of human ES cells and affirmed that their derivation is a direct result of work on mouse ES cells (Downing & Battey, 2004). This simultaneous use of ES cells from other animals and the resistance to this move highlights a tension between the rhetorical and social technologies of model organisms. Models gain their power because they provide universal rules. These rules develop through arguments from example and attendant illustrations that help illustrate the scope of that rule. At the same time, models are resource intensive: They require a great deal of money, institutional support, and a large number of interested scientists to maintain the research programs that keep a model an active part of science. The animals used as illustrations become potential contenders for the status of model. Research programs devoted to them have the potential to threaten the resources devoted to mouse ES cells, which is why the illustrations are downplayed as secondary to mouse ES cells. That said, human ES cells are often cleared of these charges because they are necessary to realize medical applications that will result in more resources for this line of research.

Another example of the material and social technologies interacting with the rhetorical technology to impact the argument from example occurs when researchers treat stem cells as a product of the laboratory. The material technology of mouse ES cells, specifically the techniques of cell culture used to create stem-cell colonies, again narrows the definition of "stem cell" to place the existence of adult stem cells in doubt. When identifying the standards for determining whether a colony of cells consists of stem cells, many research and review articles argue that prolonged time in a cell culture is necessary to establish identity (Burdon, Smith, & Savatier, 2002; Shamblott et al., 1998; Smith, 2001; Thomson et al., 1998; Thomson et al., 1995). For example, Thomson and Odorico (2000) note that the cells of the inner cell mass (ICM) from which ES cells are derived are not really stem cells until they are removed from the embryo:

> If ICM cells are removed from their normal embryonic environment and cultured under appropriate conditions, they can proliferate and replace themselves indefinitely, and yet maintain the developmental potential to form advanced derivatives of all three embryonic germ layers, thus satisfying the criteria for stem cells.
>
> (p. 53)

According to this definition, stem cells do not exist within the embryo. Instead, they only exist when they are cultured under appropriate experimental conditions. Smith (2001) makes this point even more strongly: "In reality, ES cells should be considered a cell culture phenomenon or even an artifact" (p. 449). While stem cells have their point of origin in the embryo, they only *truly* become stem cells in a petri dish, and since adult stem cells have never been isolated and grown in a petri dish (Metcalf, 2007), strict interpretations of this model would conclude that stem cells do not exist in the body.

With two exceptions, articles that explicitly use this model never address adult stem cells. The exceptions are Smith (2001) and Colman and Kind (2000), who discuss adult stem cells in their reviews; still, their discussions downplay the possibility of the existence of such cells. Both articles devote less than a paragraph to discussing adult stem cells. They also use tentative language to describe the existence and possible applications of adult stem cells. In fact, Smith argues that "adult" stem cells might in fact be embryonic stem cells *left over* from gestation. In sum, the material technology associated with the mouse ES model interacts with the rules derived vis-à-vis the rhetorical technology to produce a definition of stem cell that places the existence of adult stem cells in doubt.

Hematopoietic Stem Cells (HSCs)

Like mouse ES cells, hematopoietic stem cells, and the attendant illustrations of stem cells from other organs, act as a model for some stem-cell discourse. HSCs also provide definitions for the entire class of stem cells. The role of HSCs is established in the same way as mouse ES cells.

The material technology of HSCs builds off the cell's capacity to produce all the necessary components of blood. Human blood contains at least eight different categories of cells, from the varieties of white blood cells to platelets to red blood cells, and all of these cell types descend from one group of stem cells (Metcalf, 2007; NIH, 2001; Weissman, 2000b). This capacity to differentiate—to produce many different types of cells—becomes part of the material basis for their status as a model. As far as researchers can tell, there are more HSCs in the human body than there are stem cells for other organs (NIH, 2001; Weissman, 2000b). Also, these cells can be derived from multiple sources in the body, including circulating blood and bone marrow (Metcalf, 2007; NIH, 2001), and they are more easily accessible to researchers than stem cells found in the brain, intestines, or liver (NIH, 2001). The high differentiation capacity (i.e., the large number of cell types HSCs can become) and the relative ease of access become the basis for the model's material technology.

The social technology of HSCs has some similarities to the social technology of mouse ES cells. Research on these cells has historically been folded into research and clinical practice involving bone marrow, the primary home of HSCs (NIH, 2001; Weissman, 2000a, 2000b). Better understanding of these cells can improve medical practices involving bone-marrow transplants; thus, funding is available for HSC research through sources dedicated to bone-marrow research. For example, the National Heart, Lung, and Blood Institute supports research on HSCs and has provided funds for a set of regional institutions to support the development of therapies using hematopoietic and other adult stem cells (National Heart, Lung, and Blood Institute, 2005). Also, organizations, such as the University of Minnesota's Stem Cell Institute, focus primarily on research involving HSCs, in part because of the institute's ability to forge relationships with specialists in blood and bone-marrow transplantation at the university (University of Minnesota, 2002).

The rhetorical technology of HSCs has developed along the same lines as the rhetorical technology for mouse ES cells. Many articles lead with a discussion of HSCs. A chronological format complements this use of the example as the introduction to the article. For example, Wulf, Jackson, and Goodell (2001) discuss the history of research on HSCs and then note, "Following the chronology of discoveries, we will start from the broadening developmental potential of bone marrow-derived stem cells leading to the differentiation capacities of stem cells from nonhematopoietic tissues" (p. 1361). This move, which also appears in other reviews of adult stem-cell research (cf., Verfaillie, 2002; Weissman, 2000a, 2000b; Weissman, Anderson, & Gage, 2001), blurs the temporal priority of hematopoietic research into a logical priority. That is, because research on these cells occurred first, this becomes the main justification for treating them, even today, as a primary model for all stem-cell research.[10]

Some texts are even more explicit in their dependence on the hematopoietic model. For example, two reviews specifically use the phrase "hematopoietic stem cells as model" as a major heading within the text (Weissman, 2000b; Weissman, Anderson, & Gage, 2001). Furthermore, many scientists argue that HSCs should act as a model for research because of their (well-developed) material technology. For example, Verfaillie (2002) notes,

> The best studied adult stem cell, the hematopoietic stem cell, undergoes, at least *in vivo*, self-renewing cell divisions, differentiates at the single cell level into all mature blood elements and functionally repopulates the hematopoietic system of a myeloablated animal or human. Other adult stem cells have been more recently defined and are therefore less well studied.
>
> (p. 502; see also Jackson, Mi, & Goodell, 1999 and Weissman 2000a, p. 157)

Mitaka's (2001) review of hepatic (liver-forming) stem cells similarly argues that "it appears that we are close to answering the above question [about the nature of hepatic stem cells], owing to the great advances of hematopoietic cell research in the 1990s" (p. 1). In other words, the qualities of hematopoeitic stem cells, as well as the number of researchers working on them, has produced advances in research that justify treating them as a model for stem cells and stem-cell research (see also Alison et al., 2000; Lagasse et al., 2000; Petersen et al., 1999).

Some researchers also argue that the material similarity between the body's blood-producing system and other organs of the body such as the liver further validates the HSC as a model organism. Mitaka (2001) claims, "Hematopoiesis and the hepatic environment are known to have a close relationship at the time of hepatic development and systemic diseases" (p. 1). Along these same lines, Wulf et al. (2001) note a similarity between the endothelial cells that create blood vessels and hematopoeitic stem cells.

Cellular similarities such as these further justify the use of HSCs as model organisms.

As was the case with mouse ES cells, the interaction and coordination of the three technologies—the material, social, and rhetorical—defined "stem cells" by articulating the relationship between words, objects, and organizations. This articulation also produces simultaneous expansions and contractions of the general rules that define "stem cell" in HSC research. First, research and review articles that use the hematopoietic model incorporate the idea of stem cell "plasticity" as a key and uncontested feature of stem cells. "Plasticity" refers to the capacity of adult stem cells tied to one specific organ to produce cells that constitute other organs. For example, plasticity would mean that neural stem cells, tied to the brain and spinal cord, could potentially produce cells for the liver or pancreas (NIH, 2001). The reviews of stem-cell research written by Verfaillie (2002) and Wulf et al. (2001) are entirely concerned with the plasticity of adult stem cells. Several other research articles begin by claiming that previous studies have established the existence of high degrees of plasticity in bone marrow or HSCs, thus justifying further research (cf., Bjornson, Rietze, Reynolds, Magli, & Vescovi, 1999; Jackson et al., 2001; Jackson et al., 1999; Krause et al., 2001). These claims are grounded in the material technology of HSCs.

Researchers had reason to believe that hematopoietic and other adult stem cells had a much greater capacity for producing various types of "daughter" cells than had been thought in the early and mid-1990s. These initial reports about the material technology of HSCs justified the creation of the general concept of "plasticity" that warranted an expansive view of stem cells from adult sources and their powers, as well as justifying using HSCs to provide a definition of "stem cell" that includes cells from non-adult sources as well.[11]

While some elements of the material technology provide a more expansive or plastic definition of "stem cell," other interactions of the material, social, and rhetorical technologies provide a more limited or rigid definition. For example, some uses of the hematopoietic model discount the existence of other stem cells in bone marrow. Although bone marrow contains at least two different types of stem cells, mesenchymal stem cells and HSCs (NIH, 2001), early research that studied the power of "bone marrow stem cells" used whole bone marrow (which was marrow containing a variety of stem cells and non-stem cells) without trying to identify a specific cell type (Brazelton, Rossi, Keshet, & Blau, 2000; Ferrari et al., 1998; Gussoni et al., 1999; Mezey, Chandross, Harta, Maki, & McKercher, 2000). Therefore, researchers using the HSC model collapsed studies of "bone marrow stem cells" into HSCs by claiming, explicitly or implicitly, that these bone-marrow studies were *really* examining HSCs.

Verfaillie (2002) discusses this work as evidence of plasticity in "hematopoietic bone marrow cells" (p. 502). Jackson and coauthors

(2001) describe these studies and claim that "it is possible that hematopoietic stem cells (HSC) are directly or indirectly involved" (p. 14482). While both reports leave some ambiguity as to what types of cells are operating here, they both clearly signal the presumption that the cells showing plasticity are HSCs. Lagasse and coauthors (2000) are even more explicit: they cite the work by Ferrari et al. (1998) and Gussoni et al. (1999) to justify the claim that "bone marrow populations or bone marrow cells enriched for HSCs have the potential to give rise to muscle" (Lagasse et al., 2000, p. 1232), although the original reports only report using bone marrow without specifying the type of stem cell present.

Another example of a narrowing of the rule occurs when researchers blur the physical similarity of HSCs and other adult stem cells. While model organisms help articulate the relationships between scientists, research objects, and rhetorical strategies, some scientists fail to remember that model organisms *stand in for* a class of organisms and reduces the class to the specific organism. While Jacob and Monod treated *E. coli* as a supermodel describing everything, some treat HSCs as the *only* type of stem cell, or a super stem cell that produces every other adult stem cell. This happens most often in reports on hepatic (liver) stem cells, where the authors often claim that HSCs *are* the stem cells for the liver or they produce the stem cells for the liver. Petersen et al. (1999) note that a type of progenitor cell in the liver has a number of characteristics in common with HSCs. In later research on hepatic stem cells, this *possible* relationship becomes an *actual* relationship. Lagasse et al. (2000) claim that HSCs produce the cells that constitute the liver, and "if resident bone marrow HSC's can form a variety of cell types, they may be more multipotent than the phrase 'pluripotent hematopoietic stem cell' indicates" (p. 1232). Mitaka (2001) similarly argues that HSCs are the wellspring from which the stem cells of the liver arise.

In both cases, the claims extend beyond the available evidence, and they redefine hepatic stem cells as HSCs. Both research reports note this, but the power of the qualification diminishes because it appears only once while the claim that HSCs are the "more multipotent" source of hepatic, and perhaps other, stem cells is repeated throughout the article. These researchers use the hematopoietic model, and in using it, they transform it from a model of stem cells into the only type of stem cell.

These ways of contracting the range and type of stem cells under the hematopoietic model simultaneously highlights how social technology plays a role in shaping model organisms and how such uses of a model are scientifically productive. The claims discussed here move beyond the available evidence, but this move helps to produce future scientific work. By claiming that HSCs are a form of "super stem cell," these researchers create a research trajectory that leads from speculation to testable hypotheses. The research trajectory sets up possible research programs to see whether HSCs can form the cells of all organs. Additionally, the hematopoietic model with its standard repertoire of research techniques suggests a number of the methods and experiments to test these hypotheses.

Yet this productive aspect is threatened by the need to protect economic resources. This contracting of the general rule produced by the rhetorical technology reflects, as with mouse ES cells, the economic aspect of social technology. Researchers must protect their resources and maintain the centrality of their model to future research endeavors in order to maintain their funding. While the claims that all bone-marrow research was examining HSCs and that HSCs are a super stem cell reflect components of the material technology (i.e., the fact that HSCs produce more lineages than any other adult stem cell), testing these hypotheses might be discouraged by the social technology.

The Impact of Contrasting Models

The goal of model organisms and the technologies they articulate is to link a definition or rule to entire classes of organisms or biological artifacts through one specific exemplar. The material qualities of the exemplar organism make it useful for laboratory experiments. The strength of the argument from example helps persuade others of the general conclusions made, and the community formed around the organism—the shared vocabulary and experimental questions—help make a model organism indispensable for any area of biology. The above examination illustrates the ways in which the three technologies interact to produce facts and concepts, and how these interactions can produce limitations on the powers and capacities of each technology. Perhaps the most important limitation is the suppressing effect of social technology on the expansiveness of the rules created by the rhetorical and material technologies. Economic self-interest helps to explain this suppressing effect, particularly as it relates to the use of examples and illustrations. As described above, scientists often limit how illustrations like rat stem cells and neural stem cells expand the general rules provided by their mouse ES cells and HSCs, respectively, because they claim these cell types might not "really" be stem cells. While such a move provides a productive point of testing—scientists can treat these claims as hypotheses to be tested in future experiments—the economic self-interest of scientists who employ the model stem-cell types makes that future testing less likely. This highlights the potential tension between social technology (economic self-interest), the material technology (potential experiments with model organisms), and rhetorical technology (the general rules provided by arguments from example).

Recent research has shown that the interaction and tension does not play out in a predetermined fashion. Use of the mouse ES cell model has not changed significantly over time: the use of the model remains robust. And with the exception of human ES cells, most other illustrations associated with this example have faded from use (Downing & Battey, 2004). On the other hand, while the HSC model remains prominent, some of its features have become increasingly questioned, and researchers are making increased use of other adult stem-cell types, especially neural stem cells, in their experimental practice (Metcalf, 2007; University of Minnesota, 2002). The specific qualities of each model organism—the exact material qualities, the variations in the argument from example, and the different types of communities formed—influence how the interaction and tension between the three technologies will play out. Determining what interactions and what tensions will arise in advance would be difficult, if not impossible.

Finally, an examination of these two models highlights several interesting features of the debate about stem-cell research. While other research fields have multiple model organisms, those models do not aim to define the same phenomena, and the implications of those models do not contradict one another. In stem-cell research, the two models have the potential to conflict when pushed to their limits. The mouse ES model can be used to imply that non-ES cells do not exist. While the HSC model can be used to question the existence of other adult stem cells, it can also be used to embrace the possibility of embryonic stem cells with qualities similar to those found in HSCs (for the clearest statement of this, see Weissman, 2000b). As yet, no political, economic, or social pressure has forced scientists to repudiate either model and/or limit the conclusions they produce. Rather, many researchers and their funding agencies blend components of both models into an amalgam definition of "stem cell" (e.g., NIH, 2001). This becomes possible because of the areas of overlap between the two models. As research on stem cells continues, these amalgamations might shift, and new amalgamations (and models) can potentially arise. While predicting those new amalgamations and models would be impossible, studying the existing models and amalgamations can identify the weak points in the existing articulation of the science. These points will most likely be the places where scientists will introduce these new amalgamations, and a thorough examination of these weak spots and initial attempts to address them will allow us to identify general qualities of future science communication and scientific work on stem-cell research, even as the *specific* communication and scientific work remains unclear.

Future Directions for Science Communication

The intent of this chapter was to explore model organisms—particularly stem-cell models—as a means of articulating relationship between the three technologies of science—the material, the social, and the rhetorical. This chapter highlighted the ways in which these technologies shape how scientists practice science independently and in relation to one another.

First, this chapter illustrated the value of approaching science as a practice composed of the three technologies—and how those technologies should be articulated alongside each other. With the recognition that all three technologies are equally necessary, this approach helped eliminate the logic of representation that treats rhetoric and communication as logically and chronologically secondary to the other elements of science. It was thus argued that the absence of any of the three technologies would undermine the power of model organisms. At an even more basic level, simultaneous articulation of the three technologies reminds us that communication plays a vital role in all scientific practice. Without the existence of argument from example, the use of model organisms would not be as effective and might not be possible; argument from example allows for the creation of general rules. Future research can build on this chapter by exploring how communication and rhetoric have equal footing with the social and material technologies in other scientific arenas. Metaphors shaped genetics research (Keller, 1995), and the argumentation practice of dissociation played a role in reorganizing developmental biology to make embryonic stem cells a key model and site for scientific work (Lynch, 2006). Future research should try to identify other rhetorical and communicative practices that play key roles in developing concepts and establishing facts, alongside the material and social technologies of science.

Second, this chapter highlighted the study of model organisms. The use of models occurs in multiple biological and medical subfields. Just as mice are models for human biological development and mouse ES cells are models for human stem cells, researchers have used specific types of mice to model a broad range of human diseases. Other animals are similarly used as models for human development and human diseases, and the use of animal models in general is a necessary step for Federal Drug Administration (FDA) approval of new drugs and medical devices.

The broad use of model organisms in biomedicine suggests several avenues for communication research. Scholars could study the use of model organisms in other fields to see if it follows patterns like those found in stem-cell research. This would allow a useful comparison of communication practices associated with other model-organism-based research programs. Another research trajectory could examine the processes by which scientists argue for the adoption of specific model organisms. For example, by developing case studies in numerous scientific subfields, communication scholars could identify patterns of argument and persuasion used to advocate adopting specific models, and when in the debate those arguments and other persuasive strategies are most viable. Scholars interested in the intersection of policy, science, and communication, could examine the NIH mandates on sharing model organisms. In these studies, scholars could aim to understand the genesis of these policies, their legal justification, and the regulatory frameworks created to fulfill the mandate to share.

The challenge scientists face in linking existing words to new discoveries also provides science communication scholars endless opportunities and challenges. Scientists create new articulations of material, rhetorical, and social technology to define phenomena and establish facts, which provides scholars interested in the rhetoric and communication of science an ever-renewing source of material to study. While we can never predict what new discovery—and therefore, what combination of words and things—is just over the horizon, the examination of past and present attempts at making these connections offers us insight into scientists and the evolution of scientific practice.

Notes

1. Similar arguments appear elsewhere (e.g., Johnson, 2007; Rogers, 1998; Stormer, 2004).
2. The argument about the Marxist roots of arguments about the overwhelming power of social and economic forces and criticisms of that stance appear most clearly in the work of Ronald Greene (1998) and Davi Johnson (2007).
3. Model organisms differ from models in chemistry and physics. Chemical and physical models are abstract idealizations meant to capture features of interest to specific scientific communities and to enable prediction of physical events, while model organisms are actual, embodied creatures used as representatives of groups (Keller, 2002).
4. The work of Gregor Mendel provided the basis for the modern science of genetics. Mendel argued that any trait an individual possessed was produced because of two alleles, or versions of a gene. The inheritance and interaction of these alleles is described by two laws: the law of segregation, which says that any gamete (i.e., an egg or sperm) will receive only one allele, and the law of individual assortment, which says that the two alleles are assorted or distributed independently of each other.
5. The sources for arguments here and in the following section were developed by identifying the most widely cited review and research articles about stem-cell research from 1998 to 2002. Where possible, I have tried to limit discussion of the material and social technology to sources from this time, or review articles providing a retrospective on research from this time.
6. The term pluripotent refers to a stem cell's ability to generate other kinds of cells.
7. "EG" stands for embryonic germ cell. These cells are derived from primordial germ cells, which are the cells that will ultimately produce eggs or sperm (Shamblott et al., 1998). While EG and ES cells come from different sources, they have similar qualities, and researchers have treated them as identical (Thomson & Odorico, 2000).
8. These criteria are cited by Burdon et al. (2002) and Gorba and Allsopp (2003) in support of their own characterizations of stem cells.
9. Colman and Kind (2000) make a similar argument.
10. For more on the transformation of temporal order into a logical priority, see Burke (1966).
11. Starting in 2002, research reports have appeared that challenge the concept of

plasticity (Terada et al., 2002; Wurmser & Gage, 2002; Ying, Nichols, Evans, & Smith, 2002).

References

454 Life Sciences. (2007). *DNA and Genome Sequencing Technology and Analytical Instrumentation*. Retrieved October 17, 2007, from www.454.com/enabling-technology/index.asp.

454 Life Sciences. (2008). About 454. Retrieved December 17, 2008, from www.454.com/about-454/index.asp.

Alison, M. R., Poulsom, R., Jeffery, R., Dhillon, A. P., Quaglia, A., Jacob, J., et al. (2000). Hepatocytes from non-hepatic adult stem cells. *Nature, 406*, 257.

Battey, J. F., & Peterson, J. (2004). *Trans-NIH mouse initiatives*. Retrieved October 20, 2007, from www.nih.gov/science/models/mouse.

Bjornson, C. R., Rietze, R. L., Reynolds, B. A., Magli, M. C., & Vescovi, A. L. (1999). Turning brain into blood: A hematopoetic fate adopted by adult neural stem cells in vivo. *Science, 283*(5401), 534–538.

Bokeno, M. (1987). The rhetorical understanding of science: An explication and critical commentary. *Southern Communication Journal, 52*, 285–311.

Brazelton, T. R., Rossi, F. M., Keshet, G. I., & Blau, H. M. (2000). From marrow to brain: expression of neuronal phenotypes in adult mice. *Science, 290*(5497), 1775–1779.

Burdon, T., Smith, A., & Savatier, P. (2002). Signalling, cell cycle and pluripotency in embryonic stem cells. *Trends in Cell Biology, 12*(9), 432–438.

Burke, K. (1966). *Language as symbolic action: Essays on life, literature and method*. Berkeley, CA: University of California Press.

Ceccarelli, L. (2001a). Rhetorical criticism and the rhetoric of science. *Western Journal of Communication, 65*(3), 314–329.

Ceccarelli, L. (2001b). *Shaping science with rhetoric: The cases of Dobzhansky, Schrodinger, and Wilson*. Chicago, IL: University of Chicago Press.

Cherwitz, R. A., & Hikins, J. W. (2000). Climbing the academic ladder: A critique of provincialism in contemporary rhetoric. *Quarterly Journal of Speech, 86*(4), 375–385.

Colman, A., & Kind, A. (2000). Therapeutic cloning: Concepts and practicalities. *Trends in Biotechnology, 18*(5), 192–196.

Davis, R. H. (2003). *The microbial models of molecular biology: From genes to genomes*. New York: Oxford University Press.

Davis, R. H. (2004). The age of model organisms. *Nature Reviews Genetics, 5*(1), 69–76.

Downing, G. J., & Battey, J. F. (2004). Technical assessment of the first 20 years of research using mouse embryonic stem cell lines. *Stem Cells, 22*, 1168–1180.

Fahnestock, J. (1999). *Rhetorical figures in science*. Oxford: Oxford University Press.

Ferrari, G., Cusella-DeAngelis, G., Coletta, M., Paolucci, E., Stornaiuolo, A., Cossu, G., et al. (1998). Muscle regeneration by bone marrow-derived myogenic progenitors. *Science, 279*(5356), 1528–1530.

Gorba, T., & Allsopp, T. E. (2003). Pharmacological potential of embryonic stem cells. *Pharmacological Research, 47*(4), 269–278.

Greene, R. W. (1998). Another materialist rhetoric. *Critical Studies in Mass Communication, 15*, 21–41.

Gross, A. (1991). Rhetoric of science without constraints. *Rhetorica, 9*, 283–299.

Gross, A. (1995). Renewing Aristotelian theory: The cold fusion controversy as a test case. *Quarterly Journal of Speech, 81*, 48–62.

Gussoni, R., Soneoka, Y., Strickland, C., Buzney, E., Khan, M., Flint, A., et al. (1999). Dystrophin expression in the mdx mouse restored by stem cell transplantation. *Nature, 401*, 309–393.

Jackson, K. A., Majka, S. M., Wang, H., Pocius, J., Hartley, C. J., Majesky, M. W., et al. (2001). Regeneration of ischemic cardiac muscle and vascular endothelium by adult stem cells. *Journal of Clinical Investigation, 107*(11), 1395–1402.

Jackson, K. A., Mi, T., & Goodell, M. A. (1999). Hematopoietic potential of stem cells isolated from murine skeletal muscle. *Proceedings of the National Academy of Sciences of the United States of America, 96*(25), 14482–14486.

Johnson, D. (2007). Mapping the meme: A geographical approach to materialist rhetorical criticism. *Communication and Critical/Cultural Studies, 4*(1), 27–50.

Jorgensen, E. M., & Mango, S. E. (2002). The art and design of genetic screens: Caenorhabditis elegans. *Nature Reviews Genetics, 3*(5), 356–369.

Keller, E. F. (1995). *Refiguring life: Metaphors of twentieth century biology.* New York: Columbia University Press.

Keller, E. F. (2000). *The century of the gene.* London: Harvard University Press.

Keller, E. F. (2002). *Making sense of life: Explaining biological development with models, metaphors and machines.* London: Harvard University Press.

Krause, D. S., Theise, N. D., Collector, M. I., Henegariu, O., Hwang, S., Gardner, R., et al. (2001). Multi-organ, multi-lineage engraftment by a single bone marrow-derived stem cell. *Cell, 105*(3), 369–377.

Lagasse, E., Connors, H., Al-Dhalimy, M., Reitsma, M., Dohse, M., Osborne, L., et al. (2000). Purified hematopoietic stem cells can differentiate into hepatocytes *in vivo. Nature Medicine, 6*(11), 1229–1235.

Latour, B. (1993). *We have never been modern* (Translated by C. Porter). Cambridge, MA: Harvard University Press.

Latour, B. (2003). The promises of constructivism. In D. Ihde & E. Selinger (Eds.), *Chasing technoscience: Matrix for materiality* (pp. 27–46). Bloomington, IN: Indiana University Press.

Lynch, J. A. (2006). Making room for stem cells: Dissociation and establishing new research objects. *Argumentation and Advocacy, 42*, 143–156.

McGuire, J. E., & Melia, T. (1989). Some cautionary strictures on the writing of the rhetoric of science. *Rhetorica, 7*, 87–99.

Metcalf, D. (2007). Concise review: Hematopoietic stem cells and tissue stem cells: Current concepts and unanswered questions. *StemCells, 25*, 2390–2395.

Mezey, E., Chandross, K. J., Harta, G., Maki, R. A., & McKercher, S. R. (2000). Turning blood into brain: cells bearing neuronal antigens generated in vivo from bone marrow. *Science, 290*(5497), 1779–1782.

Mitaka, T. (2001). Hepatic stem cells: From bone marrow cells to hepatocytes. *Biochemical and Biophysical Research Communications, 281*(1), 1–5.

Mutant Mouse Regional Resource Centers. (2007). MMRRC home page. Retrieved October 21, 2007, from www.mmrrc.org.

National Heart, Lung, and Blood Institute. (2005). *Production assistance for cellular therapies*. Retrieved October 26, 2007, from www.pactgroup.net.

National Institutes of Health. (2001). *Stem cells: Scientific progress and future research directions*. Bethesda, MD: National Institutes of Health.

National Institutes of Health. (2004). *NIH policy on sharing of model organisms for biomedical research*. Retrieved May 20, 2007, from www.nih.gov/science/models/sharingpolicy.html.

Perelman, C., & Olbrechts-Tyteca, L. (1969). *The new rhetoric*. London: University of Notre Dame Press.

Peters, L. L., Robledo, R. F., Bult, C. J., Churchill, G. A., Paigen, B. J., & Svenson, K. L. (2007). The mouse as a model for human biology: A resource guide for complex trait analysis. *Nature Reviews Genetics, 8*, 58–69.

Petersen, B. E., Bowen, W. C., Patrene, K. D., Mars, W. M., Sullivan, A. K., Murase, N., et al. (1999). Bone marrow as a potential source of hepatic oval cells. *Science, 284*(5417), 1168–1170.

Rogers, R. A. (1998). Overcoming the objectification of nature in constitutive theories: Toward a transhuman, materialist theory of communication. *Western Journal of Communication, 62*(3), 244–272.

Shamblott, M. J., Axelman, J., Wang, S., Bugg, E. M., Littlefield, J. W., Donovan, P. J., et al. (1998). Derivation of pluripotent stem cells from cultured human primordial germ cells. *Proceedings of the National Academy of Sciences of the United States of America, 95*, 13726–13731.

Shapin, S., & Schaffer, S. (1985). *Leviathan and the air-pump: Hobbes, Boyle, and the experimental life*. Princeton, NJ: Princeton University Press.

Smith, A. (2001). Embryo-derived stem cells: Of mice and men. *Annual Review of Cell and Developmental Biology, 17*, 435–462.

Stormer, N. (2004). Articulation: A working paper on rhetoric and taxis. *Quarterly Journal of Speech, 90*(3), 257–284.

Terada, N., Hamazaki, T., Oka, M., Hoki, M., Mastalerz, D. M., Nakano, Y., et al. (2002). Bone marrow cells adopt the phenotype of other cells by spontaneous cell fusion. *Nature, 416*, 542–545.

Thomson, J. A., Itskovitz-Eldor, J., Shapiro, S. S., Waknitz, M. A., Swiergiel, J. J., Marshall, V. S., et al. (1998). Embryonic stem cell lines derived from human blastocysts. *Science, 282*(5391), 1145–1147.

Thomson, J. A., Kalishman, J., Golos, T. G., Durning, M., Harris, C. P., Becker, R. A., et al. (1995). Isolation of a primate embryonic stem cell line. *Proceedings of the National Academy of Sciences of the United States of America, 92*(17), 7844–7848.

Thomson, J. A., & Odorico, J. S. (2000). Human embryonic stem cell and embryonic germ cell lines. *Trends in Biotechnology, 18*(2), 53–57.

Ullmann, A. (2003). *Origins of molecular biology: A tribute to Jacques Monod* (rev. ed.). Washington, DC: ASM Press.

University of Minnesota. (2002). Stem cell institute at the University of Minnesota. Retrieved October 22, 2007 from www.stemcell.umn.edu.

Vanderbilt Center for Stem Cell Biology. (2004). Home page. Retrieved October 22, 2007, from www.vcscb.org.

Verfaillie, C. M. (2002). Adult stem cells: assessing the case for pluripotency. *Trends in cell biology, 12*(11), 502–508.

Weissman, I. L. (2000a). Stem cells: Units of development, units of regeneration, units of evolution. *Cell, 100*, 157–168.

Weissman, I. L. (2000b). Translating stem and progenitor cell biology to the clinic: Barriers and opportunities. *Science, 287*(5457), 1442–1446.

Weissman, I. L., Anderson, D. J., & Gage, F. H. (2001). Stem and progenitor cells: Origins, phenotypes, lineage commitments, and transdifferentiations. *Annual Review of Cell and Developmental Biology, 17*, 387–403.

Wulf, G. G., Jackson, K. A., & Goodell, M. A. (2001). Somatic stem cell plasticity: Current evidence and emerging concepts. *Experimental Hematology, 29*(12), 1361–1370.

Wurmser, A. E., & Gage, F. H. (2002). Cell fusion causes confusion. *Nature, 416*, 485–487.

Ying, Q.-L., Nichols, J., Evans, E. P., & Smith, A. G. (2002). Changing potency by spontaneous fusion. *Nature, 416*, 545–547.

Chapter 8

Expanding Notions of Scientific Argument

A Case Study of the Use of Scientific Argument by American Indians

Danielle Endres

Scientific arguments—or appeals to the authority of science and/or use of scientific and technical knowledge as evidence in arguments—play an important role in the deliberation of public controversies. This is evident across the many examples of environmental policy discussed in the rhetoric of science literature (e.g., Farrell & Goodnight, 1981; Fisher, 1987; Gross, 1984; Katz & Miller, 1996; Keränen, 2005; Lyne & Howe, 1986; Waddell, 1990). One area of particular interest in this body of literature is the research that has shown that scientific and technical knowledge is often valued over social, political, or pathos-based arguments in public deliberations, which results in a marginalization of these other ways of knowing (e.g., Fisher, 1987; Gross, 1984; Waddell, 1990), and in the preceding chapters of this book. This is notable because controversies over intelligent design, human genomics, and nuclear power often involve politically charged clashes that pit the authority of scientific knowledge against the authority of cultural knowledge, cultural beliefs, and religion and spirituality (see Chapters 1 and 2 in this volume). It is in this vein that this chapter examines the controversy surrounding plans to install a high-level nuclear waste site in the Yucca Mountains in Nevada (U.S. Department of Energy, 2008b).

Although the details of this site will be discussed later in the chapter, it needs to be noted here that in this particular controversy, the Department of Energy (DOE) specified the scientific and technical suitability of the Yucca Mountain site as its only criterion in considering whether or not to proceed, as evidenced in a mandate in the Nuclear Waste Policy Act (NWPA) (Nuclear Waste Policy Act, 2004). As will be argued in this chapter, this specification artificially limited the scope of a controversy that essentially bridges the public and technical spheres of argument (Goodnight, 1982) and invokes ethical, spiritual, political, cultural, and scientific arguments. During the public hearing process, public participants—specifically American Indians—appealed to the authority of science as well as the authority of their own cultural knowledge, including the narrative-based knowledge of oral traditions and religious beliefs.

While arguments based on science are typically privileged in a hierarchy of evidentiary value, the case of the Yucca Mountain high-level nuclear waste site in Nevada provides an informative study of how this dichotomy between science and culture limits our understanding of the rhetorical complexity of public debates of scientific issues. Indeed, this analysis of commentary from public hearings reinforces previous research suggesting that scientific and cultural knowledge should not be treated as mutually exclusive in public policy debates (e.g., Coleman & Dysart, 2007; van Dijck, 2003; Waddell, 1990). It also extends lines of scholarly inquiry that: (a) shift attention from the arguments of scientists to scientific arguments made by the public; (b) reveal the fluidity of boundaries between scientific and non-scientific arguments in public scientific controversies; (c) invite deeper analysis of the role of cultural arguments in environmental decision making; and (d) challenge misconceptions about the relationship between American Indian cultures and science. On this latter point, there is a tendency to both subordinate culture arguments to those of science, and underestimate the scientific literacy of American Indians.

The chapter begins with a discussion of the relationships between science, culture, religion, and American Indians; moves to an examination of the use of science and culture arguments by American Indian participants in the public comment period of the Yucca Mountain site authorization process; and concludes with a discussion of the implications of this study for our understanding of scientific argument within public scientific controversies.

Science, Culture (and Religion)

Friedman, Dunwoody, and Rogers (1986) maintain that the scope of science communication "comprises not only the biological, life and physical sciences but also the social and behavioral sciences and such applied fields as medicine, environmental sciences, technology, and engineering" (p. xv). This broad array of scientific disciplines includes both theoretical and practical fields, with a shared system of knowledge implicitly linking them together.

What further distinguishes science as a public discourse is how it has traditionally been set in opposition to culture (and to religion as a type of cultural argument). The tensions and cohesions between science and religion are a well-documented site of scholarly inquiry (e.g., Condit, 1998; Harris, Parrott, & Dorgan, 2004; Lessl, 1989, 1993, 2003, 2005; Taylor, 1992). As is alluded to above, this antagonistic relationship has been made abundantly clear more recently in public debates about evolution and whether the teaching of intelligent design should be given equal time in public schools (e.g., Condit, 1998; Johnson-Sheehan & Morgan, 2008; Martin, Trammell, Landers, Valois, & Bailey, 2006). Scientist and novelist

C. P. Snow, himself a personification of this tension, famously spoke of the "two cultures" (1993)—expressed as the sciences and humanities—with a vast gulf separating them. Snow's articulation of the competing cultures of science and the humanities implicitly lingers in much current scholarship about public understanding of science and scientific literacy.

The claims that are made in public regarding science controversies generally require some form of legitimization to become more than just groundless claims and opinions. Not surprisingly, science typically provides the grounds on which arguments in these controversies do battle. While science, or the scientific method, can be understood as a means of gaining knowledge about natural phenomena through the systematic testing of hypotheses based on observation, the way science is used in arguments about policy decisions has more to do with the scope of its perceived authority and the way it is practiced than the specific knowledge system it names.

Still, despite the fact that cultural knowledge does not arrive at truth via the scientific method of testing hypotheses, it does offer a means of arriving at truth with its own systems of logic. Culture, according to Philipsen (1997), is a "socially constructed system of symbols, meanings, premises and rules" (p. 125). This broad definition is particularly important for understanding the overlapping of science and culture arguments in public participation of environmental decisions, including the Yucca Mountain nuclear-waste siting decision. First, the definition allows for a broad, nontraditional understanding of culture that can include national, ethnic, academic, organizational, and subcultural designations. Although culture has been traditionally and popularly defined as national (i.e., American culture or Japanese culture), in this iteration culture can describe any number of social groups with shared codes of communication and ways of knowing the world.

The definition also allows for culture, understood as a system of symbols and practices, to condition or otherwise influence the practice of science and the way science is invoked to authorize claims made in defense of itself or in the defense of cultural interests. In other words, as the scholarly literature on culture and science points out, culture subsumes science in that science is (a) a culture unto itself and (b) culturally determined. The articulation of science as a culture of knowledge assumes that science is a "set of cultural activities among others" (van Dijck, 2003, p. 185). What could be called a culture of science has a general but heterogeneous set of symbols, meanings, premises, and rules that guide the practice of science across the different subfields of science such as biology, medicine, or engineering. The scientific method, then, can be understood as science's way of speaking and knowing.

The risk of accepting the science/culture dichotomy, then, is to impose limitations on each discursive field's ability to communicate with legitimacy both within and across themselves. While the public discussion of climate change and stem-cell research has dealt a blow to the authority of science (see Nisbet, this volume), in environmental public policy decisions the arguments of science enjoy privileged status, resulting in the devaluation of public arguments, cultural arguments, and spiritual arguments. Research on models of public participation in environmental decision making (e.g., public hearings) reveals that scientific argument can actually be used to silence and intimidate members of the public (Depoe & Delicath, 2004; Fiorino, 1990; Fisher, 1987; Katz & Miller, 1996; Kinsella, 2004; Ratliff, 1997). In this way, the culture of science is not only posited against the humanities (as in Snow's articulation) but is also posited against the public culture or cultural rationality. As Coleman and Dysart (2007) note, "The effect of separating scientific rationality from cultural rationality issues forth a sort of cognitive superiority that results in a marginalization of views seen as nonscientific and hence nonrational" (p. 5).

Yet, when we talk about science as a culture, it is important to understand that we are generally talking about Western science. Western science historically has a troubled relationship with marginalized, oppressed, and colonized peoples—in this case American Indians. Western scientific research is embedded within imperialism and colonialism, and can be dehumanizing to indigenous peoples (Deloria, 1997; Smith, 1999). Moreover, despite the complexity of indigenous knowledge of local ecologies and resources, indigenous beliefs and arguments are frequently portrayed and subsequently framed in the media as non-scientific or less important than scientific information. As Coleman and Dysart (2007) further suggest,

> Real-life dramas that invoke scientific rationality and progress and that affect Native American tribes—such as mineral and oil exploration, radioactive dumps, and age-old skeletal remains—relegate Indians to a preserved past in which their values are considered quaint, outmoded and scientifically irrelevant.
>
> (p. 20)

This was the framework that characterized the debate over the Yucca Mountain high-level nuclear waste site; science and scientific argument were valued over other forms of argument, including those that invoked the cultural norms and values of American Indians (Endres, 2005).[1]

Science, Culture, and American Indians

As suggested above, the view that science itself is also a cultural phenomenon has particular resonance for some American Indians and their relationship to Western science (Deloria, 1997; Hodson, 1993; Manzini, 2003). In the vein of scholarship that views science as both culture and cultural product, Manzini (2003) argues that "every culture has its own science, which can be seen as an indigenous science of that particular cultural group" (p. 193). Similarly, Deloria (1997) maintains that the way in which indigenous people hold traditional knowledge about the world can be understood as an indigenous science. In this relationship between science and culture, culture is defined more traditionally to be a national, ethnic, or racial group whose practices influence the definition of science for that culture. Of course, understanding science as a cultural practice, which is also determined by culture, shows its relevance across national, ethnic, or racial boundaries.

Speaking at a public hearing on the proposed Yucca Mountain nuclear waste site, Edward Smith of the Chemehuevi Southern Paiute said he looked "forward to the day when scientists, engineers, agencies, and policy makers give serious consideration" to the cultural value of Indian lands, rather than simply their "scientific, technological, commercial and economic value" (U.S. Department of Energy, 2001d, p. 29). While it would be accurate to say that this American Indian perspective dichotomizes science and indigenous culture, it does not dismiss the value of science, only the suitability of applying it and the motives for its use in the case of Yucca Mountain. If science is accepted as a cultural phenomenon, Smith's argument calls attention to the clash between two cultures' perceptions of the land and its value.

Another way that science and culture arguments have been applied in public debates involving American Indians is via the default frame of religion and its mutual exclusion with science. Deloria (1997) argues that any challenge to Western science by indigenous people is often perceived to be a religious objection, even though much of American Indian knowledge could also be understood as ecological and not necessarily linked to religious practice. For example, the controversy over the Kennewick Man—remains of a prehistoric man found near Kennewick, Washington in 1996—was primarily framed as a contest between Western science and American Indian religion (Coleman & Dysart, 2007). The controversy focused on whether the U.S. Army Corp of Engineers or area Indian tribes was responsible for the handling of the remains. The frame identified by Coleman and Dysart (2007) suggested that religion and science are mutually exclusive, which is typical of other public scientific controversies.

In his analysis of the debate about creationism versus evolution, Taylor (1992) noted that "while most scientists may not rigidly dichotomize scientific rationality vs. religious irrationality, the rhetorical demarcation in this case [creationism] constructed just such a division" (p. 289). Indeed, in public deliberation about policies that share a border with religion, the media often frames science as the rational choice that should be valued over religious arguments (Coleman & Dysart, 2007). And this framing can actually further entrench science and religion as mutually exclusive, reinforcing the divide between scientists and the public (Taylor, 1992).

However, just as science and cultural knowledge can provide different types of evidence to public debates, science and religious/spiritual knowledge are different ways of knowing that do not have to be in competition. In the context of public deliberation, both scientific and spiritual arguments can provide important challenges to each other. Speaking of the importance of the interplay between scientific and religious arguments, Condit (1998) notes,

> For the good of the community it is desirable for religion to attack science in order to prevent science from becoming the exclusive discourse of the public sphere. For, as many observers have noted, scientific methods are notoriously poor at offering social values. If the only discourse shared within the polity were science, that polity would lack critical ingredients for coexistence and public concordances.
>
> (p. 600)

Healthy public deliberation, then, can include both scientific and religious/spiritual claims, as long as there is an understanding of how each contributes different things to the deliberation. This holds true for all forms of cultural knowledge as well. As an example of a model of deliberation that draws from both scientific and cultural knowledge, Walker and Daniels (2004) offer the notion of civic science that calls for conversation among scientific experts, political experts, and citizen experts. The Yucca Mountain siting decision, which is detailed below, offers a means of further exploring the relationship between science, culture, and religion in public deliberation.

The Yucca Mountain High-Level Nuclear Waste Site

High-level nuclear waste (HLW) is a byproduct of nuclear fuel production or nuclear fuel reprocessing (U.S. Nuclear Regulatory Commission, 2007). High-level waste is the most dangerous of all forms of nuclear waste because it emits harmful radiation for tens of thousands of years (U.S. Department of Energy, 2008b). There are two main sources of high-level nuclear waste in the United States: the commercial nuclear power industry and the federal government (including the Department of Energy and the Department of Defense). As a result of over 60 years of nuclear power and nuclear weapons development in the United States, we are now facing a nuclear waste crisis. According to a 2002 report by former Secretary of Energy Spencer Abraham, "We have a staggering amount of radioactive waste in this country" (Abraham, 2002). By 2035, there will be approximately 119,000 metric tons of high-level nuclear waste (U.S. Department of Energy, 2008a). Through the Nuclear Waste Policy Act (NWPA) Congress vested responsibility for permanent storgage of high-level nuclear waste with the U.S. federal government. The NWPA mandates that the Department of Energy is responsible for researching and recommending a site for permanent geologic storage of high-level nuclear waste. Congress would ultimately decide on the site recommendation made by the Secretary of Energy.

Decisions about where to store nuclear waste and toxic waste are difficult and rife with controversy. The Yucca Mountain high-level nuclear waste repository site is certainly no exception. The controversy over the site began in 1978, when the Department of Energy (DOE) began researching Yucca Mountain as a potential site for an underground geologic storage site for nuclear waste (U.S. Department of Energy, 2008b). In 1984 President Ronald Reagan selected Yucca Mountain in Nevada, the Hanford Complex in Washington, and a location in Deaf Smith County, Texas as the three potential sites for geologic storage of high-level nuclear waste. Congress amended the NWPA in 1987 to direct the DOE's attention to study just one site: Yucca Mountain. In the midst of an ongoing controversy over the site, Congress and President George W. Bush officially authorized the Yucca Mountain site in 2002. Between 2002 and June 2008, the DOE prepared an application for a Nuclear Regulatory Commission (NRC) license for the site. The DOE submitted a license application on June 3, 2008 and the NRC now lists the application as docketed. An interview with an NRC official reveals that the NRC usually takes 3 to 4 years to evaluate an application.[2]

The Yucca Mountain high-level nuclear waste repository site is located in Nye County, Nevada. Yucca Mountain straddles the Nevada Test Site and Nellis Airforce Range and is about 90 miles northwest of Las Vegas. Although the Yucca Mountain site has not yet been granted a license to begin accepting high-level nuclear waste, the underground repository has been constructed. The repository consists of a series of tunnels drilled into the mountain. At present, high-level nuclear waste is currently stored in nuclear fuel rods. For storage at Yucca Mountain, the rods will be encased in casks engineered to prevent leakage and inserted into the tunnels. The capacity of Yucca Mountain is 77,000 metric tons. Although the United States is projected to have 119,000 metric tons by 2035 (as stated above), there are curently no plans for a second high-level waste-storage facility.

While the DOE stands by the safety of the repository (e.g., Abraham, 2002), opponents argue that there are risks of radioactive leaks from the repository that could damage water tables, local ecosystems, and human health (see U.S. Department of Energy, 2001c for access to public comments opposed to the Yucca Mountain site). In addition to these reasons, several American Indian nations also oppose the Yucca Mountain site because Yucca Mountain lies within the traditional boundaries of the Western Shoshone and Southern Paiute nations. Although the United

States claims that the Yucca Mountain nuclear waste site is located on federally controlled land, Western Shoshone and Southern Paiute nations claim treaty-based and spiritual rights to the land. The Western Shoshone argue that the Yucca Mountain site violates the 1863 Ruby Valley Treaty of Peace and Friendship.[3] The Southern Paiutes and others argue that the repository harms their culture and spirituality by using Yucca Mountain to store waste.

As stated above, the NWPA vested responsibility with DOE for recommending a site for permanent geologic storage of high-level nuclear waste. The NWPA outlines a detailed process for site selection including an evaluation of multiple sites, production of an Environmental Impact Statement, several public comment periods, and site characterization research (NWPA, 2004). One formal public comment period concerning the proposed site at Yucca Mountain lasted from May through December in 2001.[4] A total of 5,250 public comments were heard/collected. Statements were heard/collected at 66 public hearings throughout Nevada, delivered to a court reporter at the Yucca Mountain Information Center, and received via email messages or letters sent through U.S. mail to the center. An archive of public comments is available at the Yucca Mountain Information Center and on the Web (U.S. Department of Energy, 2001c). From this corpus of public comments, 52 statements made by 33 self-identified Americans Indians from 26 nations and two American Indian non-profit organizations were identified. Although this may be a small number of comments compared to the total number of public comments, the relative size of American Indian populations is significantly smaller than the overall population of the United States (0.8% of the U.S. population according to the 2000 U.S. Census; U.S. Census Bureau, 2000). Also, many of the 52 comments and statements were issued by American Indian governments that speak for larger numbers of individuals.

Using rhetorical criticism (e.g., Burgchardt, 2005; Foss, 2009; Hart & Daughton, 2005), in this chapter, the scientific arguments used by non-scientist American Indians are described, evaluated, and interpreted. Analysis of these comments reveals that Western Shoshone and Southern Paiute scientific arguments are characterized by two rhetorical strategies: (a) challenging the authority of Western science through invocation of Western Shoshone and Southern Paiute understandings of culture and science; and (b) using arguments based on Western scientific knowledge to contradict the government's evidence in support of the Yucca Mountain site. The remainder of this section evaluates these strategies.

Challenging the Absolute Authority of Western Science

The case study reveals findings consistent with earlier research focusing on the relationship between science and indigenous peoples (Coleman &

Dysart, 2007). In the public comment period, American Indians opposed to the Yucca Mountain project made arguments that challenged the scientific way of thinking about the Yucca Mountain site and offered alternative ways of thinking about Yucca Mountain based on the cultural and spiritual knowledge of the Western Shoshone, Southern Paiute, and others. Interestingly, many comments implicitly accept the legitimacy of science as a culture and practice but challenge its application and authority. For example, Edward Smith of Chemehuevi Southern Paiute nation stated in a public hearing in Las Vegas,

> We have been telling the government about the importance of Yucca Mountain area to our people since 1987. Today I tell you the same thing yet again. Yucca Mountain is sacred to our people. It is part of the lands that our Creator gave to us. It is a powerful place. We have been prevented from using it and caring for it. The government has disturbed the area for half a century.
>
> (U.S. Department of Energy, 2001d, pp. 24–25)

In his statement, Smith positions the spiritual nature of the land as an argument against the Yucca Mountain site. His argument does not directly address the scientific arguments that support the choice of Yucca Mountain as the repository of nuclear waste; instead, it challenges the absolute authority of science to evaluate, legitimate, and approve. This suggests the importance of context, a sort of pragmatic relativism, which can also be seen in Smith's appeal to the sacredness of Yucca Mountain to authorize his claim. Rather than dismissing the legitimacy of science, he says the mountain is sacred to his "people," an appeal to the legitimacy of cultural knowledge and a gesture intended to elicit cultural respect and understanding. Again, this represents a challenge to the hegemony of scientific argument and a call to weigh the merits of culture, as the particular case dictates, rather than dismissing the scientific outright.

While other challenges follow this line of argument, American Indians who issued public comments also invoked the superiority of their traditional spiritual knowledge. They argued not that science does not afford truth or insight—but that it can be misapplied, misunderstood, and used in the service of political interests. To draw again from Smith's comments, it is the government, not scientists or science itself, which has "prevented" his people from "using" and "caring" for the land their "Creator gave to" them. In another example, Calvin Meyers of the Moapa Paiute Nation, commented,

> I have read a long time ago and I believe this, because it came from the medicine man, that before the government or anybody else even messed with the—with radiation, they were told not to bother with it

because they don't know what to do with it. They don't what it can do
to them [sic]. They don't know how to get rid of it.

(U.S. Department of Energy, 2001a, p. 181)

In this statement, Meyers cites a medicine man to argue that humans
should have never even started to work with radioactive materials
because of the difficulty in disposing of the waste. What is significant
here is not the wisdom of pointing out the conundrum of nuclear waste—
all sides will freely admit to that—but the source of authority to which
the argument appeals. This appeal is to Moapa knowledge and sacred
wisdom, invoking a historical narrative pitting science against nature,
where science is cast as a tragic outgrowth of human ambition in the
modern world. The medicine man's authority thus becomes recognizable
to the non-insider as a source of reason and pure objectivity. Again, the
implication is that cultural ethics should play a part in judging the suitable parameters of science.

Similarly, Barbara Durham and Bill Helmer (2001), Tribal Administrator and Environmental Director, respectively, for Timbisha Shoshone
Tribe, challenge the suitability of the Yucca Mountain site by attacking the
judgment of those who practice science irresponsibly. In a letter submitted
during the public comment period, they wrote,

The unresolved dangers of the Yucca Mountain project demand that
the DOE listen and respond to the concerns of tribes and others who
may know much more than the DOE about 'site suitability.' If the
ancestors of the Timbisha Shoshones had left such a poison for future
generations we probably would be dead or not able to live here
anymore. The ancestors would never do this, and the Timbisha Shoshone Tribe of today will never approve the desecration of this land
for future generations.

(p. 10)

This comment, and Meyers' earlier comment, appeals to the wisdom of
ancestors, elders, and spiritual leaders that directly challenge the argument
made by the DOE that a scientifically and technically suitable storage site
can solve the problem of nuclear waste (Abraham, 2002). This strategy
also calls into question the technocratic reliance on Western scientific
knowledge in American public deliberation.

In similar appeals to American Indian cultural authority, the anthropo-
centric focus of the DOE's scientific evidence was also called into question.
Western Shoshone Carrie Dann stated in a Crescent Valley hearing:

And I look at all of these things, there's not only going to be suffering
from human kind, but suffering from all the animals, the birds. Of

course, the plant life too will suffer, only we can't see them suffer, but they will. They will wilt and they will die.

(U.S. Department of Energy, 2001e, p. 28)

Dann challenges the DOE to consider animal and plant health in addition to human health. Her argument reflects the tendency of some American Indian cultures to value the earth and the symbiotic relationships between all living things (Deloria, 1997; Mander, 1992).[5] Dann's perspective is not merely based on cultural and religious beliefs. Deloria (1997) argues that much indigenous knowledge is based on the oral tradition, which "represented not simply information on ancient events but precise knowledge of birds, animals, plants, geologic features, and religious experiences of a group of people" (p. 36). This argument about the effects on plants and animals by the Yucca Mountain site, therefore, does not include traditional Western "scientific evidence" but it still represents a challenge to the Yucca Mountain site. In that way, it further expands the boundaries of the scientific controversy to include spiritual and cultural concerns.

The above public comments serve to highlight three ways that American Indians used cultural—and by extension spiritual—arguments to challenge the Yucca Mountain site. In these comments we see evidence of (a) spirituality as a competing criterion to science; (b) cultural knowledge as a challenge to the authority of science and responsible practice; and (c) a challenge to the anthropocentrism of Western science. While none of these are traditional scientific arguments, they do engage science. And they engage science in a different way than direct refutation of scientific evidence. These examples demonstrate how cultural and spiritual knowledge can be invoked to dispute scientific knowledge; although in this case, this challenge was not entirely successful. In the Yucca Mountain site authorization decision, the DOE essentially ignored these arguments when it decided to go forward with the Yucca Mountain site (Endres, 2009). The DOE's reluctance to accept cultural and spiritual arguments as relevant contrary evidence is consistent with the dominance of scientific rationality over cultural and spiritual "irrationality" in public deliberation.

Yet, despite their lack of traditional Western scientific evidence, the arguments posed by these non-scientist American Indians presented significant objections and questions that are worthy to consider. Can technology solve the problem of radioactive nuclear waste? Does the focus on Western scientific argument exclude consideration of whether nuclear technologies that emit dangerous levels of radiation for hundreds of thousands of years should be pursued? Should plant and animal life be considered as important as human life? While these questions are beyond the scope of this chapter, they do suggest that multiple forms of knowledge can make public policy deliberation richer and ultimately more complex and inclusive.

Using Scientific Argument

While American Indian arguments in the Yucca Mountain public comment period invoked culture, spirituality, and traditional knowledge as support for opposition to the Yucca Mountain project, American Indian arguments also used traditional Western scientific arguments. As Fabj and Sobnosky (1995) argue, not only are non-scientists capable of engaging in scientific argument but public scientific controversy involves interplay between scientific argument and other forms of argument. Keränen (2005) states, "Participants engage in an argumentative process in which competing perceptions of science forged by scientists, citizens, policy makers, journalists, and others vie for ascendancy and acceptance in ways that reconstitute the borders between the public and the technical" (p. 97). In cases of public scientific controversy, publics can and do use scientific arguments in addition to other forms of argument. This section explores how American Indian participants in the public comment period invoked scientific arguments in their opposition to the Yucca Mountain site.

In their comment letter, Durham and Helmer (2001) from the Timbisha Shoshone Tribe made an argument about the potential for radiation leakage from the Yucca Mountain site. Their letter responds to the DOE's reliance on the Environmental Protection Agency's (EPA) 10,000-year standard for radiation compliance,[6] upon which the models of the radiation leakage from the site were based. They argue that the 10,000-year standard is insufficient and that potential radiation doses need to be monitored for a longer period of time. To support their claim, Durham and Helmer refer to some of the DOE's other studies on Yucca Mountain and studies by scientists. They wrote:

> The 10,000 year regulatory compliance period is insufficient because groundwater contamination from leaked radionuclides is predicted by the DOE to occur after 10,000 years (other scientists have predicted leakage within a thousand years). The predictive models for 10,000 years are extremely abstract and virtually worthless, since they are based on data that is constantly being revised as new data is accumulated.
>
> (2001, p. 3)

This argument challenges the scientific findings of the DOE and the technical radiation standard offered by the EPA. Similarly, Smith (U.S. Department of Energy, 2001d) questions the models that were used to create EPA and NRC standards related to radiation. He argues that models are "based on assumptions, scientific uncertainties, and degrees of uncertainty" (p. 3) Although Durham and Helmer, or Smith did not offer original scientific findings to support their claims, their arguments do reveal a familiarity with scientific concepts and an ability to critically examine the scientific arguments put forth by the DOE. Unlike the examples in the previous section which challenged the legitimacy of scientific arguments by positing cultural arguments as another form of legitimate argument, these arguments challenge the legitimacy of the Yucca Mountain project by using the DOE's own findings and standards of scientific and technical suitability. After the hearings, the U.S. District of Columbia Court of Appeals ruled that the EPA must change the radiation standard for the Yucca Mountain site (U.S. Environmental Protection Agency, 2008).

In addition to challenges to EPA models and radiation standards, there are also arguments based in geological and hydrological science. In an argument that challenged the geological findings of the DOE, Marlene Begay of the Walker River Paiute stated at a public hearing in Hawthorne, Nevada,

> Yucca Mountain is in a very active earthquake zone with a number of volcanic cinder cones visible a short distance away. The highly fractured and fissured rock allows rain water infiltration at a fast rate, which will corrode waste containers and wash their deadly contents into the ground water, contaminating the drinking water supply for nearby communities. As pointed out to the DOE three years ago by over 200 environmental groups, this fast flow of water should disqualify Yucca Mountain for further consideration, for it violates DOE's own repository citing guidelines.
>
> (U.S. Department of Energy, 2001b, pp. 1–2)

This argument posits that the geological and hydrological features of Yucca Mountain should disqualify it as a site. She argues that the volcanic and seismic features of the mountain will allow water to flow through the mountain quickly and result in radiation contamination. Although Begay does not offer original scientific data to support her claims, she does challenge the DOE's scientific and technical findings related to the Yucca Mountain site. Begay's comment calls into question the legitimacy of the DOE's findings. However, the comment does not call science into question; rather, it implies that competing scientific findings lead to a different conclusion.

The Timbisha Shoshone Tribal Council also objects to the scientific and technical suitability of the Yucca Mountain site. In Resolution 18–2001, the Timbisha Shoshone Tribal Council expresses concern over the potential contamination of groundwater from nuclear waste at Yucca Mountain. The resolution states,

> Whereas the Timbisha Shoshone Tribe will be directly affected by the proposed Yucca Mountain project since the Furnace Creek parcel of

the Tribe is down-gradient from the groundwater of Yucca Mountain, and the predicted radionuclide leakage from the storage casks will eventually reach the Timbisha Shoshone; and the proposed Yucca Mountain project would adversely affect the future members of the Timbisha Shoshone Tribe as well as all living things at the site vicinity and along the proposed transportation corridors.

(Timbisha Shoshone Tribe, 2001)

The resolution concludes with a recommendation that the Secretary of Energy not authorize the Yucca Mountain site. Like Begay's comment, this comment challenges the suitability of the Yucca Mountain site by claiming that the site will not effectively contain radioactive leakage.

These examples demonstrate that American Indian participants in the public comment period relied on Western scientific arguments to oppose the Yucca Mountain site. The comments by Durham and Helmer, and Smith also contained appeals to non-scientific arguments as evidenced by the examples in the previous section. Moreover, in addition to Begay's arguments about the geological and hydrological features of Yucca Mountain, her comment also draws from cultural beliefs about Yucca Mountain

According to the Shoshone, Yucca Mountain is not really a mountain. It is a rolling hill. This means that it moves and will continue to move. Putting nuclear waste in the land is polluting it and will kill Mother Earth. We only have one earth, and one water. Everything is related: If we poison earth, then we are poisoning ourselves.

(U.S. Department of Energy, 2001b, p. 1)

Taken together, the two passages from Begay's comment use both Western scientific and cultural or indigenous scientific claims to argue against the Yucca Mountain site. The argument employs concepts from Western geologic science to argue that Yucca Mountain is seismically and volcanically active, but also draws from a cultural knowledge to argue that Yucca Mountain is a rolling hill that will move. Both arguments challenge the suitability of the Yucca Mountain site by arguing that its instability may cause radioactive leakage.

In the above examples, scientific arguments challenge the science used to support the Yucca Mountain site, and non-scientific arguments challenge the reliance on science as the only method to determine the suitability of the Yucca Mountain site. The simultaneous use of both Western scientific and cultural claims provides evidence that scientific arguments are not mutually exclusive with non-scientific cultural or spiritual arguments.

This disputes the idea that American Indians and other indigenous people do not understand Western science or that Western science is wholly incompatible with indigenous world views. One of the risks of emphasizing the differences in Western science from the science of other cultures (see Deloria, 1997) is that the emphasis may lead some people to the conclusion that indigenous people cannot understand or engage in Western science. This is a problematic assumption that serves to reinforce the marginalization of indigenous knowledge and racist beliefs about American Indian culture and intelligence. That American Indians used Western scientific arguments simultaneously with arguments from traditional knowledge and spirituality reveals that American Indians comprehend and can use Western science when it serves their purposes. This counters the assumption that all arguments made by American Indians are "quaint, outmoded and scientifically irrelevant" (Coleman & Dysart, 2007, p. 20).

This evidence also debunks the notion that Western science and indigenous knowledge, culture, and spirituality are truly mutually exclusive. Although they are different types of arguments, they can be used together to support an overarching argument, in this case opposition of the Yucca Mountain site. That is, while some of those commenting issued statements that focused on indigenous factors, and others issued statements that focused on Western science, both approaches were intended to meet the same end: to stop the waste site. And both were issued by people with a shared culture.

Certainly, there are cases in which indigenous traditional knowledge may contradict Western science (e.g., the origins of American Indian tribes) (Deloria, 1997). However, the cases of contradiction do not invalidate the compatibility of science and culture arguments, but rather suggest that relationships between scientific, cultural, and spiritual arguments are complex and must be examined through particular cases.

It is also important to note that there may be negative consequences of simultaneously issuing both scientific arguments and non-scientific arguments, as was the case in the American Indian participation in the deliberation over Yucca Mountain. There is the possibility that the nature of perceptions and stereotypes about American Indians may result in both arguments being disregarded. Deloria (1997) suggests,

> Regardless of what Indians have said concerning their origins, their migrations, their experiences with birds, animals, lands, waters, mountains, and other peoples, the scientists have maintained a stranglehold on the definitions of what respectable and reliable human experiences are. The Indian explanation is always cast aside as superstition, precluding Indians from having an acceptable status as human beings and reducing them in the eyes of educated people to a pre-human level of ignorance.
>
> (p. 7)

As a result, work still needs to be done to envision public deliberation in a way that acknowledges the contributions of American Indians.

Conclusion

Moving outward from the case study, this chapter explored the complex relationships between scientific, spiritual, and cultural arguments in public deliberation about scientific controversy. The intersection of these types of arguments often occurs in relation to politically and emotionally charged issues. When science enters the realm of public policy deliberation, it stands as one form of evidence among many others. Public scientific controversy involves more than just debates between scientists, it also involves contestation over the role of science in decision making, scientific findings versus local and cultural knowledge, and the relationship between cultural identity/spirituality and science. The study of public scientific controversy is an important area of research in science communication, especially with recent controversies over climate change, stem-cell research, the causes of autism, and intelligent design. This chapter contributes to this much-needed program of research. There are at least four implications of the findings of this case study that call for future research.

First, the findings presented here shift the focus from the arguments of scientists to scientific arguments made by the public. Although this rhetorical analysis examined comments by American Indians, some of these findings can be generalized to other non-scientist members of the public. Science communication—both the rhetoric of science and the public understanding of science—tends to focus on either how scientists communicate with each other or how scientists communicate with the public (often through mediated channels). In both cases, the focus is mainly on how scientists communicate. This chapter calls for a shift in focus to examine how publics communicate about science. By no means should the study of how scientists communicate cease, but the collective body of research in this area will be enhanced with an understanding of how non-scientist publics attempt to make scientific arguments or challenge scientific arguments with other forms of argument. Moreover, a focus on how publics engage with science in public controversy or deliberation is revealing even when not compared to how scientists communicate. This chapter expands our understanding of the relationship of science to other forms of knowledge. Future research in this area could include case studies of different public scientific controversies.

Second, in addition to better understanding how publics engage with science in public deliberation, the current analysis also helps us to understand the interplay between science, culture, and spirituality in public scientific controversy. Instead of reinforcing the polarity of science and culture/spirituality, this case study reveals the messiness of public scientific controversy in which different perspectives interact. In other words, scientific knowledge is not the only kind of knowledge that is relevant in public controversies. The findings of this study are consistent with scholars like Fischer (2000), Wynne (1996), Kinsella (2004), Walker and Daniels (2004), and others who recognize the importance of local, cultural knowledge as a part of deliberation about scientific policies. Although scientific arguments, religious arguments, and cultural arguments are different types of arguments, they are not incompatible. Moreover, multiple forms of knowledge are crucial to public deliberation. As Fabj and Sobnosky (1995) suggest, "bridges between different discourses on the same issue help to realize the full potential of democratic society" (p. 183). When science enters the realm of public deliberation, it is no longer insulated from interaction with policy concerns. To make just and democratic policies, it is crucial that not only the scientific and technical aspects of a policy are understood, but also the implications for local communities, cultural and spiritual beliefs, and the limitations of making public policy decisions using only science.

Besides this case study, which looked at American Indian scientific, cultural, and spiritual objections to the Yucca Mountain nuclear waste site, there are many other cases worthy of study. Specifically, examination of additional cases can reveal how cultural and spiritual arguments can be defined in multiple ways. For example, in the case of autism research, groups of parents object to child immunization due to its potential correlation with autism. In this case, the parents' arguments are defined as cultural arguments and are contrasted with scientific evidence. In another example, the debate over intelligent design has revealed some interesting dynamics in the interplay between science and spirituality with some scientists, such as Richard Dawkins, defending atheism and other scientists upholding the compatibility of evolution and spiritual beliefs. Further study in this area will help to build our understanding of the interplay and instances of fluidity between science, culture, and spirituality.

Third, this chapter has implications for public participation in environmental decision making. Many environmental communication scholars study the processes of public participation in environmental decision making (e.g., Depoe & Delicath, 2004). As science plays an important role in most environmental policies like siting nuclear waste facilities, it is crucial that how science intermingles or blends with other forms of evidence in public deliberation over scientific policy is understood. As research in public participation has shown, decision making often values scientific and technical arguments over cultural, spiritual, and other forms of proof (Depoe & Delicath, 2004; Katz & Miller, 1996; Waddell, 1990). This chapter not only describes how participants in a decision-making process used scientific argument, but also how they created positions against the Yucca Mountain site through combinations of scientific and non-scientific cultural and spiritual arguments. While this chapter does not offer conclusions about how to create better models of public participation that recognize the interplay between science, cultural, and spiritual arguments, it does highlight the need for science communication scholars to engage in conversation with environmental communication scholars about the role of science in public participation in environmental decision making.

Finally, because this case study focused on the arguments made by American Indians, this chapter has implications for how the relationship between indigenous knowledge and Western science is understood. It challenges misconceptions about the relationship between American Indian cultures and science. Findings reveal that while stereotypes assume that Western science is incompatible with indigenous science and knowledge, the incompatibility is a social construction that serves to continue the marginalization of indigenous peoples. As this case study shows, it is possible for American Indians to maintain their cultural/spiritual beliefs and use Western science. Although there will be situations when Western science is at odds with indigenous science, this is not always the case. The complexity of indigenous knowledge and the necessity of evaluating American Indian engagement with science must be examined on a case-by-case basis. Thus, researchers interested in the relationship between indigenous knowledge and Western science can contribute to this conversation through examining additional cases of public scientific controversy that overlap with indigenous peoples and their lands.

Notes

1. Although the general term "American Indians" is used here, it is important to recognize that there are over 500 American Indian nations in the United States (Department of the Interior, 2002). Even though some generalizations are made about American Indians as a group, care is taken to distinguish the arguments and beliefs of specific American Indian nations, in this case mostly Western Shoshone and Southern Paiutes.
2. This interview was part of the Nuclear Technology in the Great Basin Oral History Project at the University of Utah.
3. "Treaty between the United States of America and the Western Bands of Shoshone Indians," October 1, 1863, 18 Stat. 689–692.
4. There have been several other public comment periods during the research of the Yucca Mountain site. For example, there was a public comment period associated with the Draft Environmental Impact Statement in 1998.
5. It is important to note that a cultural value does not automatically translate into practice. In other words, this chapter is not meant to romanticize all American Indians as living in harmony with nature. However, many tribes explicitly place value on nature in ways that other cultures do not.
6. The Environmental Protection Agency is responsible for setting radiation standards in relation to protecting the public from radiation exposure from the Yucca Mountain site. In 2001, they set a standard for a 10,000-year compliance

period, meaning that the Yucca Mountain project would have to perform dose projections and protect the public from potential radiation exposure for 10,000 years after accepting waste. In 2004 the U.S. Court of Appeals for the District of Columbia ruled that the 10,000-year standard was inconsistent with the recommendations of the National Academy of Sciences and called for a revised standard. In 2005, the EPA released a new standard that calls for a one-million-year compliance period (U.S. Environmental Protection Agency, 2008).

References

Abraham, S. (2002). *Recommendation by the Secretary of Energy regarding the suitability of the Yucca Mountain site for a repository under the Nuclear Waste Policy Act of 1982.* Washington, DC: U.S. Department of Energy.

Burgchardt, C. R. (2005). *Readings in rhetorical criticism.* State College, PA: Strata Publishing.

Coleman, C., & Dysart, E. V. (2007). Framing of the Kennewick Man against the backdrop of a scientific and cultural controversy. *Science Communication, 27,* 3–26.

Condit, C. M. (1998). The rhetoric of intelligent design: Alternatives for science and religion. *Rhetoric and Public Affairs, 1,* 593–602.

Deloria Jr., V. (1997). *Red earth, white lies: Native Americans and the myth of scientific fact.* Golden, CO: Fulcrum Publishing.

Depoe, S., & Delicath, J. W. (2004). Introduction. In S. Depoe, J. W. Delicath, & M. A. Elsenbeer (Eds.), *Communication and public participation in environmental decision making* (pp. 1–10). Albany, NY: State University of New York Press.

Durham, B., & Helmer, B. (2001). *Letter to the Department of Energy.* Received October 10, 2001, public comment #330036. Retrieved January 20, 2005, from www.ocrwm.doe.gov/documents/sr_comm/sr_pdf/330036.pdf.

Endres, D. (2005). *The guise of deliberation: A rhetorical criticism of arguments in the Yucca Mountain site authorization controversy.* Unpublished doctoral dissertation, University of Washington.

Endres, D. (2009). The rhetoric of nuclear colonialism: Rhetorical exclusion of American Indian arguments in the Yucca Mountain nuclear waste siting decision. *Communication and Critical/Cultural Studies, 6,* 39–60.

Fabj, V., & Sobnosky, M. J. (1995). AIDS activism and the rejuvenation of the public sphere. *Argumentation and Advocacy, 31,* 163–184.

Farrell, T. B., & Goodnight, G. T. (1981). Accidental rhetoric: The root metaphors of Three Mile Island. *Communication Monographs, 48,* 271–301.

Fiorino, D. J. (1990). Citizen participation and environmental risk: A survey of institutional mechanisms. *Science, Technology and Human Values, 15,* 226–243.

Fischer, F. (2000). *Citizens, experts, and the environment: The politics of local knowledge.* Durham, NC: Duke University Press.

Fisher, W. (1987). *Human communication as narration: Toward a philosophy of reason, value, and action.* Columbia, SC: University of South Carolina Press.

Foss, S. K. (2009). *Rhetorical criticism: Exploration and practice* (4th ed.). Long Grove, IL: Waveland Press.

Friedman, S. M., Dunwoody, S., & Rogers, C. L. (1986). Introduction. In S. S. Friedman, S. Dunwoody, & C. L. Rogers (Eds.), *Scientists and journalists: Reporting science as news* (pp. xi–xvii). New York: Free Press.

Goodnight, G. T. (1982). The personal, technical, and public spheres of argument: A speculative inquiry into the act of public deliberation. *Journal of the American Forensics Association, 18*, 214–227.

Goodnight, G. T. (2005). Science and technology controversy: A rationale for inquiry. *Argumentation and Advocacy, 42*, 26–29.

Gross, A. G. (1984). Public debates as failed social dramas: The recombinant DNA controversy. *Quarterly Journal of Speech, 70*, 397–409.

Harris, T. M., Parrott, R., & Dorgan, K. A. (2004). Talking about human genetics within religious frameworks. *Health Communication, 16*, 105–116.

Hart, R. P., & Daughton, S. (2005). Modern rhetorical criticism (3rd ed.). Boston, MA: Allyn and Bacon.

Hodson, D. (1993). In search of a rational for multicultural science education. *Science Education, 77*, 685–711.

Johnson-Sheehan, R., & Morgan, L. (2008). Darwin's dilemma: Science in the public forum. *Journal of Technical Writing and Communication, 38*, 53–73.

Katz, S. B., & Miller, C. R. (1996). The low-level radioactive waste citing controversy in North Carolina: Toward a rhetorical model of risk communication. In C. G. Herndl & S. C. Brown (Eds.), *Green culture: Environmental rhetoric in contemporary America* (pp. 111–140). Madison, WI: University of Wisconsin Press.

Keränen, L. (2005). Mapping misconduct: Demarcating legitimate science from "fraud" in the B-06 lumpectomy controversy. *Argumentation and Advocacy, 42*, 94–113.

Kinsella, W. J. (2004). Public expertise: A foundation for citizen participation in energy and environmental decisions. In S. Depoe, J. W. Delicath, & M. A. Elsenbeer (Eds.), *Communication and public participation in environmental decision making* (pp. 83–98). Albany, NY: State University of New York Press.

Lessl, T. A. (1989). The priestly voice. *Quarterly Journal of Speech, 75*, 183–197.

Lessl, T. A. (1993). Toward a definition of religions communication: Scientific and religious uses of evolution. *Journal of Communication and Religion, 16*, 127–138.

Lessl, T. A. (2003). Scientific rhetoric as religious advocacy: Origins in the public schools. *Journal of Communication and Religion, 26*, 1–27.

Lessl, T. A. (2005). The mythological conditioning of scientific naturalism. *Journal of Communication and Religion, 28*, 23–46.

Lyne, J., & Howe, H. F. (1986). "Punctuated equilibria": Rhetorical dynamics of a scientific controversy. *Quarterly Journal of Speech, 72*, 132–147.

Mander, J. (1992). *In the absence of the sacred: The failure of technology and the survival of the Indian nations.* San Francisco, CA: Sierra Club Books.

Manzini, S. (2003). Effective communication of science in a culturally diverse society. *Science Communication, 25*, 191–197.

Martin, J. D., Trammell, K. D., Landers, D., Valois, J. M., & Bailey, T. (2006). Journalism and the debate over origins: Newspaper coverage of intelligent design. *Journal of Media and Religion, 5*, 49–61.

Nuclear Waste Policy Act: As amended with appropriations acts appended (No. 20585). (2004). Retrieved March 12, 2004, from www.ocrwm.doe.gov/documents/nwpa/css/nwpa_2004.pdf.

Philipsen, G. (1997). A theory of speech codes. In G. Philipsen & T. Albrecht

(Eds.), *Developing theories of communication* (pp. 119–156). Albany, NY: State University of New York Press.

Ratliff, J. N. (1997). The politics of nuclear waste: An analysis of a public hearing on the proposed Yucca Mountain nuclear waste repository. *Communication Studies, 48*, 359–380.

Smith, L. T. (1999). *Decolonizing methodology: Research and indigenous peoples.* London and New York: Zed Books.

Snow, C. P. (1993). *The two cultures.* Cambridge: Cambridge University Press (originally published in 1959).

Taylor, C. A. (1992). Of audience, expertise and authority: The evolving creationism debate. *Quarterly Journal of Speech, 78*, 277–295.

Timbisha Shoshone Tribe. (2001). *Resolution No. 18–2001.* Submitted to the Department of Energy and received on October 24, 2001 (public comment #330095). Retrieved December 30, 2008, from www.ocrwm.doe.gov/documents/sr_comm/sr_pdf/330095.pdf.

U.S. Census Bureau. (2000). *Census 2000.* Retrieved December 30, 2008, from www.census.gov/main/www/cen2000.html.

U.S. Department of Energy. (2001a). *Hearings for site recommendation consideration of the Yucca Mountain site for geologic disposal of spent nuclear fuel and high-level radioactive waste.* Reporter's transcript of proceedings taken on Wednesday, December 12, 2001, at 1 p.m. at Las Vegas, NV, reported by Heidi Konsten, RPR #516382.

U.S. Department of Energy. (2001b). *Public comments on site recommendation for the Yucca Mountain Project.* Reporter's transcript of proceedings taken on Friday, October 12, 2001, at Hawthorne, NV, reported by Nicole M. Rossy, CSR #10698.

U.S. Department of Energy. (2001c). *Site recommendation support documents: Public comments submitted during the public comment period.* Retrieved December 30, 2008, from www.ocrwm.doe.gov/documents/sr_comm/index.htm.

U.S. Department of Energy. (2001d). *U.S. Department of Energy availability session on the possible site recommendation of Yucca Mountain.* Reporter's transcript of proceedings taken on Saturday, September 29, 2001, at 10 a.m.–4 p.m. at Las Vegas Science Center, Las Vegas, NV, reported by Kevin Wm. Daniel, CCR #711.

U.S. Department of Energy. (2001e). *U.S. Department of Energy public hearing on the possible site recommendation of Yucca Mountain.* Reporter's transcript of proceedings taken on Wednesday, October 10, 2001, at 3 p.m. at Town Center, Crescent Valley, NV.

U.S. Department of Energy. (2008a). *How much nuclear waste is in the United States?* Retrieved December 30, 2008, from www.ocrwm.doe.gov/ym_repository/about_project/waste_explained/howmuch.shtml.

U.S. Department of Energy. (2008b). *Yucca Mountain repository.* Retrieved December 22, 2008, from www.ocrwm.doe.gov/ym_repository/index.shtml.

U.S. Department of the Interior: Bureau of Indian Affairs. (2002). National Archives and Records Administration (Federal Register Vol. 67, No. 134). Retrieved December, 22, 2008, from www.census.gov/pubinfo/www/FRN02.pdf.

U.S. Environmental Protection Agency. (2008). *Fact Sheet: Public health and envi-*

ronmental radiation protection standards for Yucca Mountain, Nevada (40 CFR Part 17, final rule. Retrieved December 30, 2008, from www.epa.gov/rpdweb00/yucca/2008factsheet.html.

U.S. Nuclear Regulatory Commission. (2007). *High-level Waste*. Retrieved December 30, 2008, from www.nrc.gov/waste/high-level-waste.html.

van Dijck, J. (2003). After the 'Two Cultures": Toward a "(Multi)cultural" practice of science communication. *Science Communication, 25,* 177–190.

Waddell, C. (1990). The role of *pathos* in the decision-making process: A study in the rhetoric of science policy. *Quarterly Journal of Speech, 76,* 381–400.

Walker, G. B., & Daniels, S. E. (2004). Dialogue and deliberation in environmental conflict: Enacting civic science. In S. L. Seneca (Ed.), *The environmental communication yearbook 1* (pp. 135–152). Mahwah, NJ: Lawrence Erlbaum Associates.

Wynne, B. (1996). May the sheep safely graze? A reflexive view of the expert–lay knowledge divide. In S. Lash, B. Szerszynski, & B. Wynne (Eds.), *Risk, environment and modernity: Towards a new ecology* (pp. 44–83). London: Sage.

Chapter 9

Moral Development Framing in Environmental Justice News Coverage

Kristen Alley Swain

Science and the public come together most urgently and acutely during episodes of public risk (Gregory & Miller, 2000). When landfills and factories are sited in areas where ethnic minorities and low-income citizens live, these residents can be exposed to more pollution than the population as a whole. This problem, which is at the center of the environmental justice movement, often pits civil rights concerns against economic development initiatives. As a result, environmental justice is typically a complex and emotionally charged community issue. Depoe (1997) asserts that a better understanding of this complex issue can be reached through research focused on the evolutionary development and the rhetorical appeals that help define the environmental justice movement.

The present chapter focuses on the rhetorical appeals employed by industries that were the targets of advocacy groups active in the social justice movement in the 1990s. The concept of framing assists in this endeavor. As Nisbet explains in Chapter 2 of this volume, news framing drives the dynamics of many science controversies. For example, news coverage often highlights controversy and risk, as well as ethical dilemmas rooted in conflicting principles and interests. Furthermore, the way the news media frame the ethical stances of industries involved in environmental justice disputes can shape the outcomes of those conflicts, the health of disadvantaged citizens, and future industrial development. Thus, this chapter focuses on industry rhetoric as it is framed in the media coverage of the environmental justice movement. Further heeding Depoe's advice, this chapter also turns to Kohlberg's (1973) theory of moral development as a framework for evaluating the evolution of industry rhetoric in terms of the values and moral rationale used in industry decisions and reactions to community conflicts. The overall goal of this chapter, therefore, is to illuminate (1) the moral development of industry rhetoric and (2) the story frames evident in the news coverage of the environmental justice movement that emerged between 1994 and 2001.

The Environmental Justice Movement

The premise of environmental justice is that some individuals are at greater risk of adverse health effects from exposure to industrial pollution than others. When toxic landfills and factories are built in areas where poor and ethnic minorities live, these facilities disproportionately expose these communities to disease-causing wastes. Bullard (1994) defines environmental justice as the notion that everyone has a right to a clean, safe, healthy environment and that no community should become the dumping ground for other people's waste.

Emerging from grassroots struggles over toxic contamination, the movement links environmental activism with historical movements for civil rights and social justice. One tenet of the movement is that the mainstream environmental movement, largely white, male, and middle class, has largely ignored issues of environmental justice (Heinz, 2005). As a result, several decades of regulatory decision making have failed to consider equity in the distribution of toxics among diverse communities (Woodruff, Axelrad, Caldwell, Morello-Frosch, & Rosenbaum, 1998). For example, hazardous sites situated in communities with a higher percentage of black residents are less likely to be placed on the EPA's National Priorities List; designation on that list qualifies a site for in-depth investigation and potential hazard remediation via the Superfund program (Anderton, Oakes, & Egan, 1997). In this way, irregularities in regulatory enforcement may leave some groups more exposed to toxic wastes (Weinberg, 1998).

Census data, the Environmental Protection Agency (EPA) Toxics Release Inventory data, historical land-use data, local histories, and planning reports have been used to document environmental race and class inequalities and to generate demographic and industrial maps that illustrate such inequalities (Szasz & Meuser, 2000). An additional study that examined the proximity of people to 413 commercial hazardous waste facilities in 44 states found that minorities are more likely to live within 3 km of these potentially harmful sites—and tend to live in these areas before the facilities are installed (Mohai & Saha, 2006). Additionally, Mohai and Saha (2006) concluded recently that there has been little or no progress in environmental justice since 1987, when the United Church of Christ issued their seminal study revealing the disparities (Chavis & Lee, 1987).

As it is defined here, the environmental justice movement first gained momentum and visibility in 1982, when citizens protested against a proposed burial site for soil contaminated with highly toxic polychlorinated biphenyls (PCBs) in a predominantly poor and black North Carolina county. Five years later, the United Church of Christ published its study (Chavis & Lee, 1987). In 1988, Greenpeace helped to organize a march through Louisiana's "Cancer Alley" (Hind, 2000). In 1991, the First National People of Color Environmental Leadership Summit drew delegates from all 50 states (Shepard, Northridge, Prakash, & Stover, 2002). Then in 1994, Congress passed Executive Order 12898 on Environmental Justice, authorizing all federal agencies to protect minority and low-income groups from disproportionate impacts of environmental hazards and disparate implementation of environmental regulations (President of the United States, February 11, 1994).

One of the most prominent cases in the environmental justice movement was the dispute between Shintech Inc. and the residents of Convent, Louisiana, a small, predominantly African American town located within the Louisiana Petrochemical Corridor, an 85-mile stretch along the Mississippi River, from Baton Rouge to New Orleans (Joseph, 2005). The site of more than 125 refineries and chemical plants, the corridor has been dubbed "Cancer Alley" because of its high incidence of cancer and respiratory problems (Joseph, 2005). In addition, GIS mapping has shown that polluting industries in St. James Parish, where Convent is located, are in areas with the highest percentages of African Americans, the lowest average household income, and the most residents without a high school diploma (Blodgett, 2006). In 1996, Shintech—subsidiary of the Tokyo-based chemical company Shin Etsu, the world's largest supplier of semiconductor materials—announced plans to build a $700 million polyvinyl chloride (PVC) plant in Convent. The plant would consist of three chemical factories and an incinerator.

But the small, oppressed, and seemingly powerless community persevered to defeat the plans of this multinational chemical company, which also had the backing of local and state government elites. At a public hearing regarding the proposed air permit for Shintech in December 1996, 300 citizens voiced their strong opposition. Despite a sustained multiracial grassroots campaign supported by the Sierra Club, Greenpeace, NAACP, and other groups, Shintech received land-use and air permits in spring 1997. Over time, lawsuits resulted in costs, lengthy delays, and uncertainty for the corporation (Berry, 2003). Finally, in September 1998, while the EPA was reviewing its techniques in determining disproportionate burden, Shintech backed out of its plans to build a plant in Convent. Instead, it built a smaller, $250 million PVC plant about 20 miles away in Plaquemine (University of Michigan, 1999).

The evolving construct of environmental justice played a significant part in that battle, as community groups formed coalitions with local, state, and national agents and organizations to challenge the decision to site the hazardous and noxious facility.

Framing and Environmental Justice

A study of news frames is critical to achieve a better understanding of the environmental justice movement and the industry rhetoric that helped shape that movement. According to Entman (1993), news framing is the process of organizing and packaging information. It involves selecting aspects of a perceived reality to make them more salient. It promotes a particular problem definition, assignment of responsibility, causal interpretation, ethical or moral interpretation, or recommended solution. News frames are embodied in key words and concepts emphasized in stories.

Most news content is either framed episodically, as a case study, or thematically, in which the story emphasizes general or abstract concepts. In discussing framing, Entman also identified four aspects of perceived reality such that environmental justice might be defined as a larger social issue, interpreted causes of disease and disparity, provided moral evaluations of disproportionate burden, and offered possible solutions. Building on these concepts, Gamson and Modigliani (1989) identified eight specific frames that consistently appear across policy debates: social progress, economic development, morality/ethics, scientific uncertainty, runaway science, public accountability, compromise, and conflict. Claims makers compete for legitimacy through the news media, while the news media construct, interpret, and frame the claims makers and their issues. The framing of environmental issues involves interview source selection, presentation and evaluation of conflicting arguments, and scientific uncertainty interpretations.

Through coverage or non-coverage of risks, the news media serve as filters through which people interpret risk. Risk coverage defines the significance of events, establishes a framework of expectation, shapes public attitudes, creates biases that underlie public policy, legitimizes or calls into question government policies, and stimulates demands for accountability. The timing, content, and tone of news coverage can upset or reassure the public, encourage complacency or create fear, and justify or reinforce existing views about safety (Engel, Jaffe, & Scherer, 1996).

Nelkin (1995) found that journalists tend to frame environmental justice disputes as social drama, with communities threatened by evil, health/environmental agencies failing to deal with the threat, and industries as polluting villains that must be brought into line. Risks of industrial pollution are typically framed as industrial negligence rooted in greed or racism, rather than as systemic problems in the allocation of resources or the organization or regulation of industry. On the other hand, economic pressures from local industries can contribute to a news blackout on the environmental health risks they pose. Journalists in that situation must try to unravel the complexities of unhealthy exposures without the help of sources connected to the industries they are trying to investigate.

Framing can intensify existing anxiety and exaggerate social and economic responses to a hazard (Flynn, Slovic, & Kunreuther, 2001). The ways that neighborhoods are portrayed in the news media can influence the siting of unwanted facilities. The boundary between powerless citizens living inside an impact zone and powerful ones outside it often is presented as stakeholders' attempts to reframe a controversy for their benefit (Peeples, 2003). Typical media coverage of environmental justice during the 1990s was limited, sensationalized, focused on Superfund sites, and biased against government and industry (Reath, 1994). A content analysis of coverage about a Canadian river dam found that two newspapers tended to provide either a positive or a negative stance. They also oversimplified complex issues and focused on conflict and other sensational aspects of stories. After the government responded to public protests documented in the coverage, it eventually saw the media as biased and not representative of public opinion (De Loë, 1999).

In the present study, it was useful to examine environmental justice as a social movement, to uncover the activist dynamics that may affect industry rhetoric. This approach also helped to further explore the frames at play in the movement. In sum, people who feel deprived or disenfranchised are more likely than others to organize a social movement to improve their condition (Morrison, 1978). Stewart, Smith, and Denton (1989) argue that social movements proceed through five distinct phases: genesis, social unrest, mobilization, maintenance, and termination. Mobilization, the active organizing of a movement, occurs when individuals with grievances mobilize sufficient resources to take action. After a social movement emerges, it coalesces, bureaucratizes, and eventually declines (Tilly, 1978).

The process of creating collective action frames is a central dynamic in a social movement and facilitates progress through the five phases (Benford & Snow, 2000). Sometimes challengers simultaneously engage in confrontation and negotiation with adversaries, in order to position themselves at the decision-making table with elites (Pellow, 1999). On the other hand, when trying to build consensus and gain equal power with industrialists and state actors in the policy-making process, sometimes grassroots environmental activists shift the discussion from the interpersonal level to the wider public (Kubal, 1998). For example, Futrell (2003) found that not-in-my-backyard (NIMBY) conflicts are characterized by an "information haze," in which links among diagnostic, prognostic, and motivational elements of collective action frames are unclear. Opponents of environmental justice activists, or scientific experts asked to interpret risks, often remove the NIMBY frame from public discourse as the context of a dispute shifts.

Government efforts to provide access and accountability to stakeholders in environmental justice cases often have created a racial divide in the policy process. Politicizing environmental issues within a racialized context sometimes has distracted activists and policy makers from actions that might address the economic roots of the disparities (Torres, 1996). Membership in a minority group may affect how individuals respond to media coverage of risk-related events close to where they live or work (Rosenbaum, 1996). Among low-income groups, racial factors can affect the intensity of environmental justice perceptions. Low-income African Americans are more likely to perceive health risks and less likely to perceive benefits of a nearby facility than low-income whites. African Americans also tend to be less aware of opportunities for involvement in industry community programs than are whites (Temple & Musham, 1996).

Williams, Brown, Greenberg, and Kahn (1999) found that heightened risk perception among residents living near a nuclear reactor was associated with having low family income, being poorly educated, living down river from the reactor, living in a community not economically dependent on the reactor, not being employed at the plant, and individual reluctance to accept hazardous waste into one's community for economic gain. Historically, the EPA has placed the burden of environmental hazards disproportionately on racial minorities and low-income groups because its quantitative risk-assessment methodology does not accurately reflect the risks borne by all segments of the population, and the risk aspects examined are not salient or accessible to people of color and lower incomes (Kuehn, 1996).

News coverage of toxic exposures sometimes includes an environmental justice frame alongside other types of frames. For example, childhood lead poisoning has been framed in the news as an environmental justice issue, in which some children are more at risk of exposure than others, but the problem has been framed mainly as a silent epidemic in which all children are at risk (Shibley & Prosterman, 1998). Kenix (2005) found that newspaper coverage of environmental pollution over 29 years was overwhelmingly directed to upper-socioeconomic groups. This pattern held across different ownership, socioeconomic readership, geographic location, and circulation groupings, regardless of specific issue or time. Kenix (2005) attributed this pattern to industry-wide journalistic norms and the importance of advertising revenue, rather than to racist attitudes.

The rhetoric employed in environmental justice disputes varies, depending on the means of determining where a facility would be located, the identity of community residents, and the siting of more than one polluting facility in the same geographic area (Peeples, 2003). The grassroots response to a siting controversy often takes on a tough, no-compromise, personal tone because the activists believe they are fighting for their health and survival (Sale, 1993).

News Sourcing and Environmental Justice

In an effort to promote objectivity, reporters frequently interview sources to convey at least two perspectives in a story. Particular sources often are selected based on the journalist's location, organizational routines, or topical specialization—all of which tend to carry more weight than source credentials when deadlines are looming and budgets are shrinking (Sigal,

1986). The more frequently a source is quoted, the more
source is perceived to be. The more influential a source bec
likely his or her voice will be amplified.

In environmental disputes, the journalistic process often systematicaɪ,
manages the debate on terms that favor elites over citizen activists. Overall,
news organizations tend to offer less access, recognition, and responsive-
ness to activists than to elites (Bennett et al., 2004). Activists' efforts to
control their media image have been central to the struggle for environmental justice (Spitzer, 2000). Reporters tend to interview officials from
dominant institutions in society whose views rarely stray from the status
quo (Hoynes & Croteau, 1991). A content analysis of sourcing and risk
framing in newspaper coverage of two U.S. Department of Energy (DOE)
nuclear weapons facilities found that the most frequent sources were DOE
officials, local advocacy/citizen groups, unions, local industry, and individual citizens. Most of the coverage did not provide any risk information
(Lowrie, Greenberg, & Waishwell, 2000).

Perceived risk depends on audience trust in information sources. When
journalists are unable to ascertain the level of threat to citizens, they often
merely inform the public that a controversy is occurring and identify key
players on each side (Beder & Shortland, 1992). Statements meant to
assure the public that the air or water is safe may imply deliberate distortions, which in turn can lead to polarization, confusion, and the perception
that the hazard is unpredictable and uncontrollable (Beder & Shortland,
1992).

Moral Development and Rhetoric

The present study used Kohlberg's (1973) theory of moral development as
a framework to evaluate industry rhetoric, to capture values and moral
rationale used in industry decisions and reactions to community conflicts,
and to reflect how well industries balance profit making with social respon-
sibilities. Kohlberg's six stages are grouped into three levels: pre-
conventional, conventional, and post-conventional and reflect a progression
from less to greater moral development.

In stage 1, people behave according to socially acceptable norms because
they are told to do so by an authority figure and because they are com-
pelled to avoid punishment. People operating at stage 2 believe that right
behavior means acting in one's own best interests. At stage 3, individuals
seek the approval of others and adopt a conformist good boy/girl mentality. Stage 4 is oriented to abiding by the law and responding to authority
and rules. Stage 5 decisions are rooted in social mutuality and a genuine
interest in the rights and welfare of others. Stage 6 is characterized by
respect for justice, universalization of duties, and a highly principled individual conscience that places the good of society above self-interest. In an

environmental dispute, for example, stage 6 considerations include principles of distributive justice, equity, and proportionality (Zwetkoff, 1998).

Moral development for organizations, which has parallels to Kohlberg's
categorization of the levels of individual moral development, emphasizes
company culture and social performance. Since moral development theory
is rooted in Kantian principles, it assumes that an action is truly moral
only if it is self-sacrificial, performed out of duty, and motivated by altru-
ism. Organizations are embedded in societal and institutional environments that create expectations and standards of behavior (Campbell &
Christopher, 1996).

Parallel to Kohlberg's six stages of individual moral development, the
Reidenbach and Robin (1991) model of corporate moral development
posits five corporate stages: amoral, legalistic, responsive, emergent ethical,
and ethical. Lower stages are characterized by an unbalanced concern for
profit. Amoral organizations are characterized by an outlaw culture that
strives to avoid getting caught, win at any cost, and get what they can and
get out. The notion that corporations should be accountable for their
actions only if it maximizes profits represents pre-conventional moral
development. Legalistic organizations work the gray areas, comply with
the letter rather than spirit of the law, and assert that if an action is legal,
it is acceptable.

Responsive organizations in the Reidenback and Robin model try to
embrace a responsible citizen attitude but often have a reactive rather than
proactive mentality. Emergent ethical organizations actively strive for ethical
outcomes and a culture rooted in core values, but decisions often lack philo-
sophical reasoning and long-term planning. Ethical organizations are perme-
ated with core values and reasoned decision making, and they systematically
anticipate problems and analyze alternative outcomes. Post-conventional
decisions seek to preserve quality of life and sustainability. Promoting post-
conventional ideals not only can be good corporate public relations but also
can benefit the bottom line. Many companies have found that reducing
adverse environmental impact often has positive effects on profitability.
However, such green business practices are morally neutral because the
driving forces behind them are legal and economic, not ethical. In some
instances, managers do undertake green business initiatives with the notion
of doing something positive for future humans and for the natural environment, a morally admirable motivation (Hendry & Vesilind, 2005).

In industrial siting disputes, ethical issues often are clouded by agendas,
biases, greed, and power. Once in the open, spin, political correctness, and
a cynical media may distort deliberations. Some decisions about siting and
emissions support protection of economic interests over people, which do
not provide the greatest good for the greatest number. In some cases, it
may be more appropriate for a corporation to be merciful than to seek
justice, such as when a corporation makes reparations or helps the local

economy prosper (Spitzeck, 2005). Companies may be more likely to pollute disadvantaged communities when they have more to gain than lose by doing so and are less likely to move into these areas if sanctions might reduce potential profits. Companies that operate at a pre-conventional level might be pressured to protect disadvantaged communities from toxic exposures through environmental regulations or boycotts, while companies with a conventional approach might be motivated by social praise since they are more concerned about their reputation (Spitzeck, 2005). Stage 1 motives such as avoiding litigation or regulatory penalties can prompt corporations to knowingly contaminate disadvantaged communities in the interest of making enough profit to offset the risk (Rausser, Simon, & Zhao, 1998).

Examining News Coverage of Environmental Justice

To illuminate the moral development of industry rhetoric and story frames evident in news coverage of the environmental justice movement, seven propositions were developed after considering the literature reviewed above. These propositions were used to explore dynamics in the coverage and in the relationship between industries and the community that may have affected industry rhetoric. Specifically, they examined differences between commercial companies and public utilities, emphasis on conflict, predominant racial groups, status of facilities, the amount of play devoted to stories containing pre-conventional rhetoric, the strength of activism indicated by social movement stages, and overall bias for or against industry and activists. A more detailed discussion of the proposed relationships and definition of terms is offered below. A list of the full set of seven propositions can be found in Table 9.1.

Method

Using content analysis, 480 stories taken from 88 U.S. newspapers were examined. Although the Clinton era began in January 1992, the first story about environmental justice did not appear until January 11, 1994, a *New York Times* feature discussing the emerging movement. Thus, the time frame of the news coverage of stories used here was January 1, 1994 through January 20, 2001, the final day of the Clinton–Gore administration. The time frame was divided into three phases: the genesis phase (1994–1995), when President Clinton issued Executive Order 12989 on Environmental Justice and interagency public hearings about the order were held; the social unrest phase (1996–1998), when the Shintech controversy arose; and the mobilization phase (1999–2001), when more than 1,000 environmental justice groups had emerged.

Table 9.1 Propositions for Environmental Justice News Coverage Analysis

Proposition	Rationale
P1: Coverage of commercial industries will contain moral development rhetoric more often than coverage of public utilities.	Siting and operations of commercial industries that profit private interests provoke outrage, while public utilities purport to serve the community as a whole.
P2: Stories containing a conflict theme will be characterized by pre-conventional industry rhetoric emphasizing commercial interests.	Pre-conventional rhetoric sparks conflict when industries marginalize affected residents and disallow public participation in decision-making.
P3: African Americans will be the top racial group mentioned in stories containing pre-conventional rhetoric.	Residents living near polluting industries are often low-income minorities, and the environmental justice movement in the 1990s was characterized by African American struggles.
P4: Pre-conventional rhetoric will appear more often in coverage of commercial industries that plan to site a facility in a community, while post-conventional rhetoric will appear more often in coverage of public utilities that already operate in the community.	Public reaction to the status of an industrial facility can affect the tone of news coverage. Proposed siting can incite more public outrage than chronic polluting by existing facilities or toxic clean-up of previously sited facilities. Existing public utilities often are assumed to be necessary providers of residential necessities, even when they pollute the community.
P5: Stories containing pre-conventional industry rhetoric will receive higher play than stories containing conventional or post-conventional rhetoric.	Pre-conventional rhetoric, which places corporate interests above other stakeholder interests, would receive higher play if it provoked more conflict and thus attracted more coverage.
P6: Coverage during the genesis phase of the movement will emphasize pre-conventional rhetoric, while mobilization phase coverage will emphasize post-conventional rhetoric.	Social movements gather strength through the first three stages; it was assumed that industries would react differently to weaker public pressure than organized protest.
P7: Stories containing anti-industry or pro-environmental justice stances will contain more pre-conventional rhetoric than stories supporting industry or opposing EJ advocates.	Stories supporting industry highlight their positive contributions or criticize their opponents, both of which fail to promote the little guy vs. evil corporation conflict that can spark pre-conventional rhetoric.

The unit of analysis was an individual news story selected using the Lexis-Nexis Academic Universe "U.S. Newspapers" full-text database that mentioned "environmental justice" or "environmental racism" in the headline or lead. Lexis-Nexis searches rendered 597 news stories that fit these inclusion criteria. The final sample represented one out of every 1.2 articles in the universe. Story corrections, opinion articles, abstracts, letters to the editor, non-U.S. publications, obituaries, reprints, sports stories, and digests/round-up summaries were excluded, as were stories less than 150 words and material originating from another publication.

To evaluate search terms and categorization schemes, 20 stories were randomly downloaded and analyzed by two coders. The results of this pilot test were used to further refine the original coding instrument. Two coders independently coded the final sample, and 20% of the sample was double-coded. The overall intercoder reliability coefficient (Cohen's *kappa*) was 0.87. All coded categories in the final instrument were considered to be mutually exclusive. For many variables, more than one subcategory could be coded, to account for mentions of multiple concepts.

Section letter and page number, recorded for each story, were recoded to indicate one of three positions in the newspaper: front page, section cover, or interior. Nine levels of play indicated the relative prominence each story received, in terms of its placement and length. These levels were calculated by combining the placement of stories (front page, section front, or interior) with word counts. Longer stories on the front page received the highest play rating, while shorter stories on interior pages received the lowest. The number of photos, maps, tables, and other graphics, as indicated in the footer text on Lexis-Nexis documents, also was recorded for each story. Stories were coded as local or non-local, depending on whether the story contained a dateline indicating a non-local location where the story originated. Coders also indicated whether a story covered an event or only an issue, in order to identify enterprise reporting. Enterprise reporting was defined as a story that a journalist initiated, as distinguished from coverage of just an event or press release.

To classify the moral development of industry rhetoric, coders looked for statements in the stories that characterized particular stages (Table 9.2). For stage 1, coders looked for statements that addressed avoidance of punishment or other painful consequences for the organization, statements about releasing toxins into the environment to the extent that the organization could get away with it, how the organization was unethically exploiting natural resources, or how it was being opportunistic. For stage 2, coders looked for statements about reciprocity, such as how an organization furthers its interests through negotiation, compromise, or cooperation with adversaries.

Stage 3 statements discussed conformity with the expectations of regulatory agencies, even if doing so reduces profits. Stage 4 statements discussed

Table 9.2 Moral Development Rhetoric in Environmental Justice Coverage

Moral development level	Kohlberg stage	Average Mentions per Story	Key Concepts	Industry Rhetoric Examples
Pre-conventional	1	292 (60.8%)	Avoid punishment	We will release toxins, to the extent that we can get away with it or avoid penalty.
	2	200 (41.7%)	Achieve reciprocity	We should try to negotiate or compromise with our adversaries, in order to get what we want.
Conventional	3	95 (19.8%)	Conform to expectations of authority	We should strive to conform with environmental regulations, even if it hurts the bottom line.
	4	112 (23.3%)	Fulfill duties to others	We should seek public input in the decision-making process.
Post-conventional	5	119 (24.8%)	Utilitarianism/ rights	We should weigh benefits vs. consequences to the community.
	6	59 (12.3%)	Justice/ compassion, universal principles	We are committed to ensuring a clean and healthy environment for the community and future generations.

actions that meet societal expectations or strived to fulfill duties to other stakeholders, such as seeking public input in the siting decision process. Stage 5 statements highlighted issues of utilitarian cost–benefit analysis or balancing of rights, such as weighing benefits versus consequences of a siting decision for the community or consideration of civil rights or human rights. Stage 6 statements addressed universal moral principles, such as distributive justice and compassion or consistency with self-selected moral principles. For example, statements coded as stage 6 might discuss a company's commitment to ensure a clean and healthy environment for future generations, provide a fair number of jobs and other benefits for residents living in the impact zone, providing voluntary restitution to affected citizens, or voluntarily restoring natural resources or habitats that are used or destroyed.

Coders also searched each story for any mention of 56 keywords, which were later collapsed into seven frames within two major themes (Table 9.3). The first theme, victimization, consisted of activism, disparity, and harm frames. The activism frame was coded for stories that mentioned intervention, grassroots efforts, and crusading. The disparity frame was coded for mentions of discrimination, disproportionate burden, poverty, racism, unfairness, victimization, and vulnerability. The harm frame included concepts of killing, setbacks, toll, and hurt. The second theme, conflict, consisted of anger, dispute, problem, and outrage frames. The anger frame represented concepts of rage, resistance, deception, and conspiracy. The dispute frame included battles, conflicts, controversy, criticism, crossfire, fighting, obstruction, protest, toughness, and accusation. The problem frame included concepts of change, dilemmas, and ethics. The outrage frame described negative public reactions to hazards, including alarm, fear, threats, worry, and anxiety.

Coders selected type of facility from a list of 48 types of polluting facilities, which were later collapsed into two industry categories: commercial and public utility. Commercial facilities included companies that manufactured or processed plastics, rubber, petroleum, chemicals, agricultural products, metals, and wood products. Public-utility facilities included hazardous waste disposal, landfills, recycling, incinerators, water treatment, and power plants. The status of a facility was coded into any of three categories: it plans to locate in or near the community, it is already in or near the community, or it is no longer in community.

Coders also recorded whether each story mentioned pro-industry, anti-industry, pro-environmental justice, and/or anti-environmental justice stances. Specifically, a pro-industry stance was defined as a story that mentioned industry as desirable for the community or that the local economy will improve if a new industry comes in, a lack of action or a laissez-faire

Table 9.3 Themes and Frames Mentioned in Environmental Justice Stories

		Themes		
		Victimization 438 (91.3)		*Conflict 329 (68.5)*
Frames	Activism	102 (21.3)	Anger	35 (7.3)
	Disparity	305 (63.5)	Dispute	195 (40.6)
	Harm	31 (6.5)	Problem	99 (20.6)
			Outrage	166 (34.6)

approach to industrial development as justified, the community as economically dependent upon industry, or the flow of capital or money into the community from industry. An anti-industry stance was one that criticized industry or its impact on the environment. A pro-environmental justice stance was defined as a story mentioning minorities or low-income individuals as heroes or as helpless/innocent victims. An anti-environmental justice stance was one that criticized environmental justice advocates or their complaints, mentioned an environmental justice complaint as the product of public ignorance or irrational fear, officials as frustrated or puzzled by opposition from environmental justice advocates, or environmental justice litigation as a drain on community productivity.

Frequencies and percentages were calculated in cross-tabulated tables to show patterns in coverage, and chi-square analyses were used to assess significant differences in the amount of coverage devoted to various topics.

Findings from the Content Analysis

Within the sample of 480 stories, coders identified 877 statements that characterized the six stages of moral development, an average of 1.8 mentions per story. Overall, pre-conventional rhetoric accounted for 56.1% of the 877 stage statements that were coded, followed by conventional rhetoric (23.6%) and post-conventional rhetoric (20.3%). Details of the frames that emerged within and alongside the stages of moral development are reported below.

The first proposition, which predicted that coverage of commercial industries would contain moral development rhetoric more often than coverage of public utilities, was supported. Coverage of commercial industries was more likely than coverage of public utilities to contain rhetoric coded for at least one stage of moral development (X^2 (5, $N = 218$) = 13.48, $p < 0.05$). Overall, 53% of moral development rhetoric mentions appeared in stories about commercial industries, while 47% discussed public utilities. Also, coverage of commercial industries was more likely to contain stage 4 (X^2 (5, $N = 72$) = 5.01, $p < 0.05$) or stage 5 (X^2 (5, $N = 82$) = 3.89, $p < 0.05$) rhetoric, while public-utility stories were more likely to include stage 2 or stage 3 rhetoric (X^2 (5, $N = 57$) = 13.48, $p < 0.05$). Nearly all (99.8%) stories mentioned at least one industrial or government facility. The top facilities mentioned in the coverage were landfills (27.5%), hazardous waste facilities (21.3%), plastics (15.2%), incinerators (11.7%), wastewater treatment (7.7%), and petroleum processing (7.5%). Stories about commercial industries were more likely to mention chemical fumes (X^2 (6, $N = 61$) = 3.95, $p < 0.05$) or water pollution (X^2 (6, $N = 92$) = 4.20, $p < 0.05$) as pollutant types, while public-utility stories were more likely to mention air or soil pollution, tainted food, or radiation (X^2 (6, $N = 17$) = 16.02, $p < 0.05$).

The second proposition, which asserted that stories containing a conflict theme will be characterized by pre-conventional industry rhetoric emphasizing commercial interests, was supported. Stories that quoted polarized sources, rather than outside officials and scientists, emphasized commercial companies. Stories containing the victimization frame were more likely than not to contain pre-conventional rhetoric. Stories highlighting the conflict theme were more likely to contain pre-conventional industry rhetoric than stories without that theme. More than half of the coverage was characterized by the conflict theme (52.2%) and victimization theme (54.5%).

The coverage of commercial industries more often quoted advocates on opposing sides, while coverage of public utilities more often quoted government officials and scientists. Public-utility stories were more likely to quote local politicians (X^2 (8, $N = 56$) $= 7.07$, $p < 0.01$) and scientists, while commercial industry stories were more likely to quote state and federal politicians, environmental agencies, industry representatives, and environmental justice advocates (X^2 (8, $N = 165$) $= 18.12$, $p < 0.05$).

Pre-conventional rhetoric appeared more often in stories that quoted environmental justice advocates, industry representatives, local environmental officials, and local politicians. On the other hand, pre-conventional rhetoric appeared less often in stories quoting federal politicians, researchers, and state politicians. The sources quoted significantly more often in post-conventional stories, as compared with conventional morality stories, were local environmental agency officials, state politicians, and industry representatives. Top interview sources were environmental justice advocates (appearing in 29.3% of the stories), followed by industry representatives (13.0%), local politicians (9.6%), local environmental officials (9.0%), EPA officials (8.7%), state politicians (7.3%), scientists/researchers (5.5%), and federal politicians (5.2%).

Among stories that included a victimization frame, significant differences appeared across coverage of all stages. Although pre-conventional rhetoric appeared more than twice as often as all other rhetoric in victimization stories, the post-conventional rhetoric was significantly more likely to appear than conventional rhetoric (X^2 (5, $N = 383$) $= 22.42$, $p < 0.0001$). Stories containing stage 3 (X^2 (1, $N = 62$) $= 12.25$, $p < 0.001$) and stage 5 (X^2 (1, $N = 108$) $= 8.99$, $p < 0.001$) rhetoric were significantly more likely to include a victimization frame than not. Commercial industry stories were significantly more likely to include disparity (X^2 (8, $N = 164$) $= 4.43$, $p < 0.05$) or harm (X^2 (8, $N = 25$) $= 4.43$, $p < 0.05$) frames, while public-utility stories more frequently included anger frames (X^2 (8, $N = 28$) $= 6.12$, $p < 0.05$).

P3, which predicted that African Americans would be the top racial group mentioned in stories containing pre-conventional rhetoric, was not supported. Most of the coverage was characterized as an African American cause; 41.0% mentioned African Americans, 13.1% mentioned Hispanics,

10.0% mentioned Native Americans, and 4.0% mentioned Asian Americans. However, Native Americans were mentioned significantly more often in pre-conventional stories than in other stories (X^2 (5, $N=64$) $=10.70$, $p<0.05$) and appeared in more pre-conventional stories than any other racial group.

P4 predicted that pre-conventional rhetoric would appear more often in coverage of commercial companies that plan to site a facility while post-conventional rhetoric will appear more often in coverage of public utilities that already operate in the community. This proposition was supported. Across all coverage, 44.9% of stories mentioned facility status. Of these, 39.8% mentioned that a facility was already sited in or near a community, 36.7% mentioned that a facility planned to locate in or near the community, and 23.5% mentioned that a facility was no longer operating in the community. Stories about commercial industries were more likely to mention facility status (X^2 (2, $N=176$) $=7.82$, $p<0.01$). Commercial industry stories more often mentioned facilities planning to locate in a community or that already operated in or near a community, while public-utility coverage tended to focus on facilities that no longer operate in the community (X^2 (2, $N=142$) $=7.29$, $p<0.01$).

More than half (56.6%) of stories that mentioned a facility's status included pre-conventional rhetoric, while 23.9% included conventional rhetoric and 19.5% contained post-conventional rhetoric. Stories containing stage 1 (pre-conventional) rhetoric were significantly more likely to mention that a facility is no longer in the community than to mention that it is already in the community or that it plans to locate there (X^2 (2, $N=207$)$=27.24$, $p<0.001$). Post-conventional rhetoric appeared more often in stories about commercial industries than public utilities sited locally at any time.

Commercial industries siting a new facility in the community were more likely than those already in or near a community or those no longer in a community to be covered in post-conventional rhetoric stories. Meanwhile, public utilities already in or near a community were more likely to be covered in post-conventional rhetoric stories than those planning to site there or that were no longer around (X^2 (10, $N=161$)$=19.62$, $p<0.05$).

P5, which posited that stories containing pre-conventional industry rhetoric would receive higher play than stories containing conventional or post-conventional rhetoric, was not supported. Nearly half (48.3%) of all stories were relatively short, between 500 and 1,000 words. Front-page stories accounted for 15.8% of the coverage, while section-cover stories accounted for 24.6%, and interior stories accounted for 59.6%. Coverage of issues indicated enterprise reporting that went beyond simple reporting of events. Overall, 77.9% of stories focused on an issue only. Issue-only coverage peaked in 1998 and 2000, which were both election years. Stories that received low play were more likely to cover commercial industries than public utilities, particularly if the stories contained post-conventional rhetoric. However, high-play stories that contained pre-conventional rhetoric were more likely to discuss public utilities (X^2 (5, $N = 193$) = 30.39, $p < 0.001$).

Across all coverage, 15.8% of stories received high play, 24.6% received medium play, and 59.6% received low play. While a quarter of stories (24.8%) received the lowest level of play (the shortest interior stories), only 1.9% received the highest level of play (the longest front-page stories). Significant differences in coverage of moral development rhetoric appeared across only the lowest stage (stage 1) in contrast with the highest stage (stage 6), as reflected in the lowest-play and highest-play stories. Typical coverage of environmental justice was a stage 1 (pre-conventional), low-play story. Low-play stories were significantly more likely to include stage 1 rhetoric than medium-play or high-play stories. High-play stories were significantly more likely to include stage 6 rhetoric than other stories, and low-play stories were the least likely to include post-conventional rhetoric. High-play stories also were more likely to include post-conventional rhetoric than conventional rhetoric.

P6 asserted that coverage during the genesis phase of the movement would emphasize pre-conventional industry rhetoric, while mobilization phase coverage would emphasize post-conventional rhetoric. This was supported. The ratio of pre-conventional to post-conventional rhetoric in the genesis phase was 5.28:1, as compared with 2.58:1 for the social unrest phase, and 2.07:1 for the mobilization phase. The genesis phase (1994–1995), which began with Clinton's executive order, accounted for 24.1% of the coverage. The social unrest phase (1996–1998), which started with the Shintech situation, accounted for 36.8%. The mobilization phase (1999–2001) accounted for 28.7% of the stories.

Across all phases, coverage was dominated by pre-conventional rhetoric. However, significant differences in coverage of stages appeared in the genesis phase, when stories were five times as likely to include pre-conventional rhetoric as post-conventional rhetoric. During the social unrest and mobilization phases, stories were more likely to contain post-conventional rhetoric than conventional rhetoric. Conventional rhetoric stories appeared most frequently in the genesis phase, while conventional and post-conventional stories were more likely to appear in the mobilization phase. Coverage of the social unrest phase was characterized by pre-conventional rhetoric about public utilities, while the third and fourth phases were dominated by pre-conventional rhetoric about commercial industries (X^2 (15, $N = 193$) = 42.31, $p < 0.001$).

P7 asserted that stories containing anti-industry or pro-environmental justice stances will contain more pre-conventional industry rhetoric than stories that supported industry or opposed environmental justice advocates. This proposition yielded mixed results. Nearly half (47.5%) of all stories mentioned a pro-environmental justice position. Less than half as many stories (21.3%) mentioned an anti-environmental justice position. While 18.8% of all stories included a pro-industry stance, 64.8% included an anti-industry statement. Nearly one in five stories (19.2%) mentioned benefits of the environmental justice movement, while 80.2% mentioned negative impacts of the movement.

Coverage of pro-industry and anti-environmental justice stances typically highlighted commercial industries and emphasized pre-conventional rhetoric. Coverage of pro-environmental justice and anti-industry stances more often mentioned public utilities and emphasized pre-conventional and conventional rhetoric (X^2 (15, $N = 273) = 36.95$, $p < 0.001$). Both commercial industry and public-utility stories were more likely to cover anti-industry than pro-environmental justice stances, as well as anti-environmental justice over pro-industry stances (X^2 (1, $N = 131) = 12.62$, $p < 0.01$ and X^2 (1, $N = 64) = 13.86$, $p < 0.01$, respectively). However, public-utility stories were more likely than commercial industry stories to include anti-industry and pro-environmental justice stances.

Stories that contained pre-conventional or conventional rhetoric were more likely to mention an anti-industry stance than a pro-industry stance and to mention a pro-environmental justice stance than an anti-environmental justice stance. However, stories that contained post-conventional rhetoric were significantly more likely to mention a pro-industry than anti-industry stance, as well as an anti-environmental justice rather than pro-environmental justice stance. Stories with a pro-industry or anti-environmental justice stance were more likely to include post-conventional rhetoric, while those with an anti-industry stance or pro-environmental justice stance tended to emphasize pre-conventional rhetoric.

Discussion and Future Research

Science communication scholars long have studied how people react to information about technological threats. Conversely, the present study explores how the entities that pose technological threats communicate with people through the media. While past science communication research about public policy has studied the roles that advocacy groups play in science communication, the present study examines the rhetoric that activist targets use in defending their stances, which in turn reflects their roles in the policy process. Past research also has explored the science policy process. To this end, the present study offers insight into how industry decisions mediate public participation in the science policy process. Though little previous research has examined the ethical framing of story sources in science news, the present study addresses this issue.

In the sample used here, stories containing conflict and victimization themes may have contained more pre-conventional rhetoric because they often characterized perceived disenfranchisement among activists. Similarly, coverage of anti-industry bias may have contained pre-conventional rhetoric more often than not because these stories emphasized community conflict. The overall coverage largely favored the environmental justice movement. Industry representatives and government officials were quoted more frequently in post-conventional stories than conventional stories, possibly indicating efforts to compromise or diffuse conflict.

As expected, stories with an anti-industry bias were more likely to contain pre-conventional rhetoric than stories supporting industry or opposing activists. Interestingly, the opposite also was true; stories that contained the highest-level rhetoric (stage 6) were significantly more likely to mention a pro-industry than anti-industry stance, as well as an anti-environmental justice rather than pro-environmental justice stance. Perhaps the stories that were more balanced or that tried to present an alternate viewpoint (i.e., that of the "evil" industries) provided more positive, public relations statements reaching out to the community rather than just defensive statements in a dispute. In other words, the pattern may reflect more about the reporters' intent and questions in covering conflicts than just industry positions on the issues.

Unexpectedly, pre-conventional rhetoric stories received more low play than high play, while post-conventional stories were more likely to receive high play. Discussion of civil rights, social justice issues, and sustainability required more in-depth coverage than regulatory issues.

More than half the facilities mentioned were municipal facilities rather than commercial industries. More than half the coverage included the conflict frame, and these stories typically focused on municipal facilities. Specifically, the coverage of hazardous waste disposal facilities, municipal landfills, and incinerators was primarily characterized by the outrage and dispute frames. It had been assumed that conflict-based stories would receive higher play, as they typically do in general news coverage, and that pre-conventional rhetoric would be pervasive in stories presenting industries as opportunistic. However, it appears that since most disputes were covered on a local level, most stories were short, frequent, and appeared in an inside section, rather than in-depth, occasional, front-page stories.

Pre-conventional industry rhetoric reflected disregard for citizens as vulnerable stakeholders in the siting or policy process. It implied that affected citizens should sacrifice their health and quality of life for the greater good of economic growth. However, post-conventional rhetoric reflected greater willingness to work with citizens and transparently evaluate risks. As predicted, stories containing conflict frames contained more pre-conventional rhetoric, especially when they emphasized victimization.

As predicted, industries reacted differently during times of weaker public pressure than in times of organized protest. Coverage during the genesis phase of the movement may have emphasized pre-conventional rhetoric because advocates lacked a place at the negotiation table and industries thus did not voluntarily try to involve them as stakeholders. Similarly, coverage in the mobilization phase emphasized post-conventional rhetoric more than the other two phases, perhaps because organized protest motivated industries to consider the needs of citizens and future generations.

Pre-conventional rhetoric may have appeared more often in coverage of commercial industries that plan to site a facility in a community than similar coverage of public utilities because a large proportion of the stories discussed the Shintech controversy. Meanwhile, post-conventional rhetoric may have appeared more often in coverage of public utilities that already operate in the community because activists in those situations are also tax-payers with access to more official venues for public protest. Stories about facilities no longer operating in a community may have been characterized by pre-conventional rhetoric partly because these stories were more than twice as likely to mention a Superfund site as other stories. Stories about Superfund sites, heavily contaminated toxic waste sites that have been abandoned, typically focus on clean-ups where the responsible facility could not pay for remediation.

Although African Americans were mentioned four times more frequently than Native Americans, Native Americans appeared in more pre-conventional stories than any other racial group. Most siting disputes involving Native Americans were for municipal facilities, including hazardous waste disposal and landfills, rather than for commercial industries. A prominent and highly charged case was a proposed storage facility for spent nuclear reactor fuel and other radioactive waste, to be sited near Shoshone and Paiute tribes living near their holy lands at Yucca Mountain in Nevada. The site is now slated to begin accepting nuclear waste in 2017.

Several limitations of the study should be considered when interpreting the results. Using moral development theory to classify industry rhetoric does not reveal disguised value judgments, such as greenwashing or other public relations tactics that communicate ideal rather than actual motives. Also, the stories analyzed were drawn systematically from the Lexis-Nexis database, rather than from a random sample of all stories about environmental justice aired or published during the time period. This may reduce the generalizability of the results, but it was assumed that stories in the database would not be qualitatively different than those not in the database.

Moral development analysis can help scholars explore ethical dimensions of science communication content and the ethical context of official responses to public outrage over imposed risks. Future science communication research also might examine the ways in which policy frames in news coverage drives the dynamics and outcomes of environmental conflicts, how different levels of morality are reflected in reactions to risk controversy among claims makers, and how journalists could use moral development theory as a tool to explore the motives of stakeholders, balance the playing field, and promote trust and cooperation in community-level conflicts tied to scientific uncertainty.

More specifically, future research might examine moral development rhetoric in environmental justice conflicts in light of environmental protection rhetoric or compare news framing of environmental justice with the ways that advocates frame their own experiences. Another study might compare the news framing with the content of news releases distributed by industries involved in past disputes, to evaluate news themes that were emphasized or omitted from the company statements. A future study might compare geographic patterns in news coverage of environmental justice in the "Cancer Alley" region with the demographics, geographic concentrations of polluting facilities, and community characteristics, to see if the rhetorical appeals of industry, policy, and advocacy groups are different in news coverage of the most severely impacted communities.

More broadly, this line of research might help journalists examine the motives of their interview sources in a variety of science stories, not necessarily for the purpose of developing story content, but in selecting sources and shaping the framing of the coverage. Without exploring the full range of corporate motives and intentions in light of their promises and social responsibility, journalists may fail to hold the powerful accountable in controversial situations. Evaluating the ethical implications of news source comments could serve as an important tool for scholars and journalists to weigh environmental policy concerns and contextualize competing technical arguments about industrial pollution and waste disposal issues. Future research could explore the ethical dimensions of rhetoric from environmental advocates as well, because these stakeholders should not be let off the hook merely because they are not commercial or government organizations.

Constructivist views about public understanding of science suggest that citizens can articulate sophisticated ideas about ethical dimensions of science policy, regardless of their level of technical knowledge. However, well-informed citizens need more than expert information to grasp science policy issues; they also need tools to sort out trade-offs and moral/ethical issues. Moral development analysis of source rhetoric might help journalists and scholars better understand the nature of ethical issues in a broad range of controversial science stories. Perhaps ethical concerns should be investigated as a key component of public understanding of science, since many science issues are value laden. Evaluating the moral development of rhetoric from all stakeholders in these complex issues, including scientists and policy makers, might ultimately promote more productive public deliberation.

References

Anderton, D. L., Oakes, J. M., & Egan, K. L. (1997). Environmental equity in Superfund: Demographics of the discovery and prioritization of abandoned toxic sites. *Evaluation Review, 21*(1), 3–26.

Beder, S., & Shortland, M. (1992). Siting a hazardous waste facility: The tangled web of risk communication. *Public Understanding of Science, 1*, 139–160.

Benford, R. D., & Snow, D. A. (2000). Framing processes and social movements: An overview and assessment. *Annual Review of Sociology, 26*, 611–639.

Bennett, W. L., Pickard, V. W., Iozzi, D. P., Schroeder, C. L., Lagos, T., & Caswell, C. E. (2004). Managing the public sphere: Journalistic construction of the great globalization debate. *Journal of Communication, 5*(3), 437.

Berry, G. R. (2003). Organizing against multinational corporate power in Cancer Alley: The activist community as primary stakeholder. *Organization & Environment, 16*(1), 3–33.

Blodgett, A. D. (2006). An analysis of pollution and community advocacy in Cancer Alley: Setting an example for the environmental justice movement in St. James Parish, Louisiana. *Local Environment, 11*(6), 647–661.

Bullard, R. D. (1994). *Unequal protection: Environmental justice and communities of color.* San Francisco, CA: Sierra Club Books.

Campbell, R. L., & Christopher, J. C. (1996). Moral development theory: A critique of its Kantian presuppositions. *Developmental Review, 16*(1), 1–47.

Chavis, B. F., & Lee, C. (1987). *Toxic wastes and race in the United States: A national report on the racial and socio-economic character of communities with hazardous waste sites.* New York: Commission for Racial Injustice, United Church of Christ.

De Loë, R. C. (1999). Dam the news: Newspapers and the Oldman River Dam project in Alberta. *Journal of Environmental Management, 55*(4), 219–237.

Depoe, S. (1997). Environmental studies in mass communication. *Critical Studies in Mass Communication, 14*, 368–370.

Dula, A., Kurtz, S., & Samper, M. L. (1993). Occupational and environmental reproductive hazards education and resources for communities of color. *Environmental Health Perspectives, 101*(2), 181–189.

Engel, D., Jaffe, C., & Scherer, C. (1996). *Social and scientific conceptualizations of risk in the mass media.* Paper presented at the Society for Risk Analysis annual meeting.

Entman, R. M. (1993). Framing: Toward clarification of a fractured paradigm. *Journal of Communication, 43*, 51–58.

EPA. (2000). *What is environmental justice?* Washington, DC: U.S. Environmental Protection Agency. Retrieved from http://es.epa.gov/oeca/main/ej/faq.html.

Flynn, J., Slovic, P., & Kunreuther, H. (2001). *Risk, media and stigma: Understanding public challenges to modern science and technology.* London: Earthscan Publications.

Futrell, R. (2003). Framing processes, cognitive liberation, and NIMBY protest in the U.S. chemical-weapons disposal conflict. *Sociological Inquiry, 73*(3), 359–386.

Gamson, W. A., & Modigliani, A. (1989). Media discourse and public opinion on nuclear power: A constructionist approach. *American Journal of Sociology, 95*, 1–37.

Gregory, J., & Miller, S. (2000). *Science in public: Communication, culture, and credibility*. New York: Basic Books.

Heinz, T. L. (2005). From civil rights to environmental rights: Constructions of race, community, and identity in three African American newspapers' coverage of the environmental justice movement. *Journal of Communication Inquiry, 29*(1), 47–65.

Hendry, J. R., & Vesilind, A. P. (2005). Ethical motivations for green business and engineering. *Clean Technologies and Environmental Policy, 7*(4), 252–258.

Hind, R. (2000). George Armstrong lecture 2000. *Pediatrics, 106,* 876–879.

Hoynes, W., & Croteau, D. (1991). The chosen few: Nightline and the politics of public affairs television. *Critical Sociology, 18,* 19–36.

Joseph, P. (2005). Race and poverty are out of the closet. *Sierra, 90*(6), 28–29.

Kenix, L. J. (2005). A comparison of environmental pollution coverage in the mainstream, African American, and other alternative press. *Howard Journal of Communications, 16*(1), 49–70.

Kohlberg, L. (1973). The claim to moral adequacy of a highest stage of moral judgment. *Journal of Philosophy, 70,* 630–646.

Kubal, T. J. (1998). The presentation of political self: Cultural resonance and the construction of collective action frames. *The Sociological Quarterly, 39,* 539–554.

Kuehn, R. R. (1996). *The environmental justice implications of quantitative risk assessment*. Paper presented at the Society for Risk Analysis annual meeting.

Lowrie, K., Greenberg, M., & Waishwell, L. (2000). Hazards, risk and the press: A comparative analysis of newspaper coverage of nuclear and chemical weapons sites. *Risk, 11*(1), 49–68.

Mohai, P., & Saha, R. (2006). Reassessing racial and socioeconomic disparities in environmental justice research. *Demography, 43*(2), 383–399.

Morrison, D. E. (1978). Some notes toward theory on relative deprivation, social movements, and social change. In L. E. Genevie (Ed.), *Collective behavior and social movements* (pp. 202–209). Itasca, IL: Peacock.

Nelkin, D. (1995). *Selling science: How the press covers science and technology*. New York: W. H. Freeman & Co.

Peeples, J. A. (2003). Trashing South Central: Place and identity in a community-level environmental justice dispute. *Southern Communication Journal, 69*(1), 82–95.

Pellow, D. N. (1999). Framing emerging environmental movement tactics: Mobilizing consensus, demobilizing conflict. *Sociological Forum, 14*(4), 659–683.

President of the United States. (1994, February 11). Federal actions to address environmental justice in minority populations and low-income populations. Executive order 12898. *Federal Register, 59*(32).

Rausser, G. C., Simon, L. K., & Zhao, J. (1998). Information asymmetries, uncertainties, and cleanup delays at Superfund sites. *Journal of Environmental Economics and Management, 35*(1), 48–68.

Reath, V. (1994). The media's perspective. *St. John's Journal of Legal Commentary, 9*(2), 531–533.

Reidenbach, R. E., & Robin, D. P. (1991). A conceptual model of corporate moral development. *Journal of Business Ethics, 10*(4), 273–284.

Reese, S. D., Grant, A., & Danelian, L. H. (1994). The structure of news sources:

A network analysis of *CBS News, Nightline, MacNeil/Lehrer,* and *This Week with David Brinkley, Journal of Communication, 44,* 84–107.

Rosenbaum, W. A. (1996). *The influence of cultural "filters" in shaping the media's impact on risk perception: Some preliminary findings from focus group studies at DOE nuclear weapons sites.* Paper presented at the Society for Risk Analysis annual meeting.

Sale, K. (1993). *The green revolution: The American environmental movement, 1962–1992.* New York: Hill and Wang.

Shepard, P. M., Northridge, M. E., Prakash, S., & Stover, G. (2002). Preface: Advancing environmental justice through community-based participatory research. *Environmental Health Perspectives: Supplement 2, 110,* 139–140.

Shibley, M. A., & Prosterman, A. (1998). Silent epidemic, environmental injustice, or exaggerated concern? Competing frames in the media definition of childhood lead poisoning as a public health problem. *Organization & Environment, 11*(1), 33–58.

Sigal, L. V. (1986). Sources make the news. In R. K. Manoff & M. Schudson (Eds.), *Reading the news.* New York: Pantheon Books.

Sjoeberg, L., & Torell, G. (1993). The development of risk acceptance and moral valuation. *Scandinavian Journal of Psychology, 34*(3), 223–236.

Spitzeck, H. (2005). *Society's case for corporate responsibility.* Paper submitted to the EURAM 2005 Pre-Conference Event, Munich.

Spitzer, H. (2000). Shooting the movement. *Alternatives Journal, 26*(4), 39.

Stewart, C. J., Smith, C. A., & Denton, R. E. (1989). *Persuasion and social movements.* Prospect Heights, IL: Waveland Press.

Szasz, A., & Meuser, M. (2000). Unintended, inexorable: The production of environmental inequalities in Santa Clara County, California. *American Behavioral Scientist, 43*(4), 602–632.

Temple, J. Z., & Musham, C. (1996). *Risk perception assessment from an environmental justice perspective.* Paper presented at the Society for Risk Analysis annual meeting.

Tilly, C. (1978). *From mobilization to revolution.* Reading, MA: Addison-Wesley.

Torres, G. (1996). The future of environmental regulation: Environmental justice— The legal meaning of a social movement. *Journal of Law and Commerce, 15,* 597.

University of Michigan. (1999). *Environmental justice case study: Shintech PVC plant in Convent, Louisiana. University of Michigan Environmental Justice Initiative.* Retrieved from www.umich.edu/~snre492/shin.html#Background.

Weinberg, A. S. (1998). The environmental justice debate: A commentary on methodological issues and practical concerns. *Sociological Forum, 13*(1), 25–32.

Williams, B. L., Brown, S., Greenberg, M., & Kahn, M. A. (1999). Risk perception in context: The Savannah River site stakeholder study. *Risk Analysis, 19*(6), 1019–1035.

Woodruff, T. J., Axelrad, D. A., Caldwell, J., Morello-Frosch, R., & Rosenbaum, A. (1998). Public health implications of 1990 air toxics concentrations across the United States. *Environmental Health Perspectives, 106*(5), 245–251.

Zwetkoff, C. (1998). Mediation in environmental conflicts: The Belgian methodology. *9 Risk: Health, Safety & Environment,* 361–377.

Part III

The Future

Chapter 10

An Interdisciplinary Approach to Science Communication Education

A Case Study

Amy R. Pearce, Aldemaro Romero, and John B. Zibluk

In January 2007, Alan Leshner, chief executive officer of *Science* magazine issued a call for increased communication training for graduate students of science. Only two months later, the U.S. House of Representatives considered the Scientific Communications Act (HR 1453), a bill to request funding from the National Science Foundation to support communication training for future scientists (GovTrack.us, 2007). Although HR 1453 did not pass, these calls to action underscore recognition of the need for more serious attention to science communication education.

Academic programs that focus on science communication do exist at the university level; a directory published by the University of Wisconsin, home to one of the oldest science communications programs in the United States, lists 47 universities nationwide that offer programs and/or courses for students interested in science communication (University of Wisconsin, n.d.). However, only five of those universities offer communication courses that are housed within or explicitly affiliated with science programs. The programs offered at the remaining 42 universities are typically housed within communications or journalism departments and programs, although a sampling of course offerings and scholarship can also be found across a range of other disciplines. For example, technical writing might be taught in engineering or English departments, science writing might be taught in journalism or political science departments, and so forth. The program tree presented in Figure 10.1 reflects the taxonomy of science communication programs listed on the University of Wisconsin–Madison *Directory of Science Communication Courses and Programs*.

To meet the demand for science communication education, some science programs—like the program at Arkansas State University, Jonesboro—have begun to develop communications curricula within their own courses and departments. Yet, offering communication education under the auspices of a science program can be a formidable challenge. For example, scientists who venture out of the classroom, laboratory or field to work with the media (or who become employed by media outlets) may lack sufficient media training to understand the adversarial role of the free press (Cooke,

English
Technical writing

Health, nursing
Health communication

Speech
Health communication

Political science
Science grant writing

Business
Risk management
technology marketing

Journalism
Health communication
science writing, reporting

Science
Working with media
Academic presentations

All science communication programs

Figure 10.1 Taxonomy of Science Communication Programs Listed on the University of Wisconsin–Madison *Directory of Science Communication Courses and Programs.*

2007). They may also lack an understanding of the responsibility of the media to the public and the media's function as "watchdog" via criticism and oversight of major institutions (Benn, 1979). And they may have a limited understanding of what makes a story newsworthy. As a result, science writers trained in a science program may face unanticipated consequences and reactions to their work.

At the same time, however, science communication courses offered by traditional journalism departments may fail to meet the exacting and varied technical demands of the scientific community. Although some flagship institutions like the University of Wisconsin may be able to offer a broad set of courses and programs that allow for specialization ranging from risk management for financial managers to training in the hard sciences for journalists, science communication courses and programs nested in journalism departments at smaller academic institutions face challenges posed by the constraints of more limited course offerings and budgetary confines. Given those constraints, it can be difficult to offer students a broad array of communication training that prepares them to meet the demands of the scientific community.

In this chapter, an argument is made for the creation of more interdisciplinary science communication programs. Such programs allow for a pooling of resources, and can draw from the expertise of both trained science and journalism/communication educators. The result, it is argued here, is an educational model that is accessible to upstart science communication programs at smaller universities and that better poises educators to help students overcome the aforementioned challenges that surface when training occurs within the confines of only one discipline. A case study illustrating a science communication curriculum taught at Arkansas State University, Jonesboro is presented, along with reflections on how this curriculum can serve as a model for developing and delivering interdisciplinary science communication courses at other universities.

The Paradigm Problem

In science communication, the need for effective communication strategies is particularly crucial. The communicator, whether scientist or journalist, often must translate highly technical information to language that a less-specialized audience can understand. However, when a communicator alters specific terminology to produce understandable content for a general audience, the changes may not accurately convey the original information. And yet, if that information is presented using the exact terminology of the scientists, the message may be so nuanced and complex that it cannot be understood or appreciated by the general audience; general audience members often lack an understanding of terms commonly found in scientific or academic research. This creates a delicate balancing act for the communicator who, in order to be effective, must be true to the science, but also write for optimum reader accessibility.

The task of communicating science is made more difficult because, as alluded to above (and as covered in several of the earlier chapters in this book), journalists and scientists tend to approach science communication from different perspectives. For example, journalism practitioners place a high priority on developing stories that are newsworthy and that meet the needs and tastes of an often diverse mass audience (Russell, 2008). Thus, journalists may freely question, criticize, rewrite, and reinterpret scientific research programs or studies. They also may question or criticize the motives, backgrounds, or funding sources of scientists whose work they are covering.

Scientists, on the other hand, may regard science communication in terms of public relations (Russ-Mohl, 2007) or public education (Bhattacharjee, 2006; Gropp, 2006). In terms of public relations, scientists might perceive the media as a tool for bolstering public support for their institutions or their personal research agendas. Or they may attempt to influence public opinion on policy issues that impact their research agendas, such as intelligent design or embryonic stem-cell research. Public education, on the other hand, may have persuasive elements but tends to focus more on building public knowledge—and the media are often the chosen conduit for this task. Yet a scientist without formal training in journalism may think that all scientific work is of interest to the public simply because it is of interest to science. This is not necessarily the case. Proper training in communication can help scientists better understand how to overcome potential obstacles to media and public interest.

In addition to the challenges inherent with balancing the needs of communicators and scientists, each situation and each institution has its unique issues, opportunities, and challenges. Indeed, the challenge of developing curriculum to prepare future scientists to communicate effectively with a range of different audiences is further complicated by the inherent differences among institutions of higher education: public versus private; postgraduate education versus 4-year baccalaureate institutions; primarily educational versus research-intensive institutions, etc. According to Sharon Dunwoody, who has taught science communication at the University of Wisconsin for more than 20 years, when it comes to developing science communication courses and programs, "there is no one-size-fits-all model out there … There are many different needs" (personal communication, October 24, 2007). In other words, no one science communication course can meet the varied list of challenges outlined above. However, any attempt to develop an effective science communication course that meets even a handful of those challenges will certainly be more effective when different perspectives and disciplines are recognized.

Such a collaborative effort is under way at Arkansas State University, Jonesboro, where researchers from three different academic disciplines and diverse backgrounds have worked together over a span of 3 years to design and implement a science communication curriculum using an interdisciplinary approach. The following case study details that effort. However, before presenting the details of the case, the following section reviews the related literature and serves as a framework for the case study.

The Interdisciplinary Approach: A Brief Literature Review

Given the inherently different perspectives underlying many science communication endeavors, any participant—whether teacher, student, scientist, communicator, or audience member—can benefit from an improved understanding of the different points of view he or she encounters. As a result, an interdisciplinary approach involving instruction by multiple faculty across different relevant academic disciplines, including science and journalism, is particularly appropriate to science communication. This approach is underscored by de Semir (2000):

Since most of public knowledge is derived from mass media, it is easy to see why the general public tends to be poorly informed about scientific issues. The reporting of science news via the mass media is anything but easy, but it is becoming increasingly important. Fortunately, both journalists and researchers are realizing that their fields are becoming increasingly intertwined, and are exploring new ways to work together. The evolution of this partnership is likely to be fruitful.

(p. 128)

An interdisciplinary approach is especially important in the development of education policy and curriculum related to scientific issues that cross several subject areas. Saito and colleagues (2007) summarized the results of a conference dedicated to developing multidisciplinary approaches to studying and teaching aquatic ecology models. They reported that there is a consensus among scientists and educators that "the solution to environmental problems require interdisciplinary approaches" (2007, p. 48). For example, when addressing related issues in hydrology, it is necessary to draw upon chemistry, physics, geology, and even the social sciences, and to consider perspectives and information from all those areas. Yet, as indicated earlier in the chapter, no existing science communication courses or programs appear to explicitly use such an interdisciplinary approach. This limitation is illustrated in Saito et al.'s closing, which says that although there is a need for interdisciplinary collaboration, "environmental scientists are often still trained in a disciplinary fashion" (2007, p. 48).

In support of the interdisciplinary approach to education more generally, McClure (2007) notes, "Interdisciplinary studies, the thinking goes, will better equip students to solve problems creatively and to deal with increasing complexity" (p. 70). Drake and Burns (2004) concur that an interdisciplinary approach facilitates creative teaching and the time is right for integrating curricula.

While there is an increasing demand for science communication education, the field of communication itself is going through rapid change—and traditional approaches to communication education are changing as well. In *The Scientist*, Nisbet and Scheufele (2007) challenge traditional science communication. They state that for too long, scientists have embraced the media-centric "popular science model," which puts the news media in charge of educating the public about science that is controversial such as embryonic stem-cell research. Nisbet and Scheufele (2007) argue that in the world of MySpace and YouTube, audiences eschew traditional media and seek their own sources of information.

If audiences seek varied new media sources for their information, science communication educators must also address those trends within their courses. Ways must be found to incorporate new teaching material into existing courses, while balancing the need to continue to teach more traditional material as well. Science journalism may be found on the Web on blogs, multimedia presentations and even as YouTube videos. Science communicators—or any professionals dealing with modern media—need to be conversant with multiple technologies while maintaining a grounding in critical thinking, concise writing, and journalism laws and ethics.

As the media undergo rapid change, the inherent flexibility of the inter-disciplinary approach can be a good way to address science communica-tion across an array of channels, including online, broadcast, speech, print, and other forms of message delivery. Faculty from the sciences bring their background and knowledge of their subject to the seminar table, and com-munications faculty bring their familiarity with the ever-changing media. Faculty members with both scientific and media expertise are rare at best, but most universities may achieve the necessary expertise to address the needs of science communication by using several faculty members. More-over, the different perspectives offered by different faculty members can only bring more information and ideas to a class than the knowledge base of individual faculty members. Further, students need help finding and developing their own voice and interaction with different faculty through interdisciplinary teaching provides them with concurrent exposure to varied communication styles on the same subject matter.

However, use of an interdisciplinary approach is not free from chal-lenges. In an economic climate of declining financial resources for universi-ties, supporters of the interdisciplinary approach may face increasing political opposition to instructional methodology that requires a more intensive commitment of time and personnel than a standard laboratory-lecture teaching method. There are also pedagogical consequences, includ-ing potential disagreements between science and communication educators over structural issues like course content, assignments, the nature and format of faculty and student presentations, grading, and other issues.

Additional caveats are offered by documentation of attempts at integrat-ing interdisciplinary work in the K–12 curriculum, experiences nonetheless relevant at institutions of higher learning. For instance, implementing inte-grated curriculum takes time as instructors choose their content, gather resources, discuss course assignments, consider student learning needs, and coordinate their schedules (Lake, 1994). Considerations should also be made by involved faculty to avoid the potential pitfalls of introducing inappropri-ate or ineffective interdisciplinary approaches (McClure, 2007). Although many of these problems can be overcome with ample planning, integration should not be forced if the mix of disciplines results in irrelevant course activities and inappropriate content delivery (Lonning & DeFranco, 1997).

Complicating the demands even further, as Nisbet and Scheufele (2007) argue, there is an increasing need in science communication to partner with audiences (also see Brossard & Lewenstein, Chapter 1, and Nisbet,

Chapter 2, this volume). Fuller (2002) makes a similar assertion, arguing that journalists, scientists, and the general public should work together to create a forum for feedback and to enter into dialogue. Fuller (2002) takes the argument one step further, asserting that the field of science communication should build trust and rapport with people so that people not only become more involved in the issues, but also begin to see science as an accessible, viable career path.

Given these varied perspectives, an interdisciplinary approach to teaching science communication was deemed appealing to and beneficial for Arkansas State University, Jonesboro students—particularly students who were involved in two or more disciplines combining natural sciences, social sciences, and/or the humanities. At the same time, it was reasoned that the resulting course projects (such as packaged news stories), if properly publicized via media outlets, could create opportunities for the university to educate various audiences, stimulate interest in science, encourage dialogue on science issues among the general public, and make the public more familiar with the work being done at the university.

A Brief History of Interdisciplinary Science Communication at Arkansas State University

Established in 1909 as a state agricultural school, today Arkansas State University (ASU) in Jonesboro is characterized as a quality regional institution of higher education and is recognized for offering special services to the people of the Arkansas Delta, an area of the state that is characterized as agricultural and poverty stricken. Enrollment at the university is approximately 10,000 undergraduate and 1,500 graduate students in programs at the doctoral, specialist, master's, bachelor's, and associate degree levels.

As a result of the Tobacco Settlement Proceeds Act of 2000, ASU, as well as an additional four Arkansas campuses and a medical school, received substantial funding to plan and build major bioscience facilities throughout the state; the result is the collaborative Arkansas Biosciences Institute (ABI). The ASU–ABI provided the catalyst for unprecedented research initiatives in agriculture, bioengineering, tobacco-related illnesses, nutrition, and complementary fields. A major research facility was constructed on the ASU campus and a national and international call for scientists attracted diverse and skilled researchers, professors, and graduate students to this region of Northeast Arkansas.

Two of the authors, John B. Zibluk, an associate professor of journalism, and Amy R. Pearce, an associate professor of psychology conducting research at ABI who also had graduate training in science communication, began developing a communication course. The third author, Aldemaro Romero, then chair of the ASU Department of Biological Sciences, later became a participant as a frequent guest speaker.

The intent of the course was to inspire students from various disciplines to explore the possibilities of new research initiatives and to communicate ABI and other university research outcomes with a wider, more general audience. At the time, problems not uncommon to many small colleges and state campuses arose. Little support was offered for team-teaching throughout the university and seemingly insurmountable issues arose about exactly how to handle faculty compensation and teaching loads that were shared between colleges and departments. For these reasons, the journalism faculty member was the teacher of record and the course was not cross-listed among other academic fields. The course was offered in the fall semester of 2005 and incorporated a fairly standard model of a science communication course, inspired by a similar course taught at Johns Hopkins University (course details follow).

This undergraduate course, "JOUR: Science Communication," was offered through the Honors College and the Department of Journalism in order to attract qualified students as well as expose the students to a field of prospective graduate study. The course attracted 10 students, mostly from the social sciences. The honors course featured a general overview of various media and required students to "translate" information from scientific journals and other sources into scripts and stories suitable for media presentations. As a final project, students were required to present a media plan, which included identifying audiences, budgets and facilities considerations, and developing appropriate media presentations tailored to various audiences.

While the course was generally successful, it failed to attract the interest of science students. Originally, the instructors intended to require students to take their own research and prepare it for media presentation, but since the majority of the class members were not involved in any research, much less their own, the students did not have a great personal stake in this work.

Meanwhile, over a few years ABI had grown and many affiliated research faculty and their graduate students were developing connections in the region. The ASU central administration asked constituencies to focus efforts and resources in order to cooperate with new campus-wide science research and other interdisciplinary projects.

The Department of Biological Sciences began exploring ways to work with the media in order to bolster public understanding of projects under way at ABI as well as some projects of the department's own initiative. The department began encouraging students and faculty to write for newspapers. They did so intermittently, and in order to better organize outreach efforts, the department in 2005 entered into an agreement with the local newspaper, the *Jonesboro Sun*, to publish weekly articles produced by faculty and students. The challenge was to tailor these scientific messages into newsworthy and educational stories that were suitable for a general lay audience. To address this need, in 2006 Pearce and Romero extended the science communication curriculum further by offering a half-day science communication training workshop for both faculty and graduate students in the sciences. The workshop focused on two components: (a) an overview of the need for science communication in the community and (b) advice on the practice of science communication.

Products of the workshop were a series of print articles written by participants that focused on the science that was being produced at the university. With the help of the workshop, participants conveyed their own research (or research in their fields) in a format and language suitable for the general public and ready for publication in the local newspaper. Upon review of the workshop evaluations and informal oral feedback, the venture was deemed a success. Graduate students and faculty in the sciences soon requested that a formal course on writing for the general public and for public presentations be offered.

The following year, the biology department launched a radio show, "Science in the Natural State," produced in cooperation with the school's National Public Radio outlet. Each week, the radio show presented a short documentary on projects and issues involving ASU faculty and staff. At about the same time, Romero began producing short videos promoting the department's effort that were presented on two local television stations (ASU-TV and KAIT), and posted on the department's website and YouTube representing the majority of the university's viral video presence. An archive of articles, radio shows, and TV shows are posted on the website of the Department of Biological Sciences at http://biology.astate. edu/Outreach/outreach.htm and continue to be distributed for free by the ASU Public Relations Office to about 50 media outlets nationwide.

The need for professionalizing the approach was soon realized. With established outlets for their work, current faculty and students saw the opportunity to immediately see their broadcasting and writing efforts in print, on the air, and online. Yet, scientists, or those in training, were not always the best of communicators. It became apparent that an additional means was needed to generate stories to meet the practical need of providing stories to the media outlets as well as providing contributors the opportunity of controlled media exposure while continuing to generate sustained interest in the overall endeavor.

Given the infrastructure of established media outlets, and given the interest and need for scientists and science students to be able to navigate the media environment, the biology department was well suited to carry out a more formal science communication initiative.

In the spring of 2007, Romero revisited the recommendation to offer a semester-long science communication course, this time with focus on graduate students in the sciences. Romero teamed up with Pearce and Zibluk, and also consulted with the chair of the graduate program in environmental sciences, to develop a science communication course cross-listed through biology and environmental sciences (Romero, Pearce, & Zibluk, 2007). In addition to training scientists to better communicate with the public and the media, the course sought to fulfill three additional objectives: (1) to publicize the activities of the faculty and students in the host department—the Department of Biological Sciences, (2) to increase the profile of the department and thus enhance student recruitment and extramural funding efforts, and (3) to improve the morale of faculty and students within the department to enhance the working environment.

Romero submitted a graduate course proposal for "Science Communication for Scientists." To offer a variety of perspectives, Pearce and Zibluk would co-teach the course with him. Pearce offered expertise as a neuroscientist, science workshop organizer for educators, youth, and the lay public, and former producer of a science radio show, and Zibluk, a former National Geographic magazine faculty fellow, offered print journalism background as well as a grounding in general journalism philosophies and practices as well as insights into legal and ethical issues. (The course syllabus can be read at: www.clt.astate.edu/aromero/new_page_173.htm.)

Of the eight students who signed up for the course, one was an undergraduate and three were international graduate students representing Japan, India, and Costa Rica. When asked their reasons for taking the course, American students expressed an interest in developing their communication skills and working with various media formats. Conversations with the international students revealed their desire to improve their ability to communicate their own research in English as well as a desire to develop rapport with their research colleagues in the United States and to use any new communication skills to benefit the general public in their home countries.

The course was offered for the first time in the fall semester of 2007. The approach to the course was mostly in the form of introductory lectures or skill-development sessions followed by hands-on exercises. Students were taught the basics of science communication aimed at the general public via different media including basic techniques of radio and TV production such as recording, videotaping and editing. The textbook adopted was *A Scientist's Guide to Talking with the Media: Tips and Tools Scientists Can Use to Communicate Complex Research to a Media Audience* by Hayes and Grossman (2006). Harrower's *Inside Reporting*, (2007), a comprehensive journalism textbook, was also used extensively. After the introduction to techniques, students were then required to take their own research and present it in the various formats. They wrote news stories and press releases and developed radio and television scripts and storyboards. Each student also produced a radio program on his or her subject and created a 30-second video suitable for airing on the university and local television stations, as well as on YouTube. The students also were taught how to make presentations about their research to the general public. To that end they were asked to give the same presentation at the start and at the conclusion of the course, in order to compare their evolution as public presenters. Their presentations were videotaped and their performance was reviewed for strengths and weaknesses in areas ranging from clarity of content to body language.

The students' performance in the course was also evaluated using faculty consensus based on the quality of the products generated by the students. In addition, the instructors individually critiqued each project, with each instructor paying particular attention to student work in his or her own area of expertise. To engage the students in the critiquing process, constructive peer evaluation was practiced regularly during class discussions.

The expected student-related outcomes for this course were that students would become better communicators in terms of relaying their research to external audiences and the media, and that they would know how to approach different media formats and how to take on the role of science advocate in the media and community. Anecdotal comments early in the semester suggested that students were very excited about the skills they were learning. As the course progressed, students were impressed by the fact that their articles and radio and TV shows were being published and/or broadcast while the course was still being offered. Formal end-of-course evaluations revealed students believed the approach had increased their motivation to engage in science communication and had expanded their knowledge of and interest in the field. Students also considered the material and techniques intellectually challenging and useful. Suggestions to improve the course included using a website to facilitate course instruction and to better coordinate instructor feedback. While students did not rate the required text and readings as particularly helpful in relation to course activities, all eight students gave the highest rating to the evaluation statement "overall this was a great course." Based on the anecdotal comments and quantitative and written evaluations, it was agreed that the science communication students had a new-found appreciation for the media and for their own previously untapped abilities to influence people's understanding of science through the media.

The science communication course and related media products have been commended by university faculty and the administration. Responses from readers, listeners, and viewers have been unprecedented. This multi-faceted approach worked for ASU and particularly for its host department in Biological Sciences not only as a science communication strategy, but also as a national recruiting tool. Such promotional and educational efforts publicized current courses and research projects in which faculty and students were engaged. According to Romero, student recruitment in both undergraduate and graduate programs increased and results from recent surveys suggested that many new students decided to attend ASU after watching the Biology videos on YouTube. Additionally, because all products were freely available on the Internet, feedback has come from audiences as far away as The Netherlands. To date, a steady stream of faculty and students volunteer to write articles for the newspaper, give radio interviews, and produce videos, and science-related community outreach activities have increased. Support for the ASU Science Communication initiative currently under development is strong.

The Arkansas State University Model of Science Communication

Our experiences with team-taught interdisciplinary science communication courses, related training workshops, and continuing public outreach initiatives have been overwhelmingly positive. In 2008 our concerted efforts were recognized by the Coalition for the Public Understanding of Science (COPUS). COPUS is a national grassroots coalition intended to promote public understanding of the nature and societal value of science. The coalition links major universities, scientific societies including the American Institute of Biological Sciences, science centers and museums, government agencies including the National Science Foundation, advocacy groups, media, educators, and industry (Coalition for the Public Understanding of Science, n.d.). COPUS cited the publication of weekly articles by ASU science faculty members as exemplary outreach activity.

After 3 years of examining various programs, discussions with journalists and scientists, and the trial-and-error experience undertaken at ASU, the following tenets for developing science communication education are recommended (also see Table 10.1). These tenets are particularly relevant to universities or programs that are starting a science communication emphasis from scratch.

- Assess the individual needs of the program, including student needs and the nature of the market. For example, if a given department or university is engaged in a health-oriented initiative, tailor your program to that need.
- Assess the available personnel and faculty. Engage faculty from various departments in discussions about course development and adjust the curriculum to match the expertise of the faculty involved in the program.
- Consult the pedagogical literature for theoretical guidance and consider ways to incorporate some of the most accepted communication theories into the program.
- Keep administration (at the department level and higher) abreast of your efforts and aware of deliverables that will serve the university and the larger community.

Table 10.1 Recommendations and Considerations for Offering an Interdisciplinary Science Communication Course

1.	Examine what others are doing and find a model that works for your students, faculty and university.
2.	Involve people from multiple disciplines across your college, university, or community in both the planning and execution stages.*
3.	Decide early on what your course goals are and any products that should result from the course. Is this course specifically for training future science communicators? A graduate recruiting tool?
4.	Negotiate course content, teaching styles, course schedules, activities, and assignments with the participating faculty and appoint one person as the primary course facilitator.
5.	Determine what resources are available for use. These include both personnel and equipment resources. Examine your budget and consider ways to offset costs of expensive items such as cameras or software.
6.	Know your target audience for the course, are they students in the sciences, communication or journalism majors, graduate or undergraduate students, or a mixture.
7.	Arrange to visit media outlets such as radio stations, television stations, and newspaper headquarters. Invite reporters, producers, announcers to visit the classroom as well.*
8.	Gain hands-on experience by writing news releases, articles, radio shows, video segments, webpages, giving oral presentations, or creating science blogs.*
9.	Direct students to a wide-ranging body of resources from which to explore. Provide both exemplary and nonexemplary samples. (We used many sites from NPR, New York Times, YouTube and local radio, television and news outlets.)
10.	Develop a supportive relationship with media outlets. Are they willing to support a special student series?
11.	Allow regular opportunities in the classroom for constructive feedback from both the instructors and student peers.
12.	Embrace different perspectives brought to the experience by the journalists and scientists.
13.	Evaluate your course, the effectiveness of course products, student perceptions, and the understanding and appreciation of your efforts by the general public.
14.	Remain flexible and have fun.

Note
* We were already practicing such when we discovered Warren, Weiss, Wolfe, Friedlander, and Lewenstein, (2007).

- Involve the university's public outreach and public relations personnel.
- Engage students in work in which they are already involved. Require them to take their own work to different audiences and different media. If students are discussing their own work, they are more likely to be engaged and enthusiastic.
- Take the same projects across several media outlets. The repetition of material increases the understanding of the similarities of basic media outlets and keeps students focused.
- Have students present their work to the class and faculty. Encourage faculty and students to discuss and critique. The seminar approach encourages participation and decreases anxiety as students discover they are all facing similar issues.
- Ensure students actually produce products—articles, videos, scripts— that can be presented in media outlets. Local media outlets continually search for local material to present and students tend to be motivated when they know their work is taken seriously and professionally.
- Coordinate course assignments and exams through one instructor to limit variability in assessment criteria and to help provide consistent expectations for students.
- Participating instructors should remain in regular contact with one another to discuss challenges, criteria for course assignments, and how the integrations of differing perspectives can be managed to avoid personal conflict among students and faculty.

The interdisciplinary approach implemented at ASU is flexible and it encourages participation of students and faculty, while also providing practical experience for students. The different academic programs involved in the class benefit from increased exposure to students as well as the general public. The interdisciplinary approach followed at ASU allowed individual faculty members to concentrate on their personal strengths and afforded them the opportunity to defer to colleagues if they needed to miss an occasional class due to other obligations at the university, such as the demands of field research, etc. Benefits to co-teaching also included offering broad perspectives and varied expertise. Furthermore, the synergies experienced via this interdisciplinary approach (and the external praise it garnered) offered an enticing framework for campus-wide consideration of integrative teaching and learning initiatives. The tangible contributions in the form of publicized course products raised the profile of students, faculty, and university programs within the community and the state, and provided evidence for garnering future external funding.

However, the interdisciplinary approach undertaken at ASU is not without some limitations. For example, the broad overview of many media outlets precluded an in-depth exploration of any one outlet. Additionally, the hands-on emphasis does offer challenges for covering theoretical, ethical, and legal units, and also requires a major time commitment of faculty and students. Thus, our pragmatic approach prevented a substantial emphasis on communication theory, coverage of which could have helped ensure that communicators-in-training were able to model their outreach techniques on well-established models for mass communication. Furthermore, while each class needs to be small to be effective, undersized, homogenous classes may exclude more diverse groups of students from other areas of the campus who could add vigor to the course. Finally, when faced with budgetary constraints, low student-teacher ratio may be politically controversial.

The Future of Interdisciplinary Science Communication at ASU

To sustain the science communication efforts at ASU, the support network for the program needs to be expanded. Administrators must be convinced that modern and innovative communication agendas involve science, and that an interdisciplinary model has much to offer all affiliated parties. A better understanding of the benefits derived from an interdisciplinary approach to science communication education will provide stability from which to expand programs and guarantee the necessary opportunities and funding for long-term success.

At ASU, further promotion of science communication will need to include additional undergraduate and graduate courses (including communication theory). A longer-term vision is that these courses will contribute to a minor or degree program eventually to be housed under the auspices of an interdisciplinary Center for Science Communication. In the meantime, the development and enhancement of the interdisciplinary science communication network will be continued and current collaboration with biology, environmental sciences, chemistry, and biosciences will be extended to include other disciplines such as math, psychology, health, and nursing.

The future also includes strengthening regional partnerships among private and academic sectors through volunteer outreach activities, promotional events and media publications. Furthermore, both faculty and students will increase collaborations with other state institutions and established organizations such as the National Association of Science Writers and the American Association for the Advancement Science.

These future directions will provide an exemplary experiential laboratory for students to learn and practice science communication, maintain its interdisciplinary spirit and foster collaborations within and among other learning institutions, all the while raising awareness of important work being conducted at ASU-ABI within the community and beyond.

Conclusions

The interdisciplinary approach to science communication is prudent and reasonable given the interdisciplinary nature of modern science and modern communication. A next essential step in professionalizing this growing field is to assess the effectiveness of individual science communication courses and programs. To date, there is a paucity of published literature in this area.

One recent case study (Markowitz & DuPré, 2007) provided biomedical students with practical teaching and communication skills in an effort to better relate scientific content and improve the students' teaching abilities. The hope for that program is that scientists trained in the theory, principles, and concepts of science education will develop communication skills to employ throughout their careers. Evaluations of the course projects, classroom discussions, online reflections, and written surveys all suggested that the course was effective in improving communication and teaching strategies. A similar case study (Moni, Hryciw, Poronnik, & Moni, 2007) reported improvements in how bioscience students write for the lay public after instruction in the explicit teaching of science concepts. This study's particular strength lay in surveys employed to gauge perceptions of student writing quality among both students and the general public.

Although it remains difficult to evaluate the needs of an ever-changing market, for science communication to truly become professionalized as a field, it is important to know how the public is responding to efforts by scientists to connect and engage potential supporters. Therefore, a broad-based evaluation plan is needed to qualitatively and quantitatively analyze current efforts and provide ideas on improving the dissemination and understanding of scientific advances. Program evaluation can also provide evidence to strengthen solicitation of external funding from sources such as the National Science Foundation, a crucial step for continued support and expansion of programs.

The interdisciplinary approach offers a bridge over these potential problems. If scientists better understand the media and their potential audiences, they can better use the media as partners in reaching their communities and their audiences with newsworthy information that can foster support and understanding of science. At a time when federal agencies and private foundations are encouraging better science communication, it is both pedagogically and practically sound to engage colleagues who have science and communication expertise to help the effort to involve as many constituencies as possible.

Acknowledgments

We thank the ASU Departments of Journalism, Psychology and Counseling, and Biological Sciences, and the Graduate Program in Environmental Sciences for supporting the team-taught, cross-listed course "Science Communication for Scientists." We thank Dr. Sharon Dunwoody for her valuable insights into the teaching of science communication, Drs. LeeAnn Kahlor and Pat Stout for their helpful comments to improve the manuscript and the conference team of New Agendas in Science Communication.

References

Arkansas State University Department of Biological Sciences Public Outreach website. (n.d.). Retrieved April 24, 2008, from http://biology.astate.edu/Outreach/outreach.htm.

Benn, W. A. (1979). The democratic control of science and technology. *Science, Technology and Human Values, 4*, 17–26.

Bhattacharjee, Y. (2006, November 17). Scientists get out the word. *Science, 314*(5802), 1063.

Coalition on the Public Understanding of Science. (n.d.). Retrieved April 25, 2008, from www.copusproject.org.

Cooke, J. B. (2007). *Freedom of the press from the American Revolution to the War on Terrorism.* New York: Palgrave Macmillan.

de Semir, V. (2000). Scientific journalism: Problems and perspectives. *International Microbiology, 3*, 125–128.

Drake, S., & Burns, D. (2004). *Meeting standards through integrated curriculum.* Alexandria, VA: Association for Supervision and Curriculum Development.

Fuller, S. (2002, April 4). Communication should not be left to scientists. *Nature, 416*, 475.

Gropp, R. (2006, February). Teaching the public about science. *Bioscience, 56*(2), 91.

Harrower, T. (2007). *Inside reporting: A practical guide to the craft of journalism.* New York: McGraw Hill.

Hayes, R., & Grossman, D. (2006). *A scientist's guide to talking with the media: Tips and tools scientists can use to communicate complex research to a media audience.* New Brunswick, NJ: Rutgers University Press.

Lake, K. (1994). Integrated curriculum. *Northwest Regional Educational Laboratory.* Retrieved January 7, 2009, from www.nwrel.org/scpd/sirs/8/c016.html.

Leshner, A. I. (2007, January 12). Outreach training needed. *Science, 315*(5809), 161.

Lonning, R. A., & DeFranco, T. C. (1997). Integration of math and science: A theoretical model. *School Science and Mathematics, 97*(4), 212–215.

Markowitz, D. G., & DuPré, M. J. (2007). Graduate experience in science education: The development of a science education course for biomedical graduate students. *Life Sciences Education, 6*, 233–242.

McClure, C. T. (2007, October). Linking the disciplines and achievement. *District*

Administration, 70–71. Retrieved November 11, 2007, from www.districtad-ministration.com/ViewArticle.aspx?articleid=1348.

Moni, R. W., Hryciw, D. H., Poronnik, P., & Moni, K. B. (2007). Using explicit teaching to improve how bioscience students write to the lay public. *Advances in Physiology Education, 31*, 167–175.

Nisbet, M. C., & Scheufele, D. A. (2007, October 1). The future of public engagement. *The Scientist, Article 4*. Retrieved November 18, 2007, from www.the-scientist.com/article/display/53611.

Romero, A., Pearce, A. R., & Zibluk, J. B. (2007, June 3). ASU course will teach scientists how to communicate their ideas. *Jonesboro Sun*, pp. A8, A9. Retrieved from http://biology.astate.edu/Outreach/ASUintheNews/100.ScienceComm.pdf.

Russell, C. (2008, November). Science reporting by press release: An old problem grows worse in the digital age. *Columbia Journalism Review*. Retrieved January 5, 2009, from www.cjr.org/the_observatory/science_reporting_by_press_rel.php?page=2.

Russ-Mohl, S. (2007, October). Science journalism with a spin. *European Journalism Observatory*. Retrieved January 5, 2009, from www.ejo.ch/index.php?option=com_content&task=view&id=1077&Itemid=140.

Saito, L. S., Segale, H. M., DeAngelis, D. L., & Jenkins, S. H. (2007). Developing an interdisciplinary curriculum for aquatic-ecosystem modeling. *Journal of College Science Teaching, 37*(2), 46–52.

Scientific Communications Act of 2007. (2007). Retrieved January 5, 2009, from www.govtrack.us/congress/bill.xpd?bill=h110-1453.

University of Wisconsin–Madison. (n.d.). *Directory of science communication courses and programs*. Retrieved November 19, 2007, from www.journalism.wisc.edu/dsc/allEntries.php.

Warren, D. R., Weiss, M. S., Wolfe, D. W., Friedlander, B., & Lewenstein, B. (2007, May 25). Lessons from science communication training. *Science, 316*, 1122.

Contributors

John C. Besley (Ph.D., Cornell University) is an Assistant Professor in the Electronic and Print Journalism Sequence at the University of South Carolina. Dr. Besley's research explores the relationships between media use, citizen engagement, and risk perceptions. He is particularly interested in how news and entertainment content—whether in newspapers, on television, or online—frame scientific risk and the impact of this framing on attitudes toward new technologies, health beliefs, and scientific authorities. As a teacher, Besley focuses on methods of mass communication research and science communication, including science journalism.

Dominique Brossard (Ph.D., Cornell University) is an Associate Professor in the Department of Life Sciences Communication at the University of Wisconsin–Madison. Brossard's research interests broadly focus on the intersection between science, media, and policy, and more particularly on the role of cultural authority in public opinion dynamics in the context of controversial scientific issues. She has published numerous research articles in outlets such as *Communication Research*, *Health Communication*, the *International Journal of Public Opinion Research*, *Mass Communication and Society*, *Public Understanding of Science* and *Science Communication*. In 2007, she co-edited (with Jim Shanahan and Clint Nesbitt) a book published by Oxford University Press, *The Media, the Public, and Agricultural Biotechnology*.

Sharon Dunwoody (Ph.D., Indiana University) is the Evjue-Bascom Professor of Journalism and Mass Communication and Associate Dean for Social Studies in the Graduate School at the University of Wisconsin–Madison. She is a nationally recognized expert on science communication whose research focuses on science journalism, science-related messages, and message effects. Her leadership roles have included head of the American Association for the Advancement of Science's (AAAS) section on General Interest in Science and Technology, president of the Midwest Association for Public Opinion Research (MAPOR), and president of the Association for Education in Journalism and Mass

Communication (AEJMC). She is a Fellow of AAAS and MAPOR, as well as of the Society for Risk Analysis. Before entering academia, Dunwoody worked as a newspaper science writer.

Danielle Endres (Ph.D., University of Washington) is an Assistant Professor of Communication and Faculty in the Environmental Humanities MA Program at the University of Utah. Her research examines the intersecting areas of environmental communication, social movements, scientific controversy, and American Indian studies. Her current research examines the rhetoric of nuclear waste siting decisions. Her research appears in *Communication and Critical Cultural Studies, Environmental Communication, Western Journal of Communication*, and other journals.

LeeAnn Kahlor (Ph.D., University of Wisconsin–Madison) is an Assistant Professor in the Department of Advertising at the University of Texas at Austin where she teaches courses in public relations and science and health communication. She is affiliated with UT's Center for Women's and Gender Studies and the university's Environmental Sciences Institute. Kahlor's research interests are environmental and health-risk communication with an emphasis on information seeking and processing. Her work has appeared in *Science Communication, Public Understanding of Science, Health Communication, Risk Analysis, Communication Research, Human Communication Research, Media Psychology*, and the *Journal of Broadcast and Electronic Media*.

Lisa Keränen (Ph.D., University of Pittsburgh) is an Assistant Professor of Communication at the University of Colorado Denver. Her publications concerning the rhetoric of science, medicine, and bioethics appear in places such as *Academic Medicine, Accountability in Research, Argumentation & Advocacy, Journal of Medical Humanities*, and the *Quarterly Journal of Speech*. Keränen's first book, *Scientific Characters: Rhetoric, Politics, and Trust in Breast Cancer Research*, is forthcoming from the University of Alabama Press. Keränen served on the clinical ethics committee at Boulder Community Hospital from 2006–2009, and directs the National Communication Association Forum (NCA-F), a group dedicated to improving the quality of public deliberation about social issues.

Bruce V. Lewenstein (Ph.D., University of Pennsylvania) is Professor of Science Communication in the Departments of Communication and of Science and Technology Studies at Cornell University, Ithaca, New York. He works primarily on the history of public communication of science, with excursions into other areas of science communication. He has also been very active in international activities that contribute to education and research on public communication of science and technology. He was co-chair of a National Research Council study, Learning Science in Informal Environments: People, Places, and Pursuits (2009).

John Lynch (Ph.D., University of Georgia) is an Assistant Professor in the Department of Communication at the University of Cincinnati. His research focuses on the intersection of science and politics in debates about stem-cell research and research on genetics, race, and medicine. He teaches courses in rhetoric of science. His work has appeared in the *American Journal of Health Behavior, Argumentation & Advocacy, Health Communication, Journal of Communication Inquiry, New Genetics & Society, Social Science and Medicine*, and *Western Journal of Communication*. Lynch is the research ethicist for the NIH-funded Center for Clinical and Translational Science and Training.

Barbara Miller (Ph.D., University of North Carolina at Chapel Hill) is an Assistant Professor in the School of Communications at Elon University. She teaches courses in public relations and communications research. Her research focuses on issue advocacy, effective science, and risk communication strategies, and health news coverage. Her work has appeared in the *Journal of Advertising* and the *Journal of Computer-Mediated Communication*.

Matthew C. Nisbet (Ph.D., Cornell University) is an Assistant Professor in the School of Communication at American University in Washington, DC and is an affiliated researcher with George Mason University's Center for Climate Change Communication. Nisbet's research examines strategic communication in science and environmental policy debates, with a focus on how publics make sense of complex science questions and how citizens come to be actively involved in the resolution of science disputes. Over the past 5 years, he has authored more than 20 journal articles and book chapters, using focus groups, content analysis, in-depth interviews, case studies, and surveys to study the communication dynamics of policy debates. He has also served as a consultant to the National Academies, the National Science Foundation, Centers for Disease Control, Howard Hughes Medical Institute, and other science organizations.

Amy R. Pearce (Ph.D., Australian National University) is an Associate Professor of Psychology, Adjunct Assistant Professor of Biology and a research affiliate of the Arkansas Biosciences Institute at Arkansas State University. Pearce earned a Ph.D. in neuroscience and a certificate in Science Communication and is a former producer and host of "Fuzzy Logic," a long-running science education show on Australian community radio. She is a regular contributor to journals, newspapers, and radio, and promotes public understanding and awareness of science at national and international forums and to audiences of all ages through science fairs, seminars, and professional development workshops.

Aldemaro Romero (Ph.D., University of Miami) is Dean of the College of Arts and Sciences at the University of Southern Illinois Edwardsville. He has published more than 550 pieces of work including books, peer-reviewed articles, and articles in non-peer-reviewed publications. His academic interests range from environmental and evolutionary biology to history and philosophy of science and science outreach. He has won several awards for his writing of popular science and the writing, production, and direction of both radio and TV shows about science.

Bret R. Shaw (Ph.D., University of Wisconsin–Madison) is an Assistant Professor in the Department of Life Sciences Communication at the University of Wisconsin–Madison and an Environmental Communication Specialist with UW Cooperative Extension. Shaw's research explores how to develop effective social marketing and communication campaigns to encourage pro-environmental behaviors. He has also published extensively on topics related to online health communication in *Journal of Health Communication*, *Journal of Health Psychology*, *Journal of Broadcast and Electronic Media*, and *Health Communication*.

Janas Sinclair (Ph.D., University of Florida) is an Assistant Professor in the School of Journalism and Mass Communication at the University of North Carolina at Chapel Hill. She teaches courses in advertising and media planning. Her research focuses on advocacy advertising and the role of trust in the effectiveness of advertising and science communication campaigns. Her work has appeared in the *Journal of Advertising*, *Science Communication*, and the *Journal of Applied Communications*. Her work has been funded by the Arthur W. Page Center and the U.S. Fish and Wildlife Service.

Patricia A. Stout (Ph.D., University of Illinois Urbana-Champaign) is Professor and John P. McGovern Regents Professor in Health and Medical Science Communication in the Department of Advertising at the University of Texas at Austin. She teaches courses in persuasive communication and health communication. Her research focuses on viewer response to mediated messages and the role of different message variables in communicating about mental illness stigma, breast cancer screening, HIV prevention, and other health-related issues. Her research has been supported by the National Institute of Mental Health, the Hogg Foundation for Mental Health, and the U.S. Centers for Disease Control and Prevention, among others. Stout is former co-director of the Center for Health Promotion Research (CHPR) in the School of Nursing at UT Austin.

Kristen Alley Swain (Ph.D., University of Florida) is an Assistant Professor in the School of Journalism and New Media at the University of Mississippi. Her research emphasizes science and health communication, including news coverage of bioterrorism, international news flow about AIDS in sub-Saharan Africa, stem-cell research, sea-level rise and AIDS prevention in the African American church. Swain directed the Science Journalism Center at the University of South Florida–St. Petersburg, has taught a variety of science communication courses, and has written for a variety of news media through the U.S.

John B. (Jack) Zibluk (Ph.D., Bowling Green State University) is Associate Professor of journalism at Arkansas State University, where he is the primary teacher in the photojournalism sequence. He was the National Geographic magazine faculty fellow in 2002, and he has won the National Press Photographers Association Garland "educator of the year" award in 2005 for his scholarship on journalism ethics. His research focuses on law, ethics, and copyright. His work has been published in *Visual Communications Quarterly*, *Journalism Ethics*, the *Chronicle of Higher Education*, and other publications. A native of New Haven, Connecticut, he is a former newspaper writer, photographer, and editor.

Index

and levels of 34–5; in environmental issues 203–4; fairness in research on 71–2; model of PUOS 16, **17**, 23, 29, 31; new paradigm in 41; outreach to increase 43

public relations, benefits of 89

publics, communication about science by 202

public understanding of science (PUOS): analysis methods for HGP case studies 19; "A Question of Genes" documentary 27–9; assumptions behind outreach projects 11; conferences for minority communities 23–7; contextual model of 13–15, 16–17, **17**, 23, 25–7, 29, 31; deficit model of 12–13, 14, 16–17, **17**, 22–3, 26–7, 29, 41–3; definition of knowledge needed 33–4; definition of public(s) of interest 32; funding for HGP projects 18; *Geneletter* 21–3; interpersonal processes of communication 35; lay expertise model of 15–16, **17**, 29; new concepts of 11; overlap between models 31–2, **33**; public engagement model of 16, **17**, 23, 29, 31; selection of case studies 18–19; target audiences for outreach projects for 20; two categories of projects 12

"Question of Genes, A" (documentary) 27–9

radio shows in Spanish 30–1

Rawls, John 68

Reidenbach, R. E. 216

relapse 117–18

religion and science 191–2

reluctant apologist *persona* 144–8

Renn, O. 71–2

representation and articulation 163–4

Republican War on Science, The (Mooney) 57

research in science communication: interdisciplinary 2; recent 1–2

rhetoric: analysis of *personae*, *ethos* and voice 155–6; ethos, meanings of 135–6; perceptions of character cultivated by 135; *persona, meaning of* 136–7; and science, articulation of 162–70; voice 137, 138; *see also* industry rhetoric

rhetorical technology 165; coordination with other technologies 173–5, 177–9; of hematopoietic stem cells (HSCs) 175–6; of model organisms 169, 170; and mouse embryonic stem (ES) cells 172

risk: and distributive justice 82; future research into fairness and justice 81; judgement of and audience motives 104; and justice 76–7; justice perceptions 78

Robin, D. P. 216

Rogers, C. L. 188

Rogers, E. M. 122

Romero, Aldemaro 241, 243–4

Rowe, G. 72

Ryan, A. 68

Saito, L. S. 239

Schaffer, S. 164–6

Schellenberger, M. 58

Scheufele, D. A. 240

Schlenker, B. R. 100

Schwerin, Noel 27–9

science: as a culture 189–91; as interrelated technologies 164–6; as in opposition to culture 188–9; and rhetoric, articulation of 162–70

Science, Evolution, and Creationism booklet 40–1, 53–4

science-based controversies: analysis of role of characters in 155–6; *see also* Fisher controversy

scientific argument: American Indians challenge to authority of Western science 194–7; American Indians' use of traditional Western scientific arguments 198–202; future research 202–4; and public participation in environmental issues 203–4; relationship between indigenous and Western knowledge 204

scientists: approaches to communication 237–8; challenges of communication between 161

Self-Reliance Foundation (SRF) 30–1

Sethi, S. P. 94

Shapin, S. 164–6

Smith, A. 174–5

Smith, C. A. 213

Snow, C. P. 189

Sobnosky, M. J. 198, 203